Culture and Customs of the Central African Republic

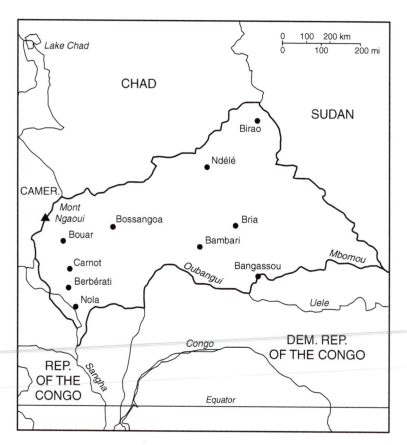

Central African Republic. Cartography by Bookcomp, Inc.

Culture and Customs of the Central African Republic

∽o∾

JACQUELINE WOODFORK

Culture and Customs of Africa
Toyin Falola, Series Editor

GREENWOOD PRESS
Westport, Connecticut • London

Library of Congress Cataloging-in-Publication Data

Woodfork, Jacqueline C.
   Culture and customs of the Central African Republic   /   Jacqueline Woodfork.
      p. cm. — (Culture and customs of Africa, ISSN 1530–8367)
   Includes bibliographical references and index.
   ISBN 0–313–33203–7
   1. Central African Republic—Civilization. 2. Central African Republic—Social life and customs.
I. Title. II. Series.
   DT546.34.W66 2006
   967.41—dc22   2006017936

British Library Cataloguing in Publication Data is available.

Library of Congress Catalog Card Number: 2006017936
ISBN: 0–313–33203–7
ISSN: 1530–8367

First published in 2006

Greenwood Press, 88 Post Road West, Westport, CT 06881
An imprint of Greenwood Publishing Group, Inc.
www.greenwood.com

Printed in the United States of America

The paper used in this book complies with the
Permanent Paper Standard issued by the National
Information Standards Organization (Z39.48–1984).

10   9   8   7   6   5   4   3   2   1

To my mother and the memory of my father

Aux peuples Centrafricains

Contents

Series Foreword

AFRICA IS A vast continent, the second largest, after Asia. It is four times the size of the United States, excluding Alaska. It is the cradle of human civilization. A diverse continent, Africa has more than fifty countries with a population of over 700 million people who speak over 1,000 languages. Ecological and cultural differences vary from one region to another. As an old continent, Africa is one of the richest in culture and customs, and its contributions to world civilization are impressive indeed.

Africans regard culture as essential to their lives and future development. Culture embodies their philosophy, worldview, behavior patterns, arts, and institutions. The books in this series intend to capture the comprehensiveness of African culture and customs, dwelling on such important aspects as religion, worldview, literature, media, art, housing, architecture, cuisine, traditional dress, gender, marriage, family, lifestyles, social customs, music, and dance.

The uses and definitions of "culture" vary, reflecting its prestigious association with civilization and social status, its restriction to attitude and behavior, its globalization, and the debates surrounding issues of tradition, modernity, and postmodernity. The participating authors have chosen a comprehensive meaning of culture while not ignoring the alternative uses of the term.

Each volume in the series focuses on a single country, and the format is uniform. The first chapter presents a historical overview, in addition to information on geography, economy, and politics. Each volume then proceeds to examine the various aspects of culture and customs. The series highlights the mechanisms for the transmission of tradition and culture across generations: the significance of orality, traditions, kinship rites, and family property distribution; the rise of print culture; and the impact of educational institutions. The series also explores the intersections between local, regional, national, and global bases for identity and social relations. While the volumes are organized nationally, they pay attention to ethnicity and language groups and the links between Africa and the wider world.

The books in the series capture the elements of continuity and change in culture and customs. Custom is not represented as static or as a museum artifact, but as a dynamic phenomenon. Furthermore, the authors recognize the current challenges to traditional wisdom, which include gender relations; the negotiation of local identities in relation to the state; the significance of struggles for power at national and local levels and their impact on cultural traditions and community-based forms of authority; and the tensions between agrarian and industrial/manufacturing/oil-based economic modes of production.

Africa is a continent of great changes, instigated mainly by Africans but also through influences from other continents. The rise of youth culture, the penetration of the global media, and the challenges to generational stability are some of the components of modern changes explored in the series. The ways in which traditional (non-Western and nonimitative) African cultural forms continue to survive and thrive, that is, how they have taken advantage of the market system to enhance their influence and reproductions also receive attention.

Through the books in this series, readers can see their own cultures in a different perspective, understand the habits of Africans, and educate themselves about the customs and cultures of other countries and people. The hope is that the readers will come to respect the cultures of others and see them not as inferior or superior to theirs, but merely as different. Africa has always been important to Europe and the United States, essentially as a source of labor, raw materials, and markets. Blacks are in Europe and the Americas as part of the African diaspora, a migration that took place primarily due to the slave trade. Recent African migrants increasingly swell their number and visibility. It is important to understand the history of the diaspora and the newer migrants, as well as the roots of the culture and customs of the places from where they come. It is equally important to understand others in order to be able to interact successfully in a world that keeps shrinking. The accessible nature of the books in this series will contribute to this understanding and enhance the quality of human interaction in a new millennium.

Toyin Falola
Frances Higginbothom, Nalle Centennial Professor in History
The University of Texas at Austin

Preface

THE CENTRAL AFRICAN REPUBLIC (CAR) is one of the least known countries in Africa, both to other Africans and people of different continents. The lack of attention paid to the CAR does not indicate a country that is uninteresting, rather it represents a trend in paying attention to those places of greater geopolitical significance to players on the world stage. This work uses the term *Centrafricans* to describe the people of the CAR; the traditional "Central Africans" more accurately describes the people of all nations of the subregion of Central Africa.

The CAR is a country of great diversity, in its geography, peoples, and cultures. There are many ethnic groups and subgroups, all of which have their own customs and traditions. The book looks at the history of the country and the changes that have taken place in the context of the cultures and their evolutions toward the present day. To do so, the book examines the cultures and customs of the CAR in a broad way, then uses examples from different ethnic groups to illustrate specific points. Certain ethnic groups were selected because of both the amount of information available and the desire not to scatter the examples too widely. This should in no way be read as a value judgment about any of the ethnic groups; rather it is a reflection of the available literature and the desire to create a narrative that is cohesive, especially for those who are new to the study of the Central African Republic.

Acknowledgments

THERE IS NOT enough room to adequately thank everyone individually, but I would like to recognize some people who have been especially helpful for this project. Molly Smith Mullally, a friend from Middlebury and a Returned Peace Corps Volunteer from the CAR, generously shared of her time, photographs, and textiles from her volunteer days. At Loyola University New Orleans, I acknowledge the committee that awarded me the Marquette Fellowship that allowed me to work on the manuscript in the summer of 2005; Patricia Doran and her staff at Interlibrary Loan, who tirelessly tracked down rare sources; and my wonderful department, especially Nancy Fix Anderson, Judith Hunt, David Moore, and Michael Ross. In Austin, Toyin Falola, and Ulrich Purbach, who always provides human and canine shelter during hurricane season, have my gratitude. A special thanks goes to Dennis Cordell and Arlette Sammy-Mackfoy for being so generous with their time and knowledge.

Chronology

Precolonial Era

c. 500 B.C.   Settled agricultural societies established in the area
                       that now composes the CAR.

c. 1600   The enslavement of the peoples of the region
                       increases dramatically with the trans-Atlantic slave
                       trade.

c. 1800–1850   Era of migrations including Banda, Manza, Gbaya,
                       Nzakara, and Zandé peoples.

1850   Apex of the Zandé and the Bandia nations.

1860s–1890s   The authority of slave raiding rulers challenged
                       successfully by the Nzakara, the Manza, and the
                       French.

Colonial Era

1891–1894   French exploration missions in the Central African
                       territory; protectorate treaties with the leaders of
                       central Ubangui and the upper Sangha.

March 15, 1894   Franco-German convention fixes the limits of the
                       French Congo and German Cameroons.

July 16, 1898	In Paris, a commission of high officials is established and charged with the partition of the French possessions in the Congo and Ubangui among the legally recognized 39 concessionary companies.
1899	The Minister of the Colonies orders the French colonial administration to completely support the action of concessionary companies. Decrees gradually put into effect between May and December.
December 29, 1903	A decree creates a new colony made up of the region of the upper Oubangui and the Chari, called Oubangui-Chari.
1902–4	Manza uprisings to protest porterage and tax demands of the colonial government.
1904–1905	Insurrection of the population against the concessionary companies leads to military occupation of the Lobaye and the Ibenga.
May 16, 1905	Pierre Savorgnan de Brazza Brazza arrives in the Congo and Ubangui and does an inspection tour.
1907	Discovery of many crimes committed by the Mpoko concession company.
1910	The subregion becomes known as Afrique Equitoriale Française (AEF) or French Central Africa.
November 4, 1911	France cedes to Germany important parts of Central Africa, including the western part of the territory of present-day CAR.
1914	First diamonds discovered near Ippy.
	France reoccupies areas ceded to Germany.
	World War I: many insurrections.
1928–1931	Many uprisings, including the Kongo Wara War (the Gbaya War); uprisings of the Gbaya and others against the French.

March 27, 1938   Ordination of the first Ubanguian Catholic priest, Barthélemy Boganda.

July 20, 1940   Defeat of Gaullist putsch at Bangui.

January 30–February 8, Brazzaville Conference.
1944

June 23, 1956   *Loi cadre* (enabling law) opens route to internal autonomy to overseas territories.

March 31, 1957   Boganda's political party, Mouvement pour l'évolution sociale de l'Afrique noire (MESAN), wins all seats in the Oubangui-Chari Territorial Assembly and Boganda is elected president of the Grand Council of French Equatorial Africa.

GOVERNMENT OF THE CENTRAL AFRICAN REPUBLIC

December 1, 1958   France proclaims a Central African Republic limited to its own territory; Barthélemy Boganda named president.

March 29, 1959   President Boganda disappears in a plane crash.

March 30, 1959   Doctor Abel Goumba becomes the interim president.

May 5, 1959   David Dacko, a nephew of Boganda, is elected president by the Assembly.

PRESIDENCY OF THE CENTRAL AFRICAN REPUBLIC

August 13, 1960   CAR gains independence from France.

November 1962   Dacko turns the CAR into a one-party (MESAN) state.

January 5, 1964   Dacko is confirmed as president in an election in which he is the sole candidate.

December 1, 1964   Colonel Jean-Bédel Bokassa named chief of staff of the army.

May 13, 1965	Dacko announces measures against widespread corruption.
December 31, 1965	Dacko is ousted by an army commander and flees.
January 1, 1966	Colonel Jean-Bédel Bokassa, head of state and of government, named general, then marshal (uses the Vichy model).
November 10, 1967	Bokassa requests French paratroop detachment (11th Intervention Division) be sent to Bangui for a "tropical country acclimatization exercise."
February 1969	De Gaulle receives Bokassa on an official visit to Paris.
April 11–12, 1969	Arrest and execution of Lieutenant-Colonel Alexandre Banza, accused of a plot against the government.
December 24, 1969	After Bokassa sends an important delegation to Moscow, the French government assures the CAR head of state of its "fraternal esteem."
March 4, 1972	Marshal Bokassa named president for life by a congress of a single party.
September 5, 1976:	Bokassa dissolves the government and creates the Council of the Centrafrican Revolution along with a new constitution. Former President Dacko becomes an advisor to Bokassa.
September 20, 1976	The Libyan head of state, Colonel Muammar Gaddafi officially visits the CAR.
October 20, 1976	Bokassa announces his conversion to Islam.
End of November 1976	Military attempt on Bokassa's life.

CENTRAL AFRICAN EMPIRE

December 4, 1976	The MESAN congress adopts a new constitution that makes the now Central African Empire a hereditary monarchy.
	In a lavish coronation ceremony, Bokassa becomes the Emperor Bokassa the First.
	Bokassa renounces Islam.

December 14, 1977   Patassé named prime minister with (theoretically) broad powers.

                       There is an imperial court and Bokassa no longer assumes direct government responsibility.

July 17, 1978   Henri Maïdou replaces Patassé as prime minister.

January 19–22, 1979   Students protest wearing obligatory uniforms sold at Bokassa's stores. Bloody repression put down with help of Zairian paratroopers. Population strikes back by shooting poison arrows at the soldiers. There are several hundred dead.

January 29, 1979   Striking teachers are joined by several high officials.

April 18–19, 1979   The government forcibly rounds up children between ages of 8 and 16. Bokassa participates in the massacre of about 100 children.

August 17, 1979   The French Minister of Cooperation announces suspension of aid to CAE, except materials relating to health, education, and food that directly affect the lives of the populace.

September 20–21, 1979 French soldiers occupy the airport and the city of Bangui while Bokassa is in Tripoli. The soldiers meet with no resistance.

September 24, 1979   Turned away from France, Bokassa finds refuges in Cote d'Ivoire.

October 10, 1979   The French newspaper the *Canard Enchaîné* reveals that French president Giscard d'Estaing received a gift of diamonds from Bokassa.

CENTRAL AFRICAN REPUBLIC

September 21, 1979   David Dacko proclaims downfall of Bokassa and the reestablishment of the republic, of which Dacko takes the presidency. Henri Maïdou named vice president and Bernard-Christian Ayandho, prime minister. This is the Second Republic.

January 9, 1981   320 French reinforcements sent to Bangui.

March 15, 1981	Election of Dacko as president.
September 1, 1981	Dacko resigns and hands power to General André Kolingba. Kolingba suspends the constitution and creates the Comité militaure de redressement national, of which he is president.
September 2, 1981	Kolingba suspends the constitution and forbids all political parties.
December 12–13, 1981	French president François Mitterand visits Bangui.
December 31,1984	Amnesty for all political party leaders declared.
October 24, 1986	Bokassa returns to the CAR.
June 12, 1987	Bokassa sentenced to death for murder and embezzlement, but this is commuted to life in prison in France.
April 22, 1991	Political parties are permitted to form.
October 25, 1992	Multiparty presidential elections. Kolingba comes in last, but the supreme court annuls the vote on the grounds of widespread irregularities.
September 27, 1993	Patassé wins presidential election, ending 12 years of military rule. Kolingba releases several thousand prisoners, including Bokassa, before he steps down.
May 22, 1996	After a rebellion in which the radio station is captured, Patassé forms a new government.
1997	More mutinies, strikes, and French military intervention.
August 4, 1997	France begins to withdraw from the CAR; African peacekeepers replace French troops.
September 11, 1999	Patassé reelected.
December 11, 2000	Civil servants strike for back pay, and they rally groups to accuse president of mismanagement and corruption. Riots ensue.

May 28, 2001	André Kolingba stages coup attempt. It is suppressed with help of Libyan and Chadian troops, along with Congolese rebels. The government tries to arrest former army chief of staff, Bozizé, which leads to fighting between government troops and Bozizé's forces.
March 15, 2003	Bozizé seizes Bangui, declares himself president, and dissolves parliament. Patassé out of the country at the time.
December 5, 2004	A new constitution is approved in a referendum.
March 13, 2005	Bozizé wins first round of presidential elections.
April 11, 2004	Ousted Haitian president, Jean-Bertrand Aristide, is offered refuge in the CAR.
May 8, 2005	Bozizé wins the presidency in a run-off election.
Early August 2005	Flooding in Bangui leaves up to 20,000 people homeless.
2006	There are continuing conflicts between government and rebel forces. Approximately 30,000 refugees fleeing violent village raids by rebels and armed gangs in the northern CAR are still in southern Chad. There are also occasional skirmishes over water and grazing rights with other pastoral populations along the border with southern Sudan.

1

Introduction

THE CENTRAL AFRICAN REPUBLIC (CAR) is one of the least known countries in the world; it is a land of many different ethnic languages and groups, with a complex history and vibrant cultures. The country has had and continues to face numerous challenges as internal, intra-African, and external factors affect its economy, diplomacy, politics, agriculture, and systems of health care and education. Cultures are continuously shifting with changes that are readily apparent as well as those that are harder to discern. Certainly there are tensions between "old" and "new" ways, and these are not even concrete categories. Those who bemoan the loss of the old customs are sometimes idealizing the past or are simply nostalgic for earlier times. But change is inevitable and Centrafricans are responding to it in the ways that are appropriate for them, or, in some cases, in the only ways that they can. Cultures and customs remain, adapt, and fade as their practitioners feel the need. Centrafricans are keenly aware of their history, and although they use the past as a way to understand and negotiate the present and the future, they are not mired in it. The CAR's geography, peoples, languages, and religions have affected its history from the earliest days to the present; in the present day, there is continuity and change in its cultures and customs.

GEOGRAPHY

In almost the precise center of the African continent lies the Central African Republic. It comprises much of the former French colony of the

Oubangui-Chari. To the north is the nation of Chad, to the northeast and east is Sudan, to the south is the Democratic Republic of the Congo (formerly Zaire), to the southwest is the Republic of Congo, and to the west lies Cameroon. The border with the Democratic Republic of the Congo is about 3,500 kilometers (2,175 miles) long, and it is partially defined by the Oubangui and Mboumu rivers. The 2,300-kilometer (1,429-mile) border with Chad is partially delineated by the Chari River. Centrafricans were not responsible for the current geopolitical borders that define their nation; European powers divided the continent, leaving borders that were not rational, for example, splitting ethnic groups between different territories. The subregion of Central Africa had different imperial powers, notably Belgium, France, and Germany; this left the region with varying colonial inheritances and occasional border disputes. The frontiers that Africa inherited were not altered at independence. The land borders with adjacent countries are scarcely clarified and patrolled; these boundaries have little meaning to the people who live along the frontiers whose daily lives are not affected or defined by them. Borders do not prevent the movement of people, livestock, and ideas, which often move as freely as they did in precolonial times.

The country's geography has had a great impact on its history. The landmass is 622,984 square kilometers (240,535 square miles), which is slightly less than that of the U.S. state of Texas. The land is fairly flat plateau, but the topography is broken up occasionally by hills. The plateau is about 600 meters (1,969 feet) high, stretching from the Chad to the Congo River basins. Three notable geographic features are the Bongo Massif, which rises to 1,330 meters (4,265 feet) near the border with Sudan; the Yadé Massif along the border with Cameroon, whose Mount Ngaoui reaches 1,420 meters (4,659 feet); and the Fertit Hills near Sudan that are 1,400 meters (4,593 feet) high. There is a lack of geographic obstacles between the Nile River Valley (especially the Upper Nile) and the Oubangui River Valley, which has led some to speculate that small, intermittent groups of people may have settled in this area from ancient Kush and Meroë, after the depleted resources of these areas in the sixth and seventh centuries A.D. sent people in search of new lands to farm and fields on which to graze their cattle. Only 3.1 percent of the land is arable, which has an enormous impact on its agricultural use and yields.

There are two main terrains in the CAR, savanna and forest, and the country lies largely in the savanna region. A fairly treeless north has a rough, scrubby terrain. Below that the savanna offers farmland, and its rivers make plant life more luxurious there. The vegetation becomes denser toward the south, melding into rainforests. For a long time, it was believed that the savannas and forests were without variety, but now it is known that they are host to great biodiversity. The densest of the forests are found along the rivers that border the Democratic Republic of the Congo and Cameroon that drain the country. One of the major challenges for the forested areas is finding means of sustainable development.

Rivers are very important to the CAR because the country is landlocked and there are no large bodies of water; this affects trade, agriculture, and transportation. Rivers are the main sources of water for people and animals, and they move people and goods as well as allowing for communication. The *priogue,* or dugout canoe, is a very popular and useful form of transportation. The Chari River flows northward to the Chad River Basin and the Oubangui River winds its way south into the Congo River Basin. The Oubangui River has a tremendous volume of water during the rainy season at 10,000 cubic meters (353,147 cubic feet) per second. The city of Bangui was established at the point where the Oubangui was no longer navigable because of cataracts. The Sangha River, which flows for 1,400 kilometers (870 miles), is also a tributary of the Congo River. Both the Mboumu and the Uele originate close to the headwaters of the Nile. Because there is no railway system and the roads are not well developed, the rivers are the lifelines of the country. The lack of arable land and lack of seaports has greatly influenced where people live and how they earn their livings.

CLIMATE

Geography and climate are closely linked, and the latter has a great impact on people's lifestyles, activities, and routines, which are adapted and timed to best produce results and comfort. The climate of the CAR is tropical with hot and dry winters (comparatively dry, that is) and hot, wet summers. In the winter, the Harmattan winds blow across the north of the country, bringing dry air and dust from the Sahara desert that covers everything with a fine layer of red powder.

There is great variation in the CAR's climate. In the north, it is hotter and drier. With less precipitation, the temperatures reach 40 degrees Celsius (104 degrees Farenheit). Here the rainy season is shorter, running from June to September. In the more humid south, the dry season is shorter, and it rains from May to October. In thickly forested areas, it rains throughout the year. Heavy rainfall in the summer makes flooding common. One of the most visible results of the heavy precipitation is that unpaved roads become vehicle-devouring muddy trenches in which tires sink and hopelessly spin. Even with all this rainfall, there is a lack of clean drinking water throughout the country.

People have adapted their lives to coincide with the physical environment. It influences where they live, how they live, when they move, what they eat, and how they understand their interactions with the natural world. Farmers and herders have adapted to the seasons that are the determining factors in planting, harvesting, and transhumance. Even the mining industry has to take the seasons into account—here modernity takes a backseat to Mother Nature.

NATURAL RESOURCES

The Central African Republic is rich in natural resources. Some of these resources are items that are necessary for everyday life, while others are luxury goods consumed mainly by the West. Gold, diamonds, copper, iron, uranium, and timber are the chief mineral resources of the land, and there is speculation that the country has oil reserves as well. Although all of these resources are lucrative, the monetary impact is fairly limited for the country's citizens. Centrafricans work in the mines and fell the trees that produce these resources, but their pay is not in line with the value of the items, especially considering what these goods cost the consumer. When the commodity is highly desirable, the natural resource can have a wide impact on communities as individuals and companies vie for control, causing scarcity and conflict. There is also the physical impact of the extraction of the resources, such as the mining scars and treeless swatches that stretch across the landscape and alter the land's usefulness to human and to animal life.

Wildlife is another sector of natural resources; some of these animals live in remote, unprotected areas as well as in national parks. The St. Floris National Park, home to many species of wildlife, is also a site where the needs of humans and the needs of animals are contested. Herders, some of whom cross the border from Sudan, graze their cattle in the park during the dry season. There are occasionally poachers who hunt in small groups with firearms, in search of bushmeat and animals such as elephants and giraffes to sell. Poaching, hunting, and the grazing of livestock in the parks has taken a toll on the wildlife within the preserves, but there is still a great variety of animals in the parks. More than 59 species have been observed in the park, including lions, hippopotami, elephants, cheetahs, and Nile crocodiles. The competition between humans and animals is but one of the reasons that people are looking for greener pastures in different areas.

The country has a low population density; the depopulation of the countryside continues as more people leave rural areas to seek opportunities in the capital city of Bangui and other urban areas. People see the cities as places with greater opportunities than the rural areas, and they strike out for urban areas, leaving the young and the aged in the countryside. The decrease in adult labor has negatively impacted farming, and the government has contemplated granting land to white farmers from Zimbabwe to increase agricultural production.

The idea of uprooting and resettling people from other areas illustrates some of the issues concerning the country's geography and its impact on people. Geography serves to separate and unite: Illogical colonial borders often separate members of ethnic groups while simultaneously creating a multiethnic geopolitical construct. Because of the country's landlocked position, the CAR is dependent on its neighbors to allow the passage of goods into and out of the country. Borders clearly do not stop the passage of goods (although they do increase the cost of them), and it is the same for people and ideas, which can move as freely as they did in precolonial times. The instability of any of its neighbors potentially unsettles the CAR economically and militarily; the government is acutely aware that it needs and is needed by other countries in the subregion as well as the rest of the continent.

INDIGENOUS LANGUAGES

In the Central African Republic, there are many indigenous languages, and some cross borders into other countries. They are classified into four language families: Nilo-Saharan, Adamawan, Bantu, and Oubanguian. Those of the Nilo-Saharan family are found in the northern part of the country, along the border with Chad and Sudan. The few Adamawan tongues are in the northwest corner, and those in the Bantu family are concentrated along the southwestern border with Cameroon and the Congo. The language family with the most members is the Oubangian, including Sango. Languages have variations or dialects, for example there are nine distinct Banda vernaculars. In all there are 68 living languages in the country. Bodo, originating in the eastern tip of the country, had only 15 speakers scattered throughout the country in 1996. None of these speakers live in the area where the language originated and not more than three were in the same village.

Because so many indigenous languages are spoken by a somewhat limited number of people and because of intergroup relations, many Centrafricans are polyglots who speak their mother tongue and are usually at least familiar with other vernaculars. These are often augmented by knowledge of French that is most widely used in urban areas such as Bangui. Also, there are non-European languages that have widespread use such as Kiswahili, Hausa, Arabic, and Sango.

SANGO

Sango is the lingua franca of the Central African Republic. It is a tonal language with three tone levels (high, medium, and low) as well as three counter tones (high-low, low-high, and mid-low). The origin of Sango is debated; its dominance in urban areas is a legacy of the colonial era and a product of modern life. Some say that Sango allows a larger group of people to directly communicate, but others counter that its use and popularity are to the detriment of the country's other indigenous languages and that its widespread use has led to a homogenization of culture. All agree, however, that the language is becoming the primary language for many in the country, especially in urban areas and among youth.

One theory about the origin of Sango is that it is the pidginization of indigenous languages produced by the foreign workers who came to the Oubangui-Chari at the end of the nineteenth century. This thesis has been refuted by those who claim that there were about 1,000 "foreign" workers in the area for the entirety of the 1890s when the language developed and that it was in use by 1893. *Sa* means "animal" and *ngu* means "water," creating "man of the water." There is the idea that "foreign" African workers cried out *sa ngu* to each other as they maneuvered their canoes, encouraging each other to paddle faster. Others believe that Sango is a simplified version of Ngbandi. People who speak Ngbandi and have no previous experience with Sango are able to understand the language, but the reverse is not true for Sango speakers, who can often only pick up some simple words.

Sango was an important tool in the nascent Oubangui-Chari. Colonial agents liked Sango because it was something they could manipulate and use to their own ends. They studied its grammar and made vocabulary lists. Colonizers who promoted Sango wanted it to be adopted by those who spoke other indigenous languages, thus encouraging one language so the French could learn to understand what the indigenous population was saying and allowing Europeans to be understood by a wider group of people.

Although colonial officials encouraged the use of Sango, Catholic missionaries originally shunned it through the first two decades of the twentieth century, deeming it a language not worthy of use for religious instruction. They chose to do their work in either French or one of the other vernaculars. Protestants did the opposite and used the language to their advantage. The language of the converts' faith and proselytizing efforts was Sango. People accepted Sango along with their new religion and Christianity helped to spread the language.

Modern Sango has considerable variation. A commission adopted a unified system of orthography in 1967, yet variety still occurs in the spoken language. Those differences are mostly dependent upon age and degree of urbanization. There are varieties that are known for the region in which they are spoken or the profession of the speaker; for example, there are Yakoma Sango, Gòdòbe Sango, as well as Pastor's Sango and Functionary Sango.

Certain groups, especially women, are more likely to use Sango. Women are the market vendors, a profession that demands knowledge and use of a lingua franca to communicate with people who use many different languages; this is especially true in Bangui. In the case of intermarriage when parents have two different vernaculars as their mother tongues, and because it is expected that children will learn the language of their father, women often speak Sango to their children. Women originating from outside of Bangui who reside in the city often make an effort to speak with a Banguiois accent to elevate their position in society and to appear more sophisticated.

Those with formal education and the youth are very likely to use Sango. Some young people in urban areas who speak only Sango have never learned the indigenous languages of their parents. Owing in part to the numerous languages present in urban areas, this is also true because Sango is used in schools. Although the linguistic medium of formal instruction is French, Sango is occasionally used to explain lessons conducted in French. The publication of books in Sango increases its use and its legitimacy, especially vis-à-vis other vernaculars.

Sango is becoming increasingly popular in the subregion where Centrafrican music brings the language to listeners in other countries, but it is not of great use outside the area. Western languages are necessary for communicating with the outside world, with Africans and non-Africans alike. For this reason, the CAR uses the language of its former colonial power as a medium to communicate with those outside its borders.

FRENCH

French maintains its importance, not so much because it is a language in which people of different ethnic groups can communicate, but because it is a way to communicate with non-Centrafricans. It is the medium of communication of government and education. French is a language of privilege, and those who speak it usually have more access to formal education; thus, speaking French well is a marker of social class or employment in a white-collar job. The formally educated are the most likely to use French, and because Sango is the lingua franca, there is not the same need for market women and others to adopt it to communicate across vernacular lines. Most people do not have more than an informal knowledge of French. One interesting aspect of French is how it is used with indigenous languages. French is used for items that did not exist before colonialism and items that developed more recently: "gasoline" and "French," for example, are words that are said in French. The young are more likely to mix Sango into their French than older people and to substitute French for Sango when the word is easier in the former language.

PEOPLES

The Central African Republic's 3.8 million people are spread over more than 622,000 square kilometers (more than 240,156 square miles), giving it one of the lowest population densities in the world. Approximately two-thirds of the population lives in the western part of the country, and the majority of the rest live in the central region; the eastern area of the country is very sparsely populated with a density of less than one person per square kilometer (.37 square miles). There are seven major ethnic groups in the country: the Gbaya (33%), the Banda (27%), the Manza (Mandja, Mandjia) (13%), the Sara (10%), the Mboum (7%), the Yakoma (4%), and the Biaka (Baaka, Aka) (4%). There are many smaller groups, such as the Zandé. Some people combine groups, for example, the Gbaya-Manza, because of their physical proximity as well as linguistic and cultural similarities. All groups have further divisions into subgroups. Our understanding, especially our historical understanding, of different ethnic groups has been hampered by poor research, great variations in orthography, exoticization, and cultural judgments.

Colonizers used anthropology as a way to construct differences between people to justify imperialism and its workings. They also used anthropology to create hierarchies among Africans people, finding some groups to be superior to others because of lifestyle, social organization, or other factors. The way Westerners perceive African ethnicity and the way that Africans do are fundamentally different. To the West, ethnicity is static: an individual has one ethnicity and the characteristics of that ethnicity are unchanging. Ethnic groups have been simultaneously lauded and reviled for their "primitiveness," discussed for their "peculiarities," and heavily criticized for their supposed extreme dislike of each other. In this sense, ethnicity is given primacy in identity construction and politics. Yet, ethnicity is but one of many building blocks that Centrafricans use to create their senses of self.

Colonizers were fond of identifying ethnic groups and noting their characteristics. They created self-important works (some with exotic pictures), including the collection of census data, that were aimed at knowing Africans better so that they could better rule them. The French erroneously classified Muslims as a "tribe" for two reasons: as a way of marking Muslims as different from other groups in the territory, and because they did not recognize that religious conversion did not erase ethnicity. This system compressed people into larger groups, not recognizing that "Oubanguians," for example, comprised many peoples with different cultures, languages, and so on.

Contrary to what the colonizers believed, ethnic groups were not hermetically sealed communities, rather there was and is a great deal of fluidity in ethnic identification. Ethnic groups share a common language, heritage, and culture, and these elements are the glue that binds people together. Far from static, languages, cultures, and customs changed over time in response to both internal and external factors. These shifts could be caused by a number of factors, including lineage, location, lifestyle (mode of production), intermarriage, and assimilation. A recent trend in Bangui sees more ethnic conflict between groups based upon political affiliations. Many blame these conflicts on military uprisings. Presently, new peripheral areas of the city are often inhabited by a single ethnic group.

Geography and lifestyle have a great impact on the market identity of ethnic groups. To this day, pygmies are relatively out of the mainstream, often considered by Westerners, other Africans, and Centrafricans to be "primitive" and "uncivilized." They fiercely guard their traditions and way of life, living in harmony with their forest environment. By virtue of their relative isolation in the forest, the pygmies remained out of the reach of foreigners until the era of independence. When their music was "discovered" and brought to the attention of the rest of the world, their obscurity to outsiders lifted, but the pygmies still retained their exotic categorization. Because of improved travel, both for others going into the forest and pygmy travels to the outside world, they have become important as "natural resources": their culture is sought-after for reasons of curiosity, study, as well as a tourist attraction and export commodity.

The term *pygmy* was a derisive term, but it is for many the preferred terminology because it refers to the collectivity of these hunter/gatherer groups that are most at home in the rainforest, but that also spend a significant amount of time in the villages of Bantu-speaking peoples at the forest's edge. They do not stop being who they are by virtue of where they are, although the temporary status as a laborer for someone else has an impact on self-perception and the psyche. Pygmies have established relationships with their neighbors of other ethnic groups that have been called clientship by some and slavery by others.

Many Centrafricans, such as the Banda who live in savanna areas, are settled farmers. Along the more arid Chadian border, there are some nomadic pastoralists, although many Mbororo people now practice mixed agriculture. These pastoralists travel during the dry season, but feel an increasing need to stay close to their fields to fend off encroachers. Riverine people, such as the Yakoma, make their livings trading along the Oubangui and other waterways. The first groups to have contact with Europeans, these peoples were also the most likely to receive Western education. Historically, these groups have been favored by colonizers and later disproportionately represented in the national government.

PRECOLONIAL HISTORY

The earliest history of the area can be done in sweeping brush strokes, and the conclusions are not concrete. The record for this era does not include written documents, thus historical re-creation is done mainly through linguistic and archeological data. The area now called the Central African Republic has been inhabited since the Stone Age, well before the great ancient Egyptian civilization came into being. The original inhabitants of the area were the hunter/gatherers. Early twentieth-century mining operations uncovered a wealth of stone tools, and the tools' locations in various strata of the ground indicated that different stone-working peoples had been in the area for many years. As agriculturalists cleared the dry, thick forest, they brought lasting change to the surface of the area. An agricultural surplus engendered a sophisticated civilization that existed from 1000 B.C. to 1000 A.D. There are rock paintings and near Bouar are megalithic sites of large granite stones that were placed into the earth near streams that generally followed the Chari and Congo watersheds. The reasons for the decline of the advanced agricultural society that created the art and the megaliths are unknown.

The expansion of Bantu-speaking peoples had a major impact on what is now the CAR. There are different theories about exactly how the expansion took place, but no matter what the precise trajectory of Bantu-speakers was, they brought great changes to the region and the people they encountered. They moved gradually from west central Africa, across central, and into eastern and southern Africa in search of new lands to cultivate. The Bantu-language speakers did not eliminate the populations that they encountered. Certainly, some people moved to avoid the new arrivals, but many others tolerated or encouraged their new neighbors. Agricultural methods, languages, and cultures all adapted to the meetings of these different peoples.

With travelers from the Muslim-speaking world, the area became known to people outside of the region, but only to those who sought out information. There were travelers such as Leo Africanus, who believed that he had located the kingdom of Gaoga where slaves, Christians, cattle, and cavalrymen all could be found. It is possible that Africanus encountered a Christian monarchy or a cluster of small states in the eastern part of the country. Other travelers searched for the mythical kingdom of Prester John; the idea of finding this Christian hero of legend in the middle of Africa, and the glory that would come with it, inspired Europeans to try to find this man and his followers.

By the beginning of the seventeenth century, there were well-established Muslim states that touched upon the northern border of the Central African Republic. Parts of the territory were incorporated into different African kingdoms, including Kanem-Borno, Bagirmi, and Darfur. Through trade, Islam was introduced to Central Africa and people converted because of religious conviction, to follow the example of their families and neighbors, and to facilitate mercantile activities. These areas also prospered through slave trading.

Slave raiding was a severe problem in the northern section of the CAR. It left the northeastern part of the country with one of Africa's lowest population densities, as raiders seized slaves and others fled the area to avoid capture. The slave buyers were often noted as "Muslims" by European sources, but non–Muslim Africans were also complicit in the trade. Slave raiding created tremendous problems between different ethnic groups; riverine people were involved in this trade, and peoples of the interior still have animosities toward them that are driven by this activity. The movement of people in the trans-Saharan trade was a trickle until the middle of the seventeenth century, when the demand to the north and across the Atlantic drained Central Africa of its people. The slave raiders were at their most powerful in the late 1870s, when the upper Oubangui was under the control of the Egyptian sultan Rabah. As the power of the slave traders declined, another group came to present an equal menace to the Central African Republic.

COLONIAL HISTORY

France first came into contact with Central Africa off the coast of what is now Gabon in 1839, and from there, French imperialism spread. European nations competed with each other to control territory in Africa, and the fever rose in the 1880s. The colonial era brought the French to the area north of the Oubangui River. The results of the Berlin Conference of 1884–85 left the Oubangui-Chari and much of Central, West, and North Africa in the hands of France. Driven by competition, notions of national supremacy, and avarice, they competed with the Belgians and other European powers in Central Africa for territories and resources. Physically, the rivalry between the French and the Belgians was divided by the Oubangui River; the city of Bangui was founded in 1889 as a counterpoint to the city of Zongo across the river in the Congo Free State. The French established themselves in the area through military conquest and trade.

Africans opposed the presence of the French in the Oubangui-Chari, as they did across the continent. Resistance to colonial rule took on many forms, including work slowdowns, migrating, and armed resistance. Much of this resistance is absent from the historical record, mostly suppressed by administrators who did want any problems made public. From 1906 to 1909, the leader Baram-Bakié used modern weapons in an attempt to maintain his authority in the area between Bambari and the Oubangui River. In the mid-1920s, a Gbaya leader named Karnu led men in rebellion, guided by a dream that his supernatural powers would protect his fighters from French bullets; they fought for two years after his death from said projectiles. In Berbérati in 1954, Africans protested when the local administrator refused to arrest a Frenchman on whose property the bodies of two men, one of whom was employed by the Frenchman, were found. The European was found not guilty, but that was not the case of the more than 100 Gbaya who allegedly shouted anti-French slogans and sang anti-French songs.

Not all the Africans who encountered the colonizers fought against them, some became their allies. Africans assessed the value of working relationships with Europeans in terms of the advantages they could gain in the realms of retaining some autonomy, working against people with whom they had pre-existing conflicts, and improving their trade. The Yakoma and other riverine peoples were the first to be recruited into the service of the French as paddlers and military auxiliaries. These alliances were very important for the traders and government, and they would produce some of the elite who would assist the colonial administration, and, later, those who would take the reins of the newly independent Central African Republic.

A series of sporadic military campaigns gave France a more secure position in the colony, but it needed to find an effective way to rule it. In 1905, the administrative responsibility for the colony was in the hands of the governor who reported to the governor-general in Brazzaville, the capital of the French Congo. However, there were too few stations and administrators for effective control. To assure power in the colony, the government looked to an alternative form of governing.

The lack of personnel to direct the Oubangui-Chari was problematic, but the establishment of concession systems was the answer for the government. The French looked enviously at King Leopold's Congo Free State, which greatly abused labor to exploit rubber and ivory; they looked toward finding a system that would allow for the successful use of resources to generate money, but with little work on the part of the government. By 1899, more than half of the territory of the Oubangui-Chari was in the hands of 17 concession companies. These newly created ventures had almost free reign in exploiting the natural and human resources of the colony. The concessions were highly authoritarian and usually quite brutal. The Lobaye and Haute-Sangha regions were most affected by these companies, and the abuses led to revolts. Even French author André Gide's 1927 *Voyage au Congo*, which chronicled the abuses that took place in Boda in the Lobaye by a concession company where the local colonial administrator turned a blind eye toward the company, did not change conditions for workers. Concessions gave the colonial government approximately 15 percent of the profits, as well as paying a fixed annual sum. The concessions made a great deal of money, and the government was able to claim control of the territory and make a profit. It was a system that worked for all parties except the Africans.

By 1911, the French believed that the Oubangui-Chari was sufficiently "pacified" to turn the colony over from a military to a civilian administration, and the colonies of Chad, Moyen-Congo, and Gabon were joined together with the Oubangui-Chari as *Afrique Equatoriale Française,* or the AEF. The main function of the administration was to ensure the colony's economic success. The concession companies fulfilled part of this function, while the collection of head taxes and customs duties generated more revenue to support the administration and its infrastructure projects. These projects, using the coerced labor of Africans, were designed to be useful to the administration, not to those who actually constructed them. The Congo-Océan railway was built between Pointe Noire and Brazzaville in what was then the Moyen-Congo between 1921 and 1934. Far from their homes, men from the Oubangui-Chari were forced to work on this project that allowed transportation to bypass the portion of the Congo River controlled solely by Belgium. The railway created a link between the Oubangui and the Atlantic Ocean that would further the misery of Centrafricans because it made the export of crops, timber, and the like faster and less expensive, bolstering the demand for the goods that the indigenous peoples produced for someone else.

It was not just the policies of the French that reduced the number of Centrafricans, but the indirect results of their presence that had deadly effects as well. Diseases, notably sleeping sickness and smallpox, weakened the population. Although sleeping sickness was endemic before the arrival of Europeans, the settlement patterns they instituted exacerbated the situation. As African labor was channeled away from hunting and the production of food for home consumption, nutritional levels plummeted. Women had a harder time conceiving and the health of the children reflected that of their mothers, who had less and less nutritious food to eat. The death rate increased not so much as a result of European military technology, but rather from the combined impact of overwork, disease, and malnourishment.

Colonialism changed much about the Oubangui-Chari. There was the loss of African authority in politics, economics, and many other aspects of life. Even group and personal relationships changed. Elder males who had great control over society lost power as the new system offered different channels of accumulating wealth for young men. The introduction of cash cropping, especially of cotton, changed the ways that Africans farmed and fed their families, as well as who controlled resources. Work that had been done communally for the compensation of camaraderie, food, and drink was now requested by colonizers who paid for the labor. The cash proved to be necessary for paying the head tax, for example, and wage labor pecked away at the solidarity of communities.

Colonial rule in Africa reflected societal norms in Europe as far as women were concerned. Women in Europe in the late 1800s and early 1900s had few avenues for gaining wealth and little autonomy, as their status reflected that of the most important man in their lives. Before colonization, African women enjoyed freedoms, especially economic and political, that European women did not. When colonial rule was established, it reinforced the notion of male superiority, which erased many of the rights of women. An African man could change his status (very few women had the opportunity) by becoming "evolved." *Evolved* was a term used to designate an African who had received a French education and had moved toward the French cultural norms of wearing Western clothes, renouncing polygyny, and all other "backward" Africans traits or activities.

During the Second World War, the Oubangui-Chari joined the other colonies of the AEF in supporting General Charles de Gaulle, who established and led Free France in opposition to the Vichy government. The colony's export of cotton and diamonds was at its peak during the war. The colony provided support for Free France in goods and in its young men who served, along with men from the rest of the AEF, in the Free French military. Veterans believed that they and their people should be compensated for their efforts that led to a French victory.

After the war, reforms were put in place that gradually, but not greatly, changed the French colonial system. In 1946, the inhabitants of French Africa gained the status of citizen, a status that very few had enjoyed before then, and there was a liberalization of African participation in government. Barthélemy Boganda, a very charismatic Catholic priest, was the first representative for the Oubangui-Chari from the French National Assembly. That year also saw the establishment of local assemblies in the colonies. In 1949, Boganda created the colony's first political party, the Movement for the Social Evolution of Black Africa (MESAN) that called for the colony's independence. The Oubangui-Chari was slowly moving toward political emancipation.

In 1956, legislation from France eliminated certain voting inequalities and created some organs of self-government. A French constitutional referendum dissolved the AEF in 1958 and on December first of that year, the Assembly announced the birth of the Central African Republic. The colony's assembly had control over domestic issues, but finances and the military were still a part of the hand France played. At the time of independence, the CAR and other new countries of the AEF signed bilateral agreements with France concerning aid, education, and cultural cooperation. France was no longer the colonial ruler, but it still had an enormous amount of influence in the fledgling nation.

POSTCOLONIAL HISTORY

The postcolonial political history of the CAR is characterized by authoritarian rule and people's responses to it. The heady days that followed independence would be dogged by inept and corrupt rule, as well as an increasingly desperate populace. Barthélemy Boganda retained his importance in the direction of the CAR, at the head of the new government until his death in a mysterious plane crash in March 1959. Boganda's successor was his nephew, David Dacko, who was handpicked by the French for the position. It was under his administration that the Central African Republic declared its independence on August 13, 1960. The Central African Republic is a veritable republic, with 14 administrative divisions, two economic prefectures (Gribingui and Sangha), and one commune (Bangui). There is a president, a unicameral national assembly, and a judicial branch. Its legal system is based upon French law. In the rural areas, traditional chiefs hold power and work in conjunction with the national government. In the countryside, traditional law is still applied.

Dacko's repressive and dictatorial rule came to an abrupt end on January 1, 1966, when Colonel Jean-Bédel Bokassa, Dacko's cousin and Boganda's nephew, led an almost bloodless coup d'état and took control of the government. The political situation in the country did not improve. Bokassa abolished the constitution of 1959, dissolved the National Assembly, and issued a decree that placed all the legislative and executive powers in the hands of the president. These moves foreshadowed events to come, as Bokassa's rule became increasing authoritarian and despotic, culminating in his self-coronation as the Emperor of the Central African Empire. The ceremony was similar to that of Napoléon Bonaparte more than a century and a half earlier. France covered much of the $20-million bill for the affair that was equal to the entirety of the country's national GDP. The regime was guilty of numerous human rights abuses to which observers called attention, but the government did not feel the need to respond, in part because France was supportive of Bokassa as the head of state. When Bokassa needed funds, he received them from French President Valéry Giscard d'Estaing. The two rulers were close; d'Estaing was a big-game hunting enthusiast, and French companies, including his father's, had significant interest in the diamonds, uranium, and ivory of the CAR.

Despite the personal relationships, France decided that it was politically expedient to switch sides after riots in Bangui, the murder of 50 to 200 schoolchildren, and Bokassa's trip to Libya in search of aid. The world was well aware of the regime's excesses and the former colonial ruler's ignoring of the problem. France then did an about-face, backing former President Dacko in his coup on September 20–21, 1979, even flying Dacko into the country. Bokassa was found guilty of murder in 1987 and sentenced to death. The sentence was commuted to life, but he was released from prison in 1993, and he died in 1996.

Dacko wanted economic and political reforms, but they never came to fruition, leading to a bloodless coup by General André Kolingba in 1981. Kolingba led the country as a military ruler until 1985, when he dissolved the Military Committee for National Recovery and put into place a new cabinet that had more civilian participation, signaling political reforms and democratization. A new political party appeared in 1986 when the *Rassemblement Démocratique Centrafrican* (African Democratic Rally) appeared, along with a new constitution. Kolingba then became the constitutional president in November 1986. Under increasing pressure to put more reforms in place, Kolingba, in 1991, announced the creation of a national commission charged with rewriting the constitution and creating a multiparty system. When elections were held in 1992, they were canceled because of severe logistical difficulties and other irregularities. Ange-Félix Patassé won a victory in the second round of these elections, and he was elected to an additional six-year term in September 1999.

The CAR faced grave problems and different segments of the population called for change. The government was in arrears with the salaries of its bureaucrats, working people desired better treatment, and the members of the military believed that the armed forces applied unequal treatment to different ethic groups. The last complaint led to three coup attempts by three different officers of three different ethnic groups in 1996 and 1997; looting and destruction of property accompanied these attempted changes of government. Unrest and the coups d'état created a charge among ethnic groups, and people began participating in and thinking about politics through the lens of ethnicity. France came to the assistance of Patassé's government, and an African peacekeeping force occupied the capital until 1998, when a United Nations peacekeeping group replaced it.

The economic woes of the country, including mismanagement and energy crises, continued to plague the Patassé government through the year 2000. The U.N. peacekeeping forces pulled out in March, making the situation less stable and ripe for the May 2001 coup attempt by the military, led by former president Kolingba. After several days of heavy fighting, the troops loyal to the Patassé government, with the help of a small number of troops from Libya and the Democratic Republic of the Congo, ended the putsch.

Yet the political strife continued. In November 2001, there was limited fighting between members of Patassé's presidential security unit and soldiers who were defending the recently fired chief of staff of the armed forces, François Bozizé, who had fled to neighboring Chad. This resulted in some border skirmishes between the two countries in the middle of the next year. Bozizé continued to pressure the Patassé government by gaining control of areas in the north and the south of the country. While people were fleeing from their homes and the marauding forces from the Democratic Republic of the Congo who crossed into the CAR, Bozizé finally toppled the Patassé regime in March 2003. Patassé was unpopular, and the country waited to see in what direction the new leader would take it.

In October 2003, Bozizé organized national reconciliation talks whose aim was to put an end to the uprisings and rebellions that beleaguered the country, and especially Bangui, for years. In December 2004, a new constitution was approved in a referendum. Riding the wave of popular participation in government, on May 8, 2005, Bozizé won a run-off election for the presidency and began his term as a civilian leader. In the months before the final presidential elections, people complained that government soldiers harassed those who did not support the sitting president, but the elections were deemed to be free and fair by observers. President Bozizé has called for a conference for national reconciliation, but hopes for national unity have recently been challenged by disturbances in the north and calls for strikes by government workers whose pay is deeply in arrears.

EDUCATION

Educating youngsters is the best hope for the future of the Central African Republic. Education has changed from the traditional to the colonial and to the postcolonial. There are significant differences between the first and the last two, because of the function of education in each of these systems. Before the arrival of Europeans, Centrafricans had educational systems in place. The goal of these organizations was to create young men and women who would be fully integrated and functioning members of their societies. These were not formal schools but were of great importance, as they included transmitting general knowledge, acculturation, and creating a sense of community. This is discussed more fully in Chapter Seven.

Under French rule, the main point of education was to create Christian Africans. The missions had a virtual monopoly on education, and the instructors were European. As more Centrafricans were formally educated, they wanted also to be teachers. The few Centrafrican teachers complained of the favoritism that Europeans enjoyed, especially their higher salaries. A French law enacted in June 1950 equalized the salaries of European and African teachers who held the same diplomas in state schools. As French rule continued to wane, the colonial government sought ways to make mental bonds between France and the colonies. Education was one method that the government employed. It created new schools, witnessed the usage of the same curricula as the metropole, prepared teaching materials, and oversaw a colonial budget that had 19.3 percent of its operating funds devoted to education.

France did not want to produce an intelligentsia that might challenge colonial rule, and it achieved its goal. After independence, there were only a handful of Centrafrican high school graduates, and France retained a great deal of influence, especially at the secondary level. Africans had replaced most French teachers at the primary level, but France continued to send many secondary teachers to its former colony. To this day, many expatriates teach in the CAR at the secondary level. In 1962, the government of the CAR chose to unify the state and private schools into one system, and all children were welcome to attend both state and religious schools. The church schools offered religious instruction after school hours. This system united Catholic, Protestant, and secular education under the same umbrella.

Centrafricans did not suffer from a lack of ability, but a lack of opportunity. In an effort to redress this problem, the University of Bangui opened its doors in 1970. In the first year, classes were given in the fields of law and economics; the sciences and letters started in the following year. The Ecole Normale Supérieure (Teacher Training Institute), as well as an institute for mines, geology, and agronomy began in 1971. This university opened without French financial support, but funds and personnel came from the former Soviet Union for the sciences and from Romania for geology and mines. In 1971, aid and personnel were sent from France. The current enrollment is around 3,000 students. Striking lecturers agreed in August 2005 to return to the classroom. They, too, were asking for the long overdue payment of their salaries.

There are many issues to take into account when looking at school attendance and the students' outcomes. Many of the schools are overcrowded and in poor condition. Students need to buy uniforms, school supplies, and pay school fees. Primary school education in the CAR is compulsory, yet many children, up to 75 percent of those who are eligible, do not attend. Approximately 10 percent of secondary school age children are enrolled. The rates of enrollment decline rapidly for females, who are most likely to attend only primary school. At the end of the twentieth century, the level of masculinity in primary schools was 148 percent, in secondary schools 195 percent, and at the tertiary level, it was 550 percent. Women have much higher rates of illiteracy than men.

The future of the Central African Republic will depend on the education of its young people, and the ability of the country to provide jobs that interest them and have sufficient financial compensation. Many Centrafricans leave the country for higher education, and a high percentage of these people choose to work outside the country, most often in France, where they can find jobs that meet their needs and expectations. The country has the natural and human resources to greatly improve its situation. The challenges are finding leadership to steer the course, securing effectively managed resources to allow for economic growth while sustaining the natural environment, having the autonomy to make the best decisions for the country, and finding the patience to wait for changes that will certainly need time to occur.

2

Religion and Worldview

RELIGION AND WORLDVIEW are very important to the ways that Centrafricans interpret the past, understand the present, and envision the future. Religion and worldview inform people about how they should interact with family, friends, neighbors, strangers, and the world around them. Although religious ceremonies are very important and attract a great deal of attention and attendance, religion and worldview permeate all aspects of daily life.

Religion is a system of beliefs, myths, and rites that develops over time and gives self-definition to individuals and groups; it helps humans to cope with the difficult challenges that life poses such as poverty, injustice, illness, suffering, and death. Religious personnel are often consulted when people have questions about philosophical difficulties as well as problems with family relationships, community issues, or other parts of life that do not neatly fall into the category of issues of faith. The respect that Centrafricans have for religion and its representatives gives these men and women revered places in society. Religion binds people together as they understand the same principles and enjoy the same moral codes. That they worship and perform rituals together helps to strengthen the bonds of the community.

Religion is not static; it is reinterpreted as time passes, and a person may find that there is another religion that suits him or her better at one time than another. In the CAR, that is often Islam or Christianity. Conversion does not imply a complete severance from the former religious and ethnic community; it is more often a widening of one's opportunities and circle of contacts. The Central African Republic is a physical crossroads that led it to be an intersection of different faiths as well. Both Islam and Christianity are very aggressive in their proselytizing efforts, and the religious map of the CAR has been drawn and redrawn. These two world religions are trying to gain converts, but they are not in the kind of competition that is found in some other African nations, and it certainly has not reached the level of what happens in Nigeria, where religious violence between Christians and Muslims is endemic and ongoing.

Many people adhere to traditional systems of religious thought while others have converted. For the vast majority of the converts, the old ways are not completely forgotten, and ideas from indigenous religions continue to influence Muslims and Christians to this day. Even with the advent of Western knowledge and using science to explain the world, people still believe the ancient wisdom. For example, a couple that wants to have a child may well know the modern scientific principles concerning conception, but the pair will not neglect to make an offering to their ancestors at this important time.

People who practice indigenous religions constitute 35 percent of the population, Christians are 50 percent of the populations with their numbers being split evenly between Catholics and Protestants, and the remaining 15 percent are Muslim. The government allows religious organizations and missionary groups to freely proselytize, actively participate in their faiths, and construct places of worship. Especially after independence, churches flourished as people became liberated from the political and theological control of the French.

An understanding of religion is transmitted in many ways. The practice of ceremonies and rites always recalls the group's religious principles and the attachment to ancestors. The art of storytelling also assists in the dissemination of religious knowledge. Creation stories and tales of the adventures of the gods provide not only entertainment, but education as well. Everyday life is an opportunity to learn of the sacred ideas, and the period of initiation training provides more in-depth knowledge. The gods and the ancestors are referenced so many times and in so many ways that it is impossible to ignore religion.

The importance of religion in the CAR cannot be overstated. No matter what the religion, people participate in services, rites, and ceremonies, not as a debt to be paid or an obligation, but as something that they look forward to with eager anticipation. Although public schools do not teach religion, there is no aversion to students' demonstration of their faiths in their places of education. There is no open hostility toward organized religion, and many of the national holidays are based on the calendar of the Catholic Church. Tensions between people of different religious faiths are few and far between;

usually, they are ethnic or economic problems. People generally believe that it is more important to have a faith than to have none; this helps them to be tolerant of people's different beliefs, even if they do not wish to follow these ideas themselves.

WORLDVIEW

Worldview refers to the general perspective with which one sees the world, a body of ideas about life and the universe that is held by an individual or by a group. In a way, worldview is a pair of corrective eyeglasses that adjusts the view of all that the wearer sees. Religion is the dominant factor in the worldview of Centrafricans, especially for Christians and Muslims. A shared worldview means that one's community interprets events in the same way, and it is comforting to people that they fundamentally agree on the roots of problems and the solutions to them.

Ancient understandings relate that deities and spirits are responsible for what happens to people, and this is a somewhat distanced way of looking at the world. But this should in no way be understood as people believing that they have no agency in their lives. To the contrary, people know that their actions have a definite impact on the events of their lives, but often the realization is through the intermediary of these nonearthly beings. People make sacrifices to the deities and to their ancestors for the express purpose of pleasing these spirits and having them take care of people's needs lest the opposite happen.

Ancestors, deities, and other spirits are otherworldly, while witchcraft, sorcery, and magic—both good and bad—originate in humans. Other people's evil actions through witchcraft can have an impact on their fellow humans. The belief in witchcraft is so strong that most communities have a "witch doctor" whose role it is to minister to the ill, especially those who have been affected by bad magic. Witch doctors are also herbalists, skilled practitioners of holistic medicine who find natural remedies for afflictions such as headaches that people believe can be caused by magic.

Especially for those who do not have formal education and do not have access to modern science, worldview can explain natural phenomena. For example, the daily rising of the sun in the east and its setting in the west is not understood as the rotation of the earth, but as a system mandated by an all-powerful god; crops grow because the god of the land has visited abundant rain on the area, not because of meteorological conditions; and an explosion happens at a factory because of witchcraft, not because of faulty electrical wiring. There are accidents that can be avoided or situations that can be encouraged through human agency.

Religion and worldview are major components of cultures. Centrafrican faiths are specific to localities and ethnic groups. Although the guiding body of ideas is commonly held, at the same time, there is flexibility in practice. As a construct, religion adapts the way other socially created institutions do. Families may alter modes of worship to suit their needs. Change also occurs when spirit mediums bring messages from the other world to their community. As more people receive formal educations, travel to different places, and encounter other religions, they find new answers to their questions. The responsibility for unfortunate events such as a lack of fecundity will not always be attributed to angry ancestors and deities that ignore prayers, but other reasons will emerge.

Some other changes in worldview have impacts that go beyond the individual, affecting the group at large. One commonly held principle is that the community is more important than the individual. This is not to say that individuals are not important, but that their significance lies in their belonging to a corporate entity.

One should act in ways that are acceptable and good for the community as a whole. The elderly and their role in society are a good demonstration of the Centrafrican worldview. To be old in the Central African Republic is not merely to have survived for many years, but it is, in a sense, to have arrived. Because of their age, people believe that the elderly are close to the venerated ancestors. Old people are revered for their wisdom and consulted when there are disagreements, and people listen to their stories with rapt attention. They live as honored members of their society. Decisions are often made by elders based on what they believe is best for the family as a group, which almost always means maintaining the status quo.

An adage states: "You take care of your children when they cut their teeth, and your children take care of you when you lose yours." Today this principle is being challenged as people leave their villages and move to cities in search of better lives. They start their own families in the city and set down roots there, leaving the elderly and their ancestral lands behind. Certainly, people keep in touch and the city-dwellers return to the village (usually laden with goods), but the intense and intimate family ties are stretched over long distances.

INDIGENOUS RELIGIONS AND WORLDVIEW

Indigenous religions explain how the world came to be, the relationship between humans and their environment, the interactions between humans, and the rules by which people live. There is a creator god who usually is distant and removed from the activities of human beings, thus the lesser deities and the ancestors play a larger role in the lives of human beings. Both forbearers and the gods are creatures whose physical forms resemble those of people. Closer still to ordinary people are the kings and chiefs who use religion or divine right to legitimize their rule. In the CAR, there are many aspects of indigenous religion that cross ethnic lines, yet each group has certain specific beliefs, customs, and rituals.

In the past, Westerners tended to denigrate indigenous religions, calling them "superstition." Even those who recognized these religions as faiths found them severely lacking in structure or morally corrupt. Westerners looked at charms (and called them "fetishes") as evidence of people's primitive nature. Christianity told the explorers, colonial officials, and missionaries that "idolatry" was wrong, but these items did more than just rouse Christian indignation. Because they looked so different and were used in ways that Westerners did not understand (in part because they made no effort to), they found these charms to be not only foreign but also menacing. The songs that accompanied religious rituals sounded distinctly unmusical to their ears, and the dances that attended them appeared to be very lewd at the least and satanic at the worst. Westerners did not understand that the systems of thought that they encountered here were every bit as complex as those of their own religions. These ideas about the inferiority of African religions have diminished, but they still exist to this day.

There is much that these religions have in common with each other: the belief in a supreme being, the veneration of ancestors, the belief in lesser deities and spirits, the desire to predict the future, and the need to enforce a social code. Some of the differences are great, others quite minor. For years, Westerners claimed that the cultures of the CAR were homogeneous, but investigating their religions advises against this claim.

Supreme Being

The supreme being or creator-god created the earth, humankind, plants, animals, and all that exists on the earth. The usual configuration has a supreme being who lives in the sky and is all-powerful. The supreme being has many names in the Central African Republic. The supreme being of the Biaka is Komba, who has some of the same foibles that humans have; for the Zandé, it is Mboli, whose name is often invoked. The supreme being of the Banda (Yilingu) and the Manza (Galé) is a distant god who is uninterested in the lives of the people he created, yet he is still the ultimate master of their destiny and their lives. He has the power to reveal himself at any time, but he chooses not to do so. In return, people do not address him with prayers. They turn instead to the lesser gods and their ancestors.

Ancestors

The family is the core unit of African life, and for this reason, ancestors play a vital role in the life of the Centrafrican. The cycle of life is not one that begins with birth and ends with death; death is a part of the continuum of life, and the ancestors are a natural part of life as well. The ancestors are the family members who have died, from the most recently deceased to the long dead. The ancestors are a part of the family, even though they are not physically present on earth. They need to be treated like other relatives: They must be remembered and included in family life. In death, they are still very much like living people in that they respond to the way they are treated. If properly looked after, an ancestor is an ally; if neglected, an ancestor can become an adversarial force. Thus, people make offerings of food, drink, prayer, and other things that the deceased enjoyed in life (such as tobacco) to placate and please their forbearers and try to curry their good favor.

Centrafricans are very mindful of their ancestors and see the relationship between the living and the dead as one of reciprocity, in much the same manner that give-and-take guides the way that people interact with each other on earth. The feeling about ancestors is appreciation mixed with fear. People are concerned that neglecting their ancestors will result in the deceased retracting support for their living relatives or even visiting malevolence upon them. People also fear that ancestors who are upset by the transgression might expose their clandestine foibles. For example, if a birth is taking too long or it is difficult, people believe that the ancestors are showing their displeasure because the mother broke a taboo or had an adulterous relationship. It is not all negative—people also venerate their ancestors for what they accomplished while they were alive.

The land of the ancestors exists in a continuum with the land of the living. Their kingdom is the mirror image of the land of the living, often separated by a body of water. It is truly a parallel universe, in which the order that exists on earth is replicated in the afterworld; even the tasks that people perform are the same in both places. The Manza believe that if a woman dies before her husband, she waits for him with her own clans and joins him and his clan upon his death, similar to what happens to a woman when she marries on earth and goes to join her husband and his people. The Manza also believe that the afterworld is egalitarian insofar as, once a person has died, there is no distinction between those who have been good and those who have not while on earth. This is because the person could have been acting badly because he or she was under the influence of a spirit. The person's soul is given clemency in the land of the ancestors.

The ancestors are the true owners of the land, and because the deceased were buried close to their homes, the association between the ancestors and the land is especially close. That the land belongs to those who passed away reinforces the idea of fecundity both in the family in creating children and in the land giving food. Offerings are made to the forbearers, often the first of the harvested food, asking for continual bountiful harvests. In general, the first of the harvest, fishing expedition, and the hunt are offered to these ancestor spirits. It is the bounty in terms of food and children for which people most often ask for the ancestors' help. This is done at the family altar. No matter what the outcome of their supplications, the ancestors are always winners. If the harvest is bountiful, the ancestors are thanked with their portion of the bounty for their assistance. If the harvest is poor, the next year the family tries to offer even more to make up for any offense they might have made.

Spirits

As with many aspects of Centrafrican culture, there are a number of similarities and variations in beliefs about spirits. Spirits are part of the worldview of all those who follow indigenous religions. Variations occur concerning the physical location of the spirits and the degree of influence that they have on people's lives. This latter is particularly true when it comes to individuals' thinking. Despite a lack of agreement about all facets of spirits, Centrafricans will agree that the spirits are ubiquitous and powerful.

Spirits can affect people as they sleep. Sleep is considered to be a state of half-death. When a person sleeps, his or her soul leaves the body and traverses the countryside. When the soul returns, the person awakes. People's dreams are the souls' adventures, otherwise the human is completely unaware of the soul's journeys. The soul can encounter a disembodied spirit on its travels who may either injure or kill it; this explains how people die in their sleep. Because people are in a state of semimorbidity, spirits take advantage of their lack of awareness. Many spirits are mischievous or malicious.

Spirits of the ancestors are called *mânes*. Ngandro to the Banda, Gbozon to the Manza and the Gbaya, they are highly feared creatures. These are the disembodied souls of the deceased that wander the countryside. They live in trees, the mountains, water, and termite mounds. They still have a corporal appearance, but their looks change with their deaths. The Banda believe that the *mânes* have white skin. According to the Manza, the *mânes* are covered with long white hair that tumbles from their small, toothless heads. Some of the *mânes* have eyes on their chests, others on the forehead or the shoulders.

They have quacking voices. Some only have one foot, and others are missing some other body part, such as a head.

The *mânes* have wide-ranging influence. Because these creatures like to wander about at night, people wear charms to protect themselves from meeting a *mâne,* which is an indicator that death is near. A *mâne* may appear to a person while he or she is sleeping, claiming offerings and causing nightmares, so the charm is needed to keep these spirits away from the person's dreams. A person asks the *mânes* about the appropriate placement of a new house, but tries desperately to keep them out once it is built. These ancestor spirits also play a role in initiation rites. In these organizations, the elders represent the role of the *mânes.* They make terrible noises, wear elaborate costumes that hide their identities, dance aggressively, and even manhandle the boys, trying and succeeding in striking fear into the young initiates. As soon-to-be ancestors, they are doing their best to ensure that they too will be venerated.

The spirit of the land is very important, especially for agriculturalists. Known as Seto or Gala-wan-To to the Manza, Wanto to the Gbaya, and Téré to the Banda, this spirit plays a great role in legends and stories. The Manza Seto is their ancestor who showed them how to farm, build their houses, and, after stealing them from other beings, gave them fire and water. Seto is a central character in their tales; he loves women, and he is a boastful trickster who loves playing jokes, but he never does so with malice. Seto is married to Nambala and has male and female children. People make sacrifices to him and ask Seto to protect the fields and make them prosperous. Seto's charm is a forked branch that is stuck in the ground, topped with a conical straw roof under which a *marmite* is placed. The charm is put in place at night so that Seto can come and advise the *indigene* while he sleeps and give him the direction that he needs to accomplish what he wants. Offerings to Seto are made early in the morning. Singing and dancing accompany the ceremonies when the Manza invoke Seto in the hopes of receiving rain.

Although some spirits can bring good, most do the opposite. For example, the Zandé, believe in *mamiwata,* water spirits that lure bathers and water collectors with their calls. They live with their families near water sources or in underwater towns, wear clothes, and, in their modern incarnations, have cars. The *mamiwata* are deceptive in part because they resemble humans, and they look like Europeans because they have light-colored skin. The *mamiwata* are intelligent, indeed literate, and are quite wealthy, although the source of their affluence is obscure. These water spirits sometimes take human spouses who have prophetic and healing powers. Their children are albinos, adding to the real-life "otherness" of those who have this ailment and their parents. These spirits have the ability to enter into the dreams of humans and can cause women, among other things, to lose their fecundity, and they generally make people go insane. These water spirits are often compared to mermaids.

The Banda version of the water spirit (Badigi) is a man with white skin who haunts rivers and streams, and who wanders alone in villages at night. He is mischievous, capsizing canoes. When he spots the home of a woman who sleeps alone, he slips inside, lies next to and then has sex with her. His children are albinos as well. Badigi is considered to be responsible for diarrhea and dysentery, two diseases that are particularly difficult for children. Things that concern water and the color white are attributed to Badigi, and offerings made to him include eggs, white hens, and *manioc* (cassava).

For the Manza, a water spirit is Ndiba who is very long, fat, black snake. He swallows his victims, which explains why drowning victims are often hard to find. Ndiba's wife, Kaya, who is a large crab, has a role in drownings. When a person falls into the water, Ndiba takes the person to his wife. Kaya interrogates the unlucky person, asking where he or she is going, from where he or she is coming, ethnicity, and names of both the father and the mother. When Kaya is done, she either sets the person free or kills him or her by plunging her two pinchers in the person's nose. That is why when a drowned person is found with blood coming from the nose, the death is attributed to Kaya.

All groups have spirits that make sense for their ethnic groups and religions. That the same spirit exists across cultures is a testament to the ubiquity of water and the fear that it inspires. Because it is a water spirit, its location does not vary, but there are variations in the shape, color, and precise actions. But across the board, its evil intentions are the same.

Witchcraft

Witchcraft is not a part of religion per se, rather it is a part of Centrafricans' worldview. Witchcraft and sorcery in the context of the CAR and the rest of Africa is different than it is in Western countries. Instead of being theologically defined as an aspect of the battle of good versus evil, witchcraft is anything that challenges the norms of the society and the way people in it should behave. This social fabric is tightly and intricately woven; thus; many actions can be interpreted as witchcraft. The African ethos dictates that the community is more important than the individual; thus, actions based on personal gain fall into the category of witchcraft. Although one gains status through the accumulation of wealth, not sharing is one of the actions that can result in an accusation of witchcraft. If a person who has food lets another person go hungry, witchcraft is noted as the source of the problem. If a person betrays his or her group to an outsider, the cause is the same. If two people are having a protracted disagreement and one falls ill, witchcraft is the culprit.

Witchcraft is the explanation for unfortunate events in people's lives. When the spirits cause unhappiness, the action is coming from the other world; when witches cause the problem, the origin of the difficulty is earthly. Spells can be cast upon an individual, or a collectivity such as a family, or an entire village. The death of a young person is considered to be the result of witchcraft because young people are not supposed to die. If a woman slips in the *manioc*-soaking pond and injures herself, that too is the result of witchcraft. People know very well that slippery surfaces can cause people to fall, but the answer to the question of why it happened to that person in that place is witchcraft. In a universe where events are ordered, there have to be reasons for all things that happen. What someone in the West understands as an accident, the Centrafrican understands as witchcraft.

The Zandé believe that witchcraft is caused by a specific substance in the body. This substance can be found in the bodies of both men and women. It is thought to be a black matter secreted by an unknown abdominal organ. The Zandé also believe that witchcraft has a genetic component and that a parent of the same gender can pass the trait on to a son or daughter. Older people are believed to be more powerful witches than younger ones because the witchcraft substance grows as the body increases in size.

Although there are genetic and biological explanations for witchcraft, there is also a component of human agency, as witches choose to take the actions that they do. Witchcraft is a deliberate action taken against someone. It finds its origins in jealousy, vengeance, a dispute with a neighbor, unpaid debt, family affairs, problems with inheritance, and other issues that arouse social tension. Witchcraft cannot be done in an unthinking way, as there are rituals to be observed in casting spells. For example, for the Banda, a wizard puts special twigs and charms into a bag and makes oscillating movements under the bag while simultaneously saying the name of his enemy. Clearly this spell cannot be cast by accident. Death by witchcraft is reputed to be long and slow. Religious leaders, spirit mediums, and *binza* (diviners and musicians who use trancelike dances to locate and expose witches) share the same goal of seeking to maintain the proper social order.

Practicing witchcraft is a criminal offense under the laws of the Central African Republic. It is extremely rare for someone to be prosecuted solely for witchcraft, however. Most of those who are charged with the offense are charged simultaneously with another crime, often murder. Some people make a distinction between witchcraft and sorcery, but both have malevolence as their desired outcome, thus deciding between the two terms is not important. Witches are usually dealt with within their communities, often harassed by their neighbors, and, in more extreme cases, they are surrounded and beaten by a crowd or even killed. Witchcraft is ubiquitous and can be deadly, both for the bewitched and the bewitcher.

Charms

Charms, amulets, or *gris-gris* play an important role in the ways in which people try to mediate the potential for harm and encourage benevolence. Charms are frequently called *fetishes*. These items have specific targets: Their use is always deliberate, and charms are made in a ritualized way. One can use a charm to bring good luck or to keep witches away; they can be used to try to bring a victory to a football team for an important match. At certain specific times in people's lives (such as after birth), people would wear a new *gris-gris,* but charms could be acquired for nonspecific reasons as well. Herbs and other objects that are known to have magical powers are combined by a "medicine man" to achieve the desired goal. Amulets come in many forms, the most common is a leather pouch stuffed with the material to affect the desired outcome. These are commonly worn around the neck, much like a cross is by Christians.

Charms can also be larger objects for group use. The charm for the *mânes* is of the utmost importance. People build installations for the disembodied spirits so that they can rest without having to go into the houses of humans and cause trouble there. The offerings to the *mânes* are pieces of the heart and the liver of animals killed on the hunt; the ancestor spirits of the Manza do not have teeth, so they must receive these choice morsels that they suck while appreciating the efforts and attentions of their living relatives.

Divination and Prophecy

Divination is trying to understand the present and predict the future. Diviners can find the source of ill will, envy, and other socially unacceptable behaviors and receive guidance in dealing with them. The process of divining changes according to ethnic group and in relation to what question the diviner poses. Similarly, prophets are men and women who receive supernatural messages that they must transfer to their group. Often the message comes through a dream. Methods of divination exist in indigenous religions and have made their way into Christianity and Islam as well.

The best-known form of oracle comes from the Zandé—the poison oracle, *benge. Benge* is also known as the poison ordeal, which is considered to be the most accurate and powerful oracle. The poison ordeal is practiced among other ethnic groups, but the Zandé have received the most attention for their practice. This test is reserved for the most serious of cases, such as adultery and death of a family member. The powerful ceremony does not take place in the village, but in an untamed area outside it. Those who attend it are those who are directly involved in the case as well as some witnesses. The person who gives the poison to the chicken is a member of the community who knows and respects its taboos. Poison is administered to the chicken, and the supplicant asks a question of the poison about the offense. If the chicken dies, suspicions are confirmed, but if the chicken does not die, it may allay fears. The poison ordeal is administered a second time to another chicken to confirm the results of the first test.

There are many other types of oracles. The Zandé also use a termite oracle when there are questions about the use of witchcraft in the community. Two branches from two different types of trees are thrust into a termite mound while a question is posed and the branch that the termites choose to eat reveals the answer. The friction oracle, *iwa,* is the most common, because it is less expensive than the poison oracle and less time-consuming than the termite oracle, and it is portable. Friction boards are made by their users and are often quite beautiful. It is assumed that a Zandé man will always be in the company of his *iwa* if the need for advice should arise. Made from wood, a friction board is divided into a female part and a male part. After it is carved, the board is prepared by scarring it with juices from plants and otherwise marring the surface of the wood. The supplicant must adhere to all of society's rules before posing a question. The rubbing instrument is applied and its movement, toward one of the two gendered sides or its simple wandering, answers the question. This oracle is also performed twice to verify the accuracy of the results. No matter what the question, but especially if the question tries to elicit an answer about current problems, witchcraft is often a part of the oracle's answer.

Prophets are also important figures in indigenous religions. The prophet is a person who has a strong connection to the other world. The prophet, who receives a message in a dream, is obligated to transmit the message to the group. The prophet's message could cause the community to take a new course of action, such as moving from one place to another or even making shifts in religious practices. Many prophets are women, giving them a level of power and authority otherwise impossible to attain in their societies. Men were powerful as political (chiefs) and family (father) heads, and prophecy gave women an opportunity to be the same in the realm of religion. Because indigenous religions as well as Christianity were used in the fight against colonialism, this gave women power that carried over into the realms that men usually controlled.

In indigenous religions, the natural order of things is what is considered to be good or desirable: security, good health, fecundity, stability, peace of mind, and harmony. These faiths want their adherents to attain these goals. Some Centrafricans find that their needs were not being met through indigenous religions and turned to the two new, imported religions to answer their questions and improve their lives. The father of a family that has suffered through continuous years of poor harvests despite numerous sacrifices to the gods and ancestors will look for a different way to improve his situation and may find that Islam or Christianity is what makes the most sense. But these family members are not likely to sever their ties to the religion of their ancestors; the ancient religions continue to have an impact on those who convert. Missionaries and other church personnel from the West often bemoan the persistence of aspects of traditional religion in the lives of Christians. For example, people will spill the first couple of drops of a drink, especially an alcoholic beverage, on the ground as a libation for the ancestors; Christians do this as well as those who follow the ancient ways. Some people believe that Islam is more accommodating to indigenous religions than Christianity.

ISLAM

Islam made its way into the Central African Republic later than it did in many other places in Africa, filtering into the area from the north and encountering preexisting indigenous religions and the people who practiced them at the beginning of the seventeenth century. One of the immediate challenges that Islam faced in gaining converts was its history in the area and the memory of Muslims as slave raiders who preyed upon the non-Muslim population, taking people captive, forcing migrations and decreasing the population. Not all contacts were so pernicious and included trading for needed and desired items. Slowly Islam came to be seen as not only an acceptable but also a desirable religion and perhaps, the best vehicle to material prosperity.

Some people argue that Islam is more suitable for Africans than Christianity because it is more in line with long-held values, and what they point to most often is that Islam allows polygyny, which is practiced in Centrafrican society. Others claim that it is an indigenous religion, even though this clearly is not true. Still others claim that it is culturally more appropriate, in part because it did not come to the CAR in the same way as Christianity did with European colonizers. Yet one cannot overlook Islam's introduction by people who brought the religion while taking human slaves. Islam now has a solid place in the CAR, mostly in the northern section of the country and in the city of Bangui.

To be a Muslim, one must accept and profess the five pillars of Islam. The first is that there is no god but God (*Allah*) and Mohammed is his prophet. This is a very simple and powerful declaration of faith. The second is that one prays five times per day in the direction of the holy city of Mecca. A *muezzin* calls the faithful to prayer based upon the position of the sun in the sky. The third is fasting for the holy month of Ramadan. People do not have sex, eat, drink, or even swallow their saliva in daylight hours during this month of abstinence and purification. The fourth is almsgiving. Giving to the less fortunate is very important as a way of spreading wealth through the community and doing it under the rules of Islam allows both the donor and the recipient to feel that participating in this action is a part of the natural and ordained order of things. The final pillar is to make the *hadj* or the pilgrimage to Mecca that all Muslims who have the means and the health must do. The *hadj* is the ultimate earthly voyage for Muslims, and people save money for years to make the trip. Some travel by airplane, others go overland, depending on their time and their means. The *hadj* is a journey of spiritual cleansing and rejuvenation. It is also a time for fellowship with co-religionists from across the globe. The tenets of Islam are very simple to follow and offer no offense to traditional values.

People convert to Islam (and to Christianity as well) because the other religion is seen as a way to improve their lives. Islam is understood as a religion of richness. Richness is primarily material, but there is a spiritual component in the idea as well. In a country where so many people live in great poverty, it is not necessarily materialism that drives the desire for more financial resources, but a desire for the safety and security of the family as well as the ability to see a better future for one's children. Muslims are known for being able to accommodate high requests for bridewealth. There is no idea in Islam about the separation of church and state, nor is there the idea that there is something inherently wrong in the accumulation of wealth. Imams preach morals and commerce. Almsgiving is also a tangible reminder of what commerce has brought to these men. The tradition of almsgiving, which also exists in Christianity, coincides with the traditional value of generosity. Islam is a universalist religion, it accepts that there is a spiritual world and sanctions beliefs in mystical powers.

Centrafricans convert because of sincere religious desire and for social and economic reasons. Muslims actively proselytize and when friends and family are Muslim, it is easy to hear the case for conversion. Because indigenous religions have a creator-god, the idea of one powerful god for polytheists was not as hard to accept as one might think. By converting to Islam in the CAR, people are becoming a part of a new community, a group whose embrace is wider than the traditional encompassing of the ethnic group. Education is one reason that people convert to Islam. Children, especially boys, attend Koranic schools where the families of three or four children go to school together. In Bangui, many people believe, as they do everywhere, that the big city is an immoral place that is likely to lead young people down the path of unrighteousness. Thus, there are mosques in all popular sections of Bangui, and these holy houses try to combat moral turpitude. Many of the people who migrate to Bangui are also trying to escape rural poverty and agricultural work. The sight of a Muslim merchant wearing a beautiful damask *grand boubou* is inspiring and something to which the recent arrival aspires to wear. People become Muslim to facilitate entry into commercial activities. Because so many businessmen are Muslim, sharing the religion makes the entrée easier. People feel more comfortable dealing with people who share their religion, and thus, their values.

There are intersections in the beliefs and practices of Islam and traditional religions. For example, Islamic holy men use amulets and charms (for protection), as is done in traditional society. The difference is that Koranic verses are substituted for herbs in the pouches. Another example is polygyny, a common traditional practice, and Islam allows for it as well. The difference is that instead of an unlimited number of wives, men are limited to four. This helps to account for Islam's popularity, and Islam is seen as being more flexible or accommodating than Christianity for this reason.

CHRISTIANITY

Christianity in its earliest days in Africa did not reach what is now the Central African Republic. Northeast and northwest Africa were heavily involved with the development of early Christianity, its traditions and philosophies, but the Greek and Roman traders, travelers, and warriors who interacted with Africans in coastal areas did not come into contact with the interior of the continent. Their Christian African counterparts also did not carry their religion over the desert. Nor did the monks who had a great impact on the Kongo Kingdom in the fifteenth through seventeenth centuries reach the CAR. Christianity arrived with the colonizing French, making Christianity an imperial religion. The colonizers had very specific ways that they wanted Centrafricans to participate in Catholicism, but the people of the CAR were able to come to terms with Christianity and have it make sense for them. The subregion of Central African is today the most Catholic area on the continent, and Christians in the country are evenly split between Catholicism and Protestant denominations.

On the heels of the explorers and the colonizers came the missionaries. Westerners wanted to convert Africans to Christianity, both to rescue the souls of Africans and to aid in their own salvation. Christianity actively seeks converts, and Frenchmen tried to bring as many people as possible into the Roman Catholic Church. St. Paul of the Rapids Church was established five years after Bangui was founded. Missionary activity started in Bangui, primarily to provide religious services to the Frenchmen who were there, but then they fanned out into the countryside to reach not only the French but the indigenous population as well. In 1923, the first mission to the Sangha Basin was founded by a Frenchman, and in 1924, Swedish Baptist missionaries made their way to the Oubangui-Chari. They were followed by missionaries of other denominations and nationalities. Converting Africans to Christianity was part of the "civilizing mission" used to justify imperialism.

Missionary activities varied from providing food and medical care to translating the Bible to teaching about their faith. But just as the earliest Europeans' Victorian attitudes shaped the way they saw and reacted to everything, missionaries who came later also were guilty of lacking cultural sensitivity; many cultural traits and practices were considered to be inappropriate for Christians (or anyone else for that matter). For example, the Biaka who have only recently been proselytized have been told that their dances are satanic.

Why would people convert from their ancestral religious traditions to the religion of the colonizers? As polytheists, those practicing traditional religions believed that they could incorporate Christian religious figures into their long-standing pantheons of gods as they sometimes did with the gods of their African neighbors. But the early Christians in the Oubangui-Chari would brook no such "heresies." Another important factor in conversion is that people believed that the missionaries and colonial officials were powerful and took them at their word when they said that their religion and their God made them so. Missionaries cleared fields and provided food to the converts. Additionally, they brought with them two very attractive things: education and health care. Listening to the words of or even converting to a new religion was seen by some as an acceptable sacrifice to make for a more secure future. Those who had ambitions to work in the clinics had to be members of the church that ran the institution. They needed to receive a formal education to be able to perform the job, thus ensuring for the missionaries that their personnel were well indoctrinated into their lives and ways of thinking. Missions had a virtual monopoly on formal education in the colony. Because Christianity has a systematic body of beliefs, it helped fill in some gaps in indigenous religious knowledge, such as the doctrine of Revelation, which explains the history of the supreme being.

Ancestor veneration, a mainstay of the African worldview, was dismissed by Christians along with other aspects of African culture and faiths. The figures that the people used to venerate their ancestors were heaped into the pile of "suspicious mumbo jumbo," and the Christians encouraged converts not only to ignore their ancestors but also to build pyres in which the charms would be burned. The ways that Africans dressed (or did not dress) and danced, and the fact that they had premarital sex and drank alcohol were all frowned upon by the missionaries in varying degrees, depending upon the denomination. It was not only a religion that the missionaries brought but also the culture that sustained it. Considering all that the missionaries found objectionable about African religion and culture in general, it is remarkable that Christianity found as many converts as it did. It was not Christianity that found Centrafrican society objectionable, it was the people who brought it.

Although the message that came from the pulpit was usually meant to maintain the status quo, Africans saw Christianity differently. This was especially true with those who were members of Protestant denominations that emphasized reading the Bible. Centrafricans interpreted the holy book's promise that "the meek shall inherit the earth" as a promise that Africans would some day not live under colonial rule, although not to the point that they should blindly obey authority in the hopes that doing so would ameliorate their situation.

Making Christianity more palatable to the African worldview and traditional practices was and is the goal of many. There is the desire to combine Christianity with ways that people worshiped and lived their lives on a daily basis, to make Christianity make more sense. The Africanization of Christianity was a response to the perceived lack of desire on the part of Western churches to let Africans participate on levels other than that of the congregational laity and allow more aspects of African culture into services. Centrafricans accused the churches of trying to keep Africans "in their places" because they saw that so few of their own were elevated to positions of authority.

African Christian denominations rose when there was a call from a charismatic individual to follow him or her. In Zandéland, the Mission ti Africa (MTA) churches fall into this category. According to oral tradition, the MTA began in 1934 when a young girl named Awa Marie Sibonguirete survived a severe accident. While unconscious, she met God who asked her to spread His word on earth. God decided that his white male prophets, Moses, Jesus, and Mohammad had not been able to bring Christianity to the Zandé, so He selected an African woman to accomplish the goal. He wanted her to be a healer and gave her a bottle of medicine to cure people. God proposed to make her white and send her down to earth on a wire, but His advisors convinced him to let her remain black. According to colonial documents, Awa Marie Sibonguirete's house was burned down by a Catholic priest and the colonial government jailed her. Colonial officials saw the MTA as antimissionary and antiwhite.

These churches are led by a prophet called a *nebi*. The *nebi* is usually a woman known as a *ngidi,* or occasionally a man known as a *bagidi.*

The prophet is the messenger from God who is supposed to spread His word through prayer, song, prophecy, and healing. Often the ability to communicate this way finds its onset after a serious illness where the sick person recovers from a near-death experience in which she or he met God, Jesus (Yeso), or Mary. That so many of these prophets are women continues a role that they played in Zandé religion: as prophets, they brought change to their communities, including Christianity.

The MTA holds services on Saturdays and Sundays; prayer and song are a large part of the event. Those who are "impure" may not enter the church: women who are menstruating or people who drank alcohol the night before the service, for example. The genders are segregated while they enter into the church, but they leave through the same exit. According to the MTA, God communicated through prophets who received His word on the palms of their hands. When divining or praying, they look into their open hands and read. They can read the word of God in Zandé, Sango, French, Lingala (spoken in the Democratic Republic of the Congo), and English. Every prophet is assisted by church officials who, after hearing his or her confession, listen to the problems of the members of the congregation and transmit them to the prophet. The prophet receives a message from God in a dream and then transmits the answer to the congregant at the next service. Many of the questions that they receive concern social interactions, health, and fecundity. These prophets do not use the traditional Zandé methods of divination of the poison, termite, and friction but do use a sand oracle.

What these prophets have done is combine aspects of traditional religion with more recently introduced religions. Prophets exist in ancient and new religions, but the way in which the prophesizing is done has changed, as in the example of the MTA. Now these communicators also receive written messages from God instead of receiving messages only in dreams or visions. Codified language came to Zandéland with the missionaries, especially the Protestants, who emphasized the need to read the Bible as a way to knowing God. Literacy, deemed appropriate only for those who went to Christian schools, was a sign of being an elite. The combination of traditional and modern in religion is not limited to leaders, but it is most evident with them.

Another variation of Christianity as Kimbanguism. The religion began in what was then the Belgian Congo in 1918, when Simon Kimbangu began to have visions in which he was called to be an apostle and a healer, and this religion has made its way into the CAR. Kimbangu and his wife had been baptized as Baptists just three years before. Kimbangu tried to escape his calling but he finally accepted and embraced his future, starting a faith healing ministry in 1921. His ministry attracted a large number of followers, and it alarmed the colonial officials who thought that the faith might be used to start a nationalist rebellion of sorts. He was arrested and beaten; his death sentence was commuted to life in prison. The fears of the Belgians were unfounded. Kimbangu preached obeisance to authority as well as the end of the use of charms, traditional dancing, and drinking alcohol, many of the same requests made by Western missionaries. Kimbangu prayed that his people would be delivered from poverty and hardship and asked for the help of the ancestors in achieving this goal.

During the colonial era, a number of Christian clubs formed in the Central African Republic. One of these is the Legion of Mary, which started in 1947. The purpose of the group was to discuss and debate issues of the club and to help the parish by visiting the ill, and other such good works. *Bè-Tâ-Ouali*, which means "the true heart of a woman," is an organization of Christian women. *Bè-Tâ-Ouali* is mostly concerned with the way that a Christian woman conducts herself in her home and it also focuses on her conduct in society at large, the love of family, and hygiene. The women in this organization are easy to identify because they wear a blue dress, a scarf, and a yellow kanderole. The Scouts began in the Oubangui-Chari in 1909 to teach the children at home what they were learning in school, but the emphasis was not on academics. There were weekly meetings that focused on agricultural work, metal work, first aid, and social life, and there were other activities and collective games. The meetings started with prayers and had choral music. The organization emphasized that Scouts should put their theoretical knowledge into practice. This gave Scouts training in occupations in which they could later find employment. In some places today, Scouting activities are being used as a substitute for traditional initiation. There are also Guides, Christian Student Youth, and Christian Youth. These groups teach different skills, but they have unity-building at their core.

The colonial government was often skeptical of religious personnel and the social justice that some preached, and missionary activity only increased when independence came. After independence, there was a growth in Christian churches. In the colonial era, Africans were not allowed to rise in the hierarchy of churches; the end of French political control meant the liberalization of Christian churches, and Africans started to play larger roles in the running of the houses and organizations of their faiths. No longer was African Christianity feared as a tool that sought to rebel against the government, but Christians sought to change how Africans and the churches interacted.

Numerous Christian churches exist in the CAR. Catholics and the long-established Protestant groups, as well as the Africa Inland Mission, Grace Brethren, Seventh Day Adventists, Jehovah's Witnesses (which was an illegal group during the colonial days), the Bahai, the Church of Jesus Christ of Latter Day Saints, and many others are active in the country. Catholicism is the single largest denomination. Missionaries who come to the CAR from France, the United States, and other Western nations are joined by those from other African nations, especially Nigeria and the Democratic Republic of the Congo. Missionaries are active across the country, from the northern part of the country with its Muslim population to the rainforests and animists of the southern part. They have not succeeded in eradicating traditional ideas and practices from Christian worship and thinking.

SYNCRETIC PRACTICES

Islam and Christianity are world religions that people practice differently depending on, for example, the particular Muslim brotherhood or Christian church to which one belongs. In the CAR, there are aspects of traditional religions that survive despite adherence to Islam or Christianity. One of the big stumbling blocks for Christianity is monogamy, although there are men who profess to be Christian who have more than one wife.

There is a debate about whether syncretism is more prevalent among Muslims or Christians. One of the reasons for this is that Islam has more aspects in common with traditional religions than Christianity does. For example, Muslim holy men in the CAR use amulets as part of their religious practices. At the same time, MTA prophets tell their followers not to use *gris-gris*—a clear indication that its use has not been eradicated from Christian circles. Centrafricans continue to be attached to their ancestors and have not stopped venerating them. This is not acceptable in orthodox Christian churches, but this aspect is retained in Africanized churches. As Christianity's parameters are expanded by Africanization, the idea of syncretism will become less prevalent. Indeed, it is mostly a concept adhered to by Westerners and the orthodox; to the Centrafrican Christian, the use of amulets or ancestor veneration is just as natural as going to church on Sunday.

To some, syncretic practices are unorthodox or even heretical; for others, they make more sense than the practice of the world religion alone. African religions are flexible and accommodating; prophets were able to change people's practices and introduce new gods. Why would someone want to ignore his or her ancestors if they have been a part of people's lives since time immemorial? Why would a community stop the practice of using amulets to ward off illness when it is a time-honored method of maintaining health? Ancestors, amulets, excision, sacrifices, augury, and other facets of traditional life coexist with these new world religions. Religions are not just about the theology, they also concern the cultures that created them, and that is why syncretic practices are so prevalent. Syncretism is the attempt to find compatibility in two different, but not adversarial, systems of thought.

Religion and worldview have and will continue to have an enormous impact on the lives of Centrafricans. Religion draws people together, and it is hoped that it will not tear people apart as it has done in other places. The CAR has shown more religious tolerance than intolerance. The government provides for freedom of religion. Yet in 2003, more than 30 churches were closed by the government, intending to curb the proliferation of houses of worship but the government allowed all of them to reopen in 2004. There is a constitutional provision that prohibits religious fundamentalism, a provision widely understood as aimed at Muslims. Visitors to Bangui note that Protestant churches are often located right next to mosques. Because religions address the same issues, it is not difficult to apply aspects of one religion to another; all religions and witchcraft can offer the same cause or solution to the same problem. For example, crop failure can be understood as a result of not making proper sacrifices to the ancestors, not donating enough money to the church, not saying daily prayers, or sabotage by a jealous person. All the answers concern doing one's part in society in order to get what one needs in return. Reciprocity rears its head again.

3

Literature and the Media

THROUGH LITERATURE, the people of the Central African Republic educate, replicate their cultures, and express their understandings of the world, their moral codes, their histories, and their hopes for the future. Precolonial literature was oral literature. When the French arrived, they brought a new and codified language with them, which increased the media through which Centrafricans could express themselves, but it heralded in a new era of less prominence for oral literature. This was especially true as formal French education became more and more prestigious and an enabler of a better life. Today, written literature is produced in indigenous languages, mostly Sango, and in French. The modern media uses these two languages as well. To control information and access to it is a way of demonstrating power and limiting or developing what people know. Just as with the written word, oral information is biased. The oral traditions and histories, legends and tales, radio broadcasts, and television shows (especially news programs), and journal articles all seek to inform and persuade.

ORAL HISTORY

The people of the Central African Republic spoke and understood many languages before the arrival of the French, but they did not read or write them. Their lack of a codified language was one of the reasons that the French falsely believed that they were superior to Africans and that Africans lacked intelligence. Westerners also held that, without written language, people did not have history. The cultures of the CAR preserved their pasts through oral means. Historical events were committed to memory and told over and over again. Living without a written language simply meant that the information had to be committed to memory instead of paper. Critics of oral history claim that because it is not written, it is open to change. Yet written history is open to interpretation, and the "validity" of older historical works is constantly challenged by new works that may use different data and reach new conclusions; thus, their malleability is equal.

Some people believe that the oral histories of the very distant past are not useful sources in re-creating history as we understand it in the West. Detractors cite the inclusion of fantastic information, for example, in traditions of origin where tales describe how the universe came to be. Traditions also tell of how certain ethnic groups were formed or how people migrated from one place to another. All religious groups have stories about the creation of the earth and its peoples that do not accord with modern scientific knowledge, yet these stories are not popularly denigrated. Although some of these stories do not seem believable to many, it is important to remember that this is how people understand themselves and their pasts.

Oral histories that can be quite useful, especially for Western-style historical re-creation, are chronologies such as king lists. These are very important to groups that had powerful leaders with centralized authority, and these names of rulers and their exploits are meticulously remembered and recounted. These chronologies do not give us precise dates because time was not reckoned by the Roman calendar but by the passing of seasons or by major events such as famine or war. One may not know exactly when a happening occurred, but one can learn of who did what, the order of the events as they took place, and a general timeframe for the occurrences. Monumental events such as the defeat of an enemy or a great hunt would be recounted as well.

In the Central African Republic, there is no real tradition of the *griot* as there is in West Africa. *Griot* is the term for a man who is a professional historian *cum* musician. The *griot* is attached to a family of standing and serves as a historical resource and political advisor in the capacity of a paid professional. In the tradition of the Zandé who had a well-developed monarchical system, there are poet musicians who perform either in front of their homes or before audiences at court. The key difference from the *griot* is that this poet musician does not receive remuneration for his services.

ORAL LITERATURE

In the words of Kenyan writer Ngugi wa Thiongo, the oral literature of Africans is *orature*. Oral literature not only entertains, it educates as well.

Stories teach their listeners about the ethnic group's religion and world-view. These stories also explain why, for example, there is a hierarchy in the animal world, how the natural elements work with and against each other, and how humans fit into the picture. All ethnic groups have explanations for these phenomena. This chapter offers a few examples of oral literature from the CAR, but its reduction to the written word will lessen the experience for the reader. The tales about how the universe was created and other stories that touch upon worldview should not be seen as fiction, because people believe in them. Just as Christians in the West may accommodate their beliefs between the theories of creationism and evolution, Centrafricans are able to analyze and find balance in different forms and sources of knowledge.

STORIES

The telling of stories is an important part of Centrafrican culture. People gather in the evenings around a fire in multigenerational groups to hear stories that inspire pride, fear, devotion, and other emotions as they teach people about their pasts and cultures. Storytelling is easier during the dry season when everyone can sit outside and listen. People come and go during the evening as they please, and people go to bed when the stories are done. In the rainy season, the audiences are more limited because the recounting of tales takes place indoors. There are numerous stories held in the communal repertoire of a family, camp, or village, and the same story is never told twice on the same evening.

Often the stories are as well known to the audience as they are to the teller. It is not unusual for someone to be murmuring the story along with the "official" storyteller, as he or she tries to commit the tale to memory. If the storyteller hesitates, a member of the audience will give a prompt to help the story move along. If the storyteller truly falters, someone else will spontaneously pick up the story and complete it. This can happen to any storyteller, young or old, female or male.

People want to have explanations about why things are the way they are—from the most profound to the most mundane. Ethnic groups have a body of legends that provide explanations for phenomena. The Banda do so often with a quadrumvirate of characters: Ngandré, the all-powerful but distant creator-god, and his three sons, Olokoda, Brakalé, and Téré. The two oldest sons play less of a role in Banda legends than Téré, and their offspring are not discussed. Téré in some ways is closer to humans because he has problems that need solving, and he seeks his brothers for advice the way people turn to their ancestors for assistance.

The Banda people have a story that explains the gendered division of labor. The legend says that Téré had only girls to help him with his work, and Téré asked for a meeting with Brakalé to discuss his problem. Brakalé advised him that to have boys, Téré needed to take the child by the right hand, and for girls, to take the child by the left hand. Although the exact mechanism that assigned gender is obscure, the story is understood as a valid explanation. The story makes it clear that there are types of work that are done by men and other work that is done by women: the gendered division of labor. This story also makes it clear that this situation was ordained by the gods, and, thus, humans needed to accept and abide by these gender constraints.

Much of the folklore addresses issues in everyday life. Deceit, shame, rejection, pride, mistrust, relations with spouses, punishments for bad behavior and rewards for good behavior, love, loyalty, and seeking the help and guidance of spirits frequently appear. These are some of the types of stories that would be told around fires in the villages in the evening where lots of people would gather. The lessons or morals are sharp and clear. Morals, taboos, proper attitudes, and the rules of the ethnic group are transmitted through stories. Stories answer questions about proper behavior, a reference text of sorts for the unsure. Human anxieties are addressed, and possible solutions are given. Unlike many Western tales, the endings are not necessarily happy: Sometimes the ending explains the reason that certain animals remain enemies, or why some specific unhappiness persists in the world.

The stories' themes are time-honored and familiar. Some stories try to explain human nature and why people act the way that they do. Legend also tells us that the gods created the taboo against incest. According to the Banda, it was Téré who brought word of the law that humans should not have sexual relations with a sibling. At the beginning of the tale, Téré was not blessed with a large number of children. Téré told his sons that they were not to take a sister to procreate. His sons followed his order, and the advice was so sound that the population increased very quickly. Then Téré ordered each family to go live in a different country. That is also how the earth became populated with different races of people, and Téré gave each group a name. This tale explains why people have a natural aversion to incest, and it demonstrates the wisdom of heeding the advice of one's elders as Téré did to Brakalé and as Téré's sons listened to him. It also speaks to an African origin of humankind.

Among the Biaka, many of the tales concern the actions of animals and the responses of Komba, the creator-god. Komba is the creator-god who judges and punishes human behavior while sharing the same foibles as people. Many creator-gods are distant in African thought, but Biaka stories about Komba make it clear that he can be deceived and he makes mistakes. In these tales, humans and animals often mock and humiliate Komba, but he is always vindicated in the end. In one tale, Komba has a son-in-law, Mbewe Salumbe, who steals *mobei* fruit from a cherished tree. When Komba finds out about the theft, he punishes his son-in-law by turning him into the kind of worm that eats the fruit that he had stolen. Biaka stories are often recounted in a chanting, rhythmic way, and tellers add rhythmic accents to illustrate the sounds of the story.

In the telling of stories, there is often a good deal of repetition, especially in longer stories. The repetition helps both the teller and the listener. The cadenced, songlike quality that many storytellers employ helps to make the repetition more integral to the narrative, like a refrain in a song. The marriage of narrative, rhythm, and tune are engaging and entertaining, but it is also a mnemonic device that allows the story to be remembered more easily because there are more clues. The young, the old, and those in-between are recounters. Tales are passed along from teller to teller, and even young boys are given an opportunity to try their hand at entertaining an audience with a tale. Occasionally women tell stories, and, although they do so less frequently, the audience listens to them with equal respect. Anyone can tell narratives that educate and entertain others.

Storytelling is not simply done by talking; it is a more expansive art form that involves not only the storyteller but the audience as well. Certainly, there is simple storytelling, such as that which might occur while walking to the spring to fetch water, but usually music and audience participation accompany the recounting of myths, fables, and tales. Storytelling is also a community event. The performance of stories very often is in the form of a call and response, where the soloist tells the story and the audience chimes in. This is done in a regularized way and people know when and how they should participate, but also people sometimes will interject spontaneous comments about the actions of the protagonist or other characters in the story. Additionally, it is a communal effort because many people actively participate by telling stories. When a person is done with his or her narrative, he or she cedes the storyteller's position and invites someone else to begin, usually there is an eliding from one teller to another by the use of a formulaic phrase such as "the story jumps to a new person."

There are elements of the fantastic in many of the stories and tales. One example of this is the ease with which different types of creatures come into contact and are able to communicate with one another. Animals and humans are in intimate contact as they eat together, marry, and take care of each other. Sometimes the relationships are more difficult, with an animal taking on the role of the trickster. The telling of these stories in the present day is a testament to the continued close proximity of humans and animals as well as people's sometimes fraught relationship with wildlife: People depend on game for food, but they also fear the pain and destruction wild animals can bring by eating crops in gardens and injuring and even killing humans.

Although some stories involve the mundane activities of daily life, other stories are specific to a time and a place or a certain group of people. Cooking is certainly a quotidian activity, but one can also see the prominent role of food in Centrafrican society as many stories involve a girl who prepares food for a suitor, or the importance of a woman, as a wife and a mother, making good and appealing food for her family and guests. Men tell special tales to boys, for example, when they are hunting. Some stories are recounted about specific events, such as the training the boys (especially) and girls go through when they are initiated and about circumcision as well.

The Banda also use folklore to explain how the practice of circumcision came to be. In this story, Téré saw all his children die when they were very young and he went to ask the advice of Brakalé, who said that Téré's children died and would continue to die because he was not circumcised. Brakalé then circumcised Téré. Yet Téré's children still died and he returned to Brakalé, who said to him that his children would continue to die because they were not circumcised. Brakalé advised Téré that he had to circumcise everyone: male and female. Téré followed this advice and the deaths stopped, so Téré ordered the operation for everyone. This tale explains the relationship between circumcision and two highly sought-after goals: good health and continued life. Also, it relates that these procedures are ordained by a higher authority and that it is pleasing to the ancestors. When people defend circumcision and female genital cutting, they may be arguing from this perspective.

In another Banda story about circumcision, we see the importance of the prescribed care and healing after the operation through a man named Ganzayo (*ganza* means "circumcision" and *yo* means "medicine"). After being circumcised, Ganzayo did not take the precautions to protect his penis and the wound spread to the eyes of the uncircumcised. Forgetting this formality also transformed the wound into a sore that gnawed away at his penis and testicles. Téré was upset, and he went to consult Brakalé who told Téré that, to perform the circumcision, it was necessary to gather the largest number of uncircumcised possible, and that each boy who was being operated on had to follow a prescribed course of treatment. Today there is a very strict protocol that is followed after the operation to speed healing. Because the elders are responsible for the initiation and overseeing the operation, it is also a cautionary tale about listening to and following the advice of the older generation. It speaks to the idea that the incorrect actions of an individual can have a negative impact, not just upon the one who committed the act but also on the group as a whole.

Although many legends are about society and some have an aspect of social control, there are stories that explain the natural world. People want to know why the world is ordered in the way it is; because the sun shines during the day and the moon does so at night, we accept that this is the way that it always has been and always will be. This tale tells the listeners the origin of this reality. The tale teaches that nothing happens by accident, that this is the result of certain actions that the actors undertook.

> The sun looked for an argument with the moon and the stars. The two camps warred with each other and the moon injured the eye of the sun with an arrow. The sun saved itself and since then it only shines during the day while the moon and the stars, living in the same village, only shine at night.[1]

The legend does not focus on how the sun saved itself from the moon because the most important part of the story is that, even though the sun and the moon had such problems with each other that they came to blows, they were able to reach an agreement at the end that allowed both to live in harmony. This principle is supposed to apply to humans as well.

A similar story exists about the elements. In this story, we see more of the commonly used technique of anthropomorphization. In giving the elements human traits, the story shows a positive and a negative side to human nature.

> Following discords, the rain and the wind were at war with each other. The rain fell on the wind and wet it, then the wind fell on the rain and made it blow much more weakly. The battle raged for a good while when fire, seeing the rain and wind battle, profited by burning their villages, killing practically all their men. For revenge, the rain, ending the battle, fell on the fire, which was extinguished. The moral of the story: A) when there is a fire somewhere, it is with water that one extinguishes it, and B) since this day, the winds and the rain are reconciled, to unite their force, and they always accompany each other.[2]

"The Legend of the Lake of Sorcerers" is one of the most widely told tales in the CAR. In this story, listeners can learn a great deal about the cultures and customs of the country. Instead of attributing the story to a specific ethnic group, the translator attributed it to "the Ubanguian people."[3] Coined by the colonizers, this term has some validity, as it describes the various riverine people, such as the Yakoma, and other peoples who inhabit the Ubangui Valley and share many common traits. The importance of the impact that nature has on human life is another theme for Centrafrican tales. Wind, sun, rain, fire, earth, and animals all affect the lives of people. Houses, villages, farming, hunting, and fishing are all at the mercy of the elements and the workings of nature as a whole, and people have to cope with the results.

Sometimes people are able to manipulate nature, but the results are not always what the human intended.

After eleven moons, the twelfth rises in the sky. The yellow *pagne* of the dry season covers the savanna. The winds push in front of them the gray and black smoke of the bush fires.

The savanna that is the color of gold became the color of coal.

Gray is the dust and the light from the sky. Gray is the ground and gray are the trunks of the trees.

It is hunting season.

It is the season chosen by the herders of Chad to cross the Centrafrican plains with their herds.

During this season, the thin cows try to find the rare grass on their path.

In the sky heavy birds look for the remains of an animal that died of fatigue on the side of the path and that was sold to some peasant for a few measures of peanuts, corn, or millet to the people of a village.

During this season, the children of Tagoua, the monkey with red hair and the fingers of a thief, descend from their trees to collect the ears of corn forgotten by the machetes of the peasants.

During this season the traveler hears at a distance the cries of the scarecrows placed high in the branches of trees.

The dry season has returned.

After eleven moons, the twelfth rises in the sky.

It is the dry season.

The father says: "Mother, the granaries are full. Now the child must pass the test that will make him a man. During this test he will learn to conquer fatigue and pain."

"Let us take our son to the test. There he will be alone. The eyes of his heart will look for me every day. But you are the father. Promise me to pay attention to his health."

She quiets herself and starts to cry.

For her, her child, her son, it's her body, her soul. It is her language and her words. Since he has arrived in the world, she taught him to walk, to run, to say his first words. She cared for him when he was sick. She watched over him at night, she laughed to teach him to laugh.

"Let us take our son to the test."

And the child left ...

The camp is in the heart of the forest, next to a spring. There the young boys learned to become men.

There, to prepare them for their work as men, they obeyed all the laws that came from very ancient times.

They slept at night with their legs separated and attached to the bed of branches and dry leaves. They were awakened at daybreak for a first bath in the cold water of the spring.

Dressed in a skirt of husks, they learned sacred dances, their bodies painted with white powder.

Then from morning to night they learn the plants that cure and those that kill. They learn to follow the paths that animals make. They learn to hunt, to fish, to wrestle.

The physical tests are terrible. The child goes to look for honey without fearing the sting of the bee. Lost in the bush, he must live alone and find a path to get him back to the camp.

Death will get him if he lacks courage or if fear makes him crazy.

If he quits before the end of the tests the old ones will make fun of him in a wicked way. He is punished and beaten. They refuse to feed him or give him anything to drink.

And during all this time, he will see no woman. For many weeks, no woman. Neither his mother nor his sisters will see him.

And the child is gone.

"Father, did you see the child?"

"Yes, mother."

"Does he eat well?"

"Yes, mother."

"Does he sleep well?"

"Yes, mother."

"Father, have you seen the child?"

"Yes, mother."

"Is he in good health?"

"Yes, mother."

"Does he speak of me?"

"He repeats non-stop. 'Tell my mother that I am okay and that I am facing the tests with bravery. Tell her also that I am becoming a man and that I will come back soon.... Also tell her that I think of her ...'"

The child has been gone for two moons.

The third rises in the cloudless sky.

That morning at dawn, in the camp, in the heart of the forest, a child was found dead on his bed on his bed of dried leaves. His poor skinny body was found there, lifeless, not moving, by the head of the camp.

The head of the camp said "It is the law of nature and it is the law of men."

He made the father come. This child was buried according to the law of the past, in silence, in the shade of the deep forest.

And the chief said: "The bush has its secrets. Only the ancestors have the right to know them. The wise man must keep the secret of the bush, the secret of death in his mouth. The secret of death. If he speaks, the anger of the gods will be upon his house, his wife, his children and the children of their children."

The chief and the father left. At the camp, life continues.

The father came back to the village. Silence and forgetfulness covered the bush and its mysteries.

"Father, did you see the child?"

"Yes, mother"

"Is he eating well?"

"Yes, mother."

"Is he sleeping well?"

"Yes, mother, he sleeps well."

"Is he in good health?"

"Yes, mother."

"Does he speak of me?"

"He spoke of you."

"Father, when is he coming back?"

"He will come back when the next moon rises from the bottom of the night."

"Tell him that to receive him I have repainted the walls of the hut in white. Tell him that for his rest, I have made him a new mat. Tell him that I will be there, with all the village, to receive the new man that he has become. And we will sing, and we will all dance at the festival of his return."

The moon rose from the depths of the night.

The new men, born in the camp, came back to the village. They arrived with the dawn of the new day. They walked all night, their faces and bodies painted in vivid colors.

For five days and five nights the village will have great festival.

That morning the woman came back from the fountain, her earthenware pot of water on her head. She saw the young people descend the mountain. But she did not recognize her son.

She stopped herself on the side of the road, put down her burden and says, "I do not want to be what I am. I did not ask for this sadness."

Then she started to cry and scream. Then she tore up her *pagne* and nude, totally nude, she loses herself in the bush.

"Oh! God! And you my ancestors. You have killed my child. Listen to the cries of a mother. Listen to my cries which will now live in the bush and mix with those of savage animals. Block your ears if you do not want to hear my songs which will tell and repeat my sadness."

But the bush is sometimes more mild than the law of men.

The woman walked since the morning.

Near a spring she stopped.

She tumbled in the dewy grass.

In sleepiness, she tried to forget the fatigue of her body and that of her heart.

At the foot of an old tree, she hears the voice of running water that told her: "Mother, I will carry the echo of your pain to the great waters of the plain."

Then a very old woman advanced with small steps and said to her: "I understand your hurt, my girl. But I offer to heal you and offer you vengeance."

She showed her a small tree, which kept all its green leaves despite the season and the bush fires. She asked her "This tree keeps its leaves. Can you tell me why?"

"It is the plant of good and evil. It is the plant which, attacked by fire, burned by the sun, does not die. It gives power to all that touch it. Make yourself a *pagne* of her leaves. Pick a branch that you will hold in your hand. Go to the place of the festival. You can, if you want, prevent your husband, your relatives, your friends from mixing with the people of the village."

"I want everyone to be struck by my vengeance."

"When the sun sets behind the mountain, you will make a furrow with the end of the stick around the village."

The old woman disappeared and the mother found herself at the entrance to the village where the festival had begun.

The tam-tams beat. The *balafons* resonated. The dancers turned faster and faster, jumped higher and higher. Hands beat harder and harder. The laughs and cries mounted along with the songs. The mothers showed with their fingers their sons who returned from the camp who were now men.

Then the woman, alone, started to walk slowly around the village. At the end of the stick that she picked from the tree of Good and Evil, she drew, silent and with a grave air, a little furrow.

When she came back to the spot from where she departed, the earth opened up with a terrible noise. The village, its dancers and spectators, the tam-tam and balafon players, the houses, and trees disappeared all of a sudden into a big hole.

And the hole is so deep that one cannot see the bottom. A high wave showed in a clap of thunder. The waters seemed to boil. They covered and devoured everything.

When the waters that came from the center of the earth were calmed, a lake of black waters was born.

There was nothing on its shores but a woman all alone who laughs and cries at the same time.

This lake, today, is called the Lake of Sorcerers. No one has ever been able to measure its depth. No fisherman has ever plied his canoe on its waters. In all seasons, neither the rains nor the dry season make the waters of the surface of the lake go up or down. No river empties into it. Its dead waters are inhabited only by crocodiles with fiery eyes.

There was also a white administrator at Damara, the neighboring village. One day an old man came to talk with him about the lake.

"Commandant, the black lake that sleeps behind our village is not tranquil like the others. Every night the voices of men, women and children, noise of the tam-tam and the sound of *balafons* rise from its depths and all its sides shine like a thousand fires."

The white man listened, but the story did not interest him. "In Cameroon," he said, "the blacks said that the souls of the dead flew in the air and went walking at night. One could see them and hear them around still waters. They healed lost travelers along the road and walked around sleeping villages. In the Soudan, Africans made huts in the bush for their lost souls. If they came in, they could not get out. And the souls of the living forgot them."

The white chief made a sign to the interpreter. "Tell this peasant that maybe I will go one night to see this lake he thinks is inhabited. Tell him also that if this lake stays tranquil and without life I will put him in prison for mocking me and for coming to trouble the spirit of the citizens."

One night, the white man went to the sleeping lake. At midnight the wind rose up and blew strongly in the branches. A savage music rose in the air from the bottom of the lake. It was accompanied by cries and very sad songs. Then one heard moaning voices. A wave rolled to the surface of the lake. The noise of the tam-tams and the *balafons* got louder and louder. The leaves of the trees and the grass shone with a thousand fires.

The commandant was afraid, he ran into the night, followed and enveloped by the increasingly terrible noise.

Never again did anyone see the one who did not believe in the African spirit.

The lake is dead still today in the middle of the forest. It is the place where one comes to take courage from those who suffered from losing very close loved ones. Women sometimes soak their feet to ask the gods for the happiness of mothers.[4]

This piece reveals some of the most salient aspects of the lives and traditions of the CAR. The importance of initiation is one of the central themes of the story, and we can also see that it was an exclusively male affair. Relationships between husbands and wives are shown where the man is the dominant partner in the marriage, as evidenced by the way that he brought back information for his wife and how she had to ask questions to get the knowledge that he controlled. Many Westerners believe that African women do not exercise power, but we see the opposite in this story. It is the woman, armed with the force of magic, who has the power to make the entire town suffer and disappear. Centrafricans very much believe in the presence and the power of magic. The colonial official serves to show the disdain that many Europeans had for Africans and what the desired outcome for them was. The last part was an addition to the narrative, and it clearly demonstrates how tradition was adapted in response to new situations.

The tales are often very active and intense, as much action is packed into a small space. The style of the storytelling is also unambiguous in that the narrative is clear and concise. Proverbs also give insight into people's ideas and values and may have covert meanings. With shorter pieces of wisdom such as riddle and sayings, language is very important. For example, the use of double entendres and other types of word play are as integral to the riddle as the content of the question itself. Proverbs explain situations; why, for example, one must venerate the ancestors.

The Zandé believe that there are some things that are too serious to be the subject of proverbs such as princes, witchcraft, and oracles. Zandé proverbs often use animal metaphors, wild creatures, and hunting dogs. The Zandé have a proverb, "How Hatred Began between Monkey and Dog," which, instead of teaching that trickery is necessarily wrong, teaches that intelligence and cunning can help one attain one's goals, but the same actions can earn one an enemy for life.

> Dog went for a walk in the groundnuts cultivation. When Monkey saw Dog taking a walk he asked, "Dog, my friend, why do you always cry at home?" Dog replied, "Who told you that I cry? It is the oil that I eat at home, and usually when I have not yet finished one lot they call me to eat another." Monkey asked Dog, "My friend, what can a person do to eat that sort of oil you eat?" Dog said to Monkey, "Come in one evening and lie down by the side of the homestead and when I come to you lie flat on my back and hold on to me tightly."
>
> When it was evening Monkey came near the homestead. Dog went to Monkey and said, "My friend, just lie as flat as you can on my back." Monkey lay prone on Dog's back. After that, Dog went home in the dim light of evening. When Dog reached home he ran quickly and first put his muzzle into a woman's small pot to lick it. The woman took hold of a pestle and hit Monkey with it very hard on the back of Dog. Monkey stretched himself from the pain of the blow and began to squeak, for Monkey was in unbearable pain. Dog said to Monkey, "My friend, do not cry. They did not yet begin to prepare a meal. You will surely eat oil today. When they begin cooking I shall eat oil, that for which you hear my voice at home."
>
> After that Dog went again in haste and put his muzzle into the woman's oil in a pot and gobbled it up. The woman again took up a pestle and hit Monkey with it on his back. Monkey lept up and jumped down from the back of Dog and took to his heels, running to the bush, because it hurt him so much more than the first blow. Monkey ran into a big thorny bush and stayed there in a tangle of creepers.
>
> In the morning Dog went again to walk in the groundnuts cultivation. Monkey said to Dog, "Alas! What a bad person you are. You took me to your home yesterday and people beat me till I nearly died from the blows. I did not know that you are such a trickster. You just steal the woman's things and they beat you for it, and you say you eat oil." Thus there began to be hatred between monkeys and dogs, and monkeys for their part are in tangles of creepers and dogs are in homesteads here.[5]

WRITTEN LITERATURE

Making the transition from oral to written literature faces many challenges. Written literature came to the Central African Republic with foreigners; certainly, the Arabic-speaking slave traders who were there before the European colonizers had access to codified works, but it is the French who introduced the tradition of written literature in the CAR. The environment, peoples, and cultures of the CAR inspired Westerners to write about their experiences there. Many colonial officials and other French visitors fancied themselves to be ethnographers, and, though amateurs, produced books and articles devoted to describing the peoples they encountered. The lenses through which these early Europeans saw the Oubangui-Chari and its peoples were decidedly Victorian ones, and they colored their opinions. Objectivity was limited for these writers and those of later generations, and their writings were often tainted by racism and notions of cultural superiority. They had varying degrees of success and accuracy. The colony also inspired fiction and nonfiction books and articles that touched on the tradition of Joseph Conrad's *Heart of Darkness*.

Europeans wrote in a variety of genres. Animal stories were popular during the colonial era, yet it was the physical environment and the people that gave authors the most inspiration. Many Europeans believed that the climate adversely affected both Europeans and Africans. B. Combette wrote two books about his experiences in the Oubangui-Chari. The second book, *Isolation*, written in 1929, addressed the dangers of being a low-level French businessman in the Haut Sanga region. Fissures in the foreign community were shown in Charlotte Rabbette's 1947 *Donvorro the Tornado*, which describes a group of French functionaries, businessmen, and residents who struggled with and against each other in Banda country.

Not all writings by Europeans were concerned with themselves; some were impressed with indigenous cultures and treated them in an unbiased manner. In 1908, Ernest Poichari published *Earth and Sun*, a study of Gbaya culture. Poichari used oral literature to investigate the Gbaya culture and language. He studied a Gbaya lullaby, using the same techniques of literary analysis that one would use to analyze a poem. He also compared Gbaya with Greek literary works. Félix Charles Tisserant complied an extensive resource of Banda grammar in 1930 and a Banda-French dictionary in the following year, both of which demonstrated the organization and complexity of the language. Tisserant also turned his pen to history with *What I Know about Slavery in the Oubangui-Chari* in 1955.

Rene Maran was a colonial official in the Oubangi-Chari. Of African descent, he was born in the French Caribbean. Because of his success in school, he was sent to France for further education, and he trained at the Colonial School in Paris where he met Europeans, Africans, and others from the Caribbean. As an administrator, Maran witnessed the excesses of colonial rule in his colony and wrote the book *Batoula* in 1921, which addressed the issue and the impact of colonialism on Africans and Europeans. The work painted a fairly brutish picture of humankind. *Batovala* won the prestigious *Prix Goncourt*, but it garnered a mixed reception in the metropole. Maran also wrote animal tales. Another work that received mixed reactions in France was André Gide's 1927 *Voyage to the Congo*. This book lashed out against the concession system and the *Compagnie Forestière du Congo*. Both of these works are still in print in French, English, and other languages. Félix Éboué, a colleague of Maran's, wrote ethnographic works about the people he encountered. *The Peoples of the Oubangui-Chari: Essay on Ethnography, Linguistics, and Social Economy*, which concentrated on the Banda, was originally published in 1933.

Writings by Centrafricans not only have themes that have traditional origins, but their writing styles often try to reflect classical forms as well. Centrafricans are quite prolific in theatre and poetry. One of the best-known poets is Aristide Mblanendji Ndakala, who wrote *Poems for Liberation*. Oral poetry had a long tradition in the CAR, so it is not surprising that some of the first formal written works were in this field. Writing for the theatre also lends itself more naturally to the transition from oral traditions and their dramatic presentations. In their written form, plays are easier to adapt because of the stage directions that are integral to the play as it is written that provide the kind of nuances that oral presentations have. One of the difficulties with putting oral traditions into writing is that they lose a lot in translation. The telling of an oral tradition versus reifying it into a written form necessarily renders the story flatter than it would be if told to an appreciative audience that was part of the performance. Even when the oral tradition is written in the same language in which is it spoken, it is not the same.

Writers need to choose the language in which they will communicate. In the CAR, as Sango is the lingua franca, using an African language makes it easier to reach more people than it would be in some other African nations. Yet, for some who do not speak Sango, it seems that Sango too is an imperial language because of its far-reaching range and the fact that it is a language of trade and of the capital city. By opting for French, more people have access to the written word, especially outside the country; but it is also the language of the colonizer. The choice of language is also a political one. In selecting an indigenous language, one can better represent the people in the work by using the vocabulary of the culture that created the piece. On the level of language and what it reveals about culture, some words and phrases are virtually impossible to translate and maintain the same meaning. Many languages in the CAR were codified in the twentieth century, largely because of the work of Protestant missionaries who translated the Bible into local languages. Changing the vernacular from, for example, Zandé to Sango, although "authentic" insofar as it is an African language, is not authentic because a Zandé tale is being told in a non-Zandé language. French is the language that most choose.

Very few Centrafrican writers are known outside their country. The one publishing house in Bangui is Éditions St. Paul, which publishes mostly religious texts. In terms of intellectual support, the university system is unstable, and there are few bookstores and libraries to provide inspiration to potential writers. The CAR is coming onto more radar screens in the area of literature, and Centrafrican writers are receiving recognition for their efforts. The challenges that writers face are multiplied when it comes to women. Women are less likely to go to school and get formal language training, and they have many demands placed on their time by parents, husbands, and children. Professional writing is a very male vocation.

Centrafrican writers are inspired by some of the same things that gave rise to literature about the area written by Europeans, but their interpretations are, of course, quite different. History, folklore, patrimony, politics, as well as modernity and all its appendages, such as changing ways of thinking, the role of technology, and the conflict between generations, serve as the creative stimulus for many. In a country where political instability reigns and governments clamp down on dissent, writing about politics is an interesting yet potentially dangerous vocation.

After independence, Centrafrican writers began to produce work that was recognized in their country and abroad. Centrafricans also produce comic books: This is a genre that is fairly limited in Africa as a whole, but these works are receiving more attention. Ph. Gabral and B. Nambana produce "The Chain and the Ring" and O. Bakouta-Batakpa writes *Tatara*.[6] Centrafricans are better known for more "serious" pieces. Pierre Makombo was one of the first with *Funeral Chants for an African Hero,* published in 1962. In 1972, he published *Princess Mandapu,* which incorporated history, poetics, drama, and sociopolitical criticism. Faustin-Albert Ipeko-Etomane published a series of short stories in *The Lake of Sorcerers,* whose title was an homage to the great Centrafrican oral tradition. Gérald Félix Tchicaya started writing poetry and gravitated toward the theatre. He was born in 1931, and his father was elected a deputy from the French Congo to the National Assembly in Paris. Tchicaya studied in France and was involved with education at high levels in the CAR. In 1978, the play *The Glorious Destiny of Marshall Nniku* was produced, a comedy with a sinister tone detailing the reign of a contemporary tyrant that was certainly inspired by the Bokassa years (and Bokassa had proclaimed himself Emperor during its writing), but it also speaks volumes about other authoritarian leaders in Africa and elsewhere.

Pierre Sammy-Mackfoy is a writer and a teacher. He worked for the Ministry of Education, and he is a *Chevalier* in the *Légion d'Honneur*. Remarkably dexterous as a writer, Sammy-Mackfoy writes history, pedagogical works, and fiction. In *The Blue Butterfly and the Daughter of the Devil* (1989), the conflict between the traditional and the modern takes center stage. This work is in use in secondary classrooms in the CAR. Using the character Mongou, Sammy-Mackfoy explores the daily struggle that many Centrafricans face in trying to reconcile the past with the present. He published *Mongou, Son of Bandia* in 1967, which was followed by *The Odyssey of Mongou* in 1983 and *The Illusions of Mongou* in 2002. Next, he turned his pen to history, writing *From the Oubangui to La Rochelle: Or the Route of an Infantry Battalion, June 18, 1940 to June 18, 1945*, a narrative published in 2003. This book focuses on the participation of men from the colony of the Oubangui-Chari in Second World War and how blacks and whites from the colony shared the same patriotic sentiments and fought for the Free French. His work with fiction has given him a facility with language that renders this an eminently readable history.

One of the best-known writers outside of his country is Étienne Goyémidé. Goyémidé, like many other Centrafrican writers, was involved with teaching, and he rose to the level of the Minister of Education for the CAR. His *The Last Survivor of the Caravan* is the first work by a Centrafrican to address the issue of slaving in the country. Set in Banda country near the end of the slave raiding period, it witnesses the migration of the Banda toward the Oubangui River and away from the human traffickers. The text combines oral literature, legends, tales, and song to tell the story of a chief who finally kills the head of the slavers and who dies in battle himself. Goyémidé's *The Silence of the Forest* is about an "evolved" man who chooses to give up his privileged life and live with the pygmies. This work enjoyed success as a novel and was adapted into a film in 2003.

BROADCAST MEDIA

In a country where televisions are few and far between and many people do not have electricity, the radio, usually battery-operated, is the most popular vehicle of music and information. The state-run station is Radio Centrafrique, also known as Radio Bangui. Radio Centrafrique was created in December 1958. Many Banguiois who were used to listening to programs from Brazzaville and Kinshasa (then Léopoldville) were surprised when political change also brought them their own radio station. It was truly only for them; with just a 250-watt transmitter, its broadcasting capabilities were limited, but the station was later able to broadcast much farther. By the end of 2004, the station was working with equipment that was almost 50 years old. Only on the FM dial, Radio Bangui could only transmit in the capital city, but France began to relay the transmission so that it can now be heard on short-wave as far away as Europe. The station hopes to expand its broadcast hours and raise funds for a new transmitter. Donor countries such as Japan have pledged money to the country, earmarked for the station's rehabilitation.

Radio Centrafrique broadcasts music, news, and announcements in both French and Sango. One very popular show is "Special Communications," in which part of each morning and afternoon is dedicated to allowing city dwellers to send messages to family and friends in the villages. Because the state owns this station, most of its broadcasts concern the activities of the president and other high-level officials. The director of the station is a member of the ruling party and the broadcasts tend to favor this political organization. There have been assurances on the part of the government that it would provide opportunities for dissenting voices and opposition parties on both government-owned radio and television, but there are complaints that this liberalization has not materialized yet.

For the rural areas, there is Radio Rural, which is directed by the Minister of Communication. The station began in 1985 as a way to get information to people in more remote areas. Even though the language is not understood by everyone in the countryside, almost all of its transmissions are in Sango. Thus, information from the government is not getting to its intended audience and some resent that the broadcasts are in the language of the capital city instead of their own. Many Centrafricans get their news from nongovernment radio sources. Two of the foreign stations are the British Broadcasting Corporation (BBC), which has English-language news, and Radio France Internationale, which broadcasts 24 hours a day in French and with some of its information specific to the CAR.

Some of the stations heard in the CAR send signals or are sponsored from abroad; others are under the auspices of the Catholic Church. A transnational organization, Africa Number One, is based in Libreville, Gabon, and it broadcasts to Bangui. The Catholic Church runs Radio Notre Dame and Radio Evangeline, which have programs about national news, human rights education, Church information, and legal counsel. A new community-based station in Bangui is N'Deke Luka. *N'Deke Luka* means "bird of luck" in both Sango and Lilanga, a language widely spoken in the Democratic Republic of the Congo, and, thanks to popular music, understood by a good number of people in the CAR. It is the heir to the now-defunct United Nations radio station, MINURCA, that operated from April 1998 to February 2000. MINURCA was part of a larger United Nations' mission to enhance stability and security in Bangui and the surrounding areas by working on disarmament and technical support for legislative and presidential elections. *N'Deke Luka* replaced MINURCA in 2000 and began broadcasting in Bangui on FM and later on shortwave. Its objectives are similar, desiring to promote peace and development by using programming from international and local nongovernment organizations that work in the region. Its political reporting has been called fair and balanced.

Television is much less widely enjoyed than radio, and the government runs the only station. Bokassa started *Télévision Centrafricaine*, or TVCA, which began broadcasting in February 1974. The laws of the CAR allow for private television stations, but no one has applied to start one; experts cite the unfavorable economic conditions in the country. About 40 percent of the programming is indigenous and 60 percent foreign. Most of the foreign programming comes from France. News of the government, its personalities, and activities dominate television programming. Both television and radio used to feature call-in shows that inspired people in Bangui to telephone in their opinions about various issues. Those that featured individuals who criticized the government were taken off the air.

PRINT MEDIA

In a country where literacy rates are low, transportation and shipping is infrequent and expensive, and city dwellers often do not have much disposable income, the purchase of books and magazines as well as the circulation of newspapers is limited. One person, perhaps a government employee, will purchase a paper and give it to a colleague when he is done. The colleague then shares the paper with his taxi driver, who later gives it to his houseboy. The houseboy may or may not be able to read it himself, but he will pass it along as well. Those who have read the paper will discuss its contents with those who did and did not read it. This oft-repeated scenario creates financial hardship for the print media, because it cannot generate a steady income. Additionally, the questionable level of the freedom of the press makes local news sources somewhat less credible, especially when dealing with national news or news from a donor country; this is especially true when the news items concern France.

The government owns *Centrafrique Presse*, which reflects the views of the ruling party, as does the *agence Centrafricaine de Presse*. There are more than 10 private newspapers in the CAR, although some appear only on a sporadic basis. Although the *Echo de Centrafrique* has close ties to the ruling party and reflects its views, the other private papers have offered stinging critiques of the government, its actions (or lack thereof), and its officials. Private papers that have a more certain publication schedule include *Le Citoyen*, *Le Novateur*, *L'Hirondelle*, *Be Africa Sango*, and *Le Démocrate*.

Journalists have complained that they are expected to propagandize for the state. Efforts to establish a journalists' union had long been thwarted by the administration. The government claims that freedom of expression is guaranteed in the Constitution, but journalists argue about the way in which this principle is applied. Critics of CAR's print press claim that reporters are often more concerned with using the press to settle political scores than with providing objective information. There are certain themes that are taboo, and one of them is the economy.

Freedom of the press is an issue for a country whose journalists are occasionally denounced, harassed, jailed, prosecuted, and persecuted. In July 2003, Maka Gbossoko, the editor of the private newspaper, *Le Citoyen*, was arrested and charged with creating and distributing libelous writings when he produced an article that alleged that the parastatal electric company was being improperly managed. He was eventually given a suspended sentence and fined, but with the help of the Association of CAR Journalists, he is appealing his conviction. There are hopes that with the civilian administration of François Bozizé, the tides are turning toward a more liberal arena for all of the CAR's writers and reporters.

NOTES

1. Félix Éboué, *Les Peuples de l'Oubangui-Chari: Essai d'Ethnographie, de Lingusitique et d'Economie Sociale* (Paris, 1933; repr., New York: AMS Press, 1977), p. 29.

2. Ibid., pp. 29–30.

3. Yves Igot, *Légendes Oubanguiennes* (Paris: L'École, 1975), pp. 5–6.

4. Ibid., pp. 27–38.

5. E. E. Evans-Pritchard, "Some Zande Animal Tales from the Gore Collection," *Man* 65 (May–June 1965): 71.

4

Art, Architecture, and Living Patterns

ART IS A VISIBLE representation of people, their ideas, their aesthetics, and their cultures that they produce for themselves. Looking at people's artistic production alone does not give an accurate picture; considering the cultures that produced the art, the available materials, and the use of the objects gives a fuller picture. The country's architecture reflects a combination of aesthetic sensibilities along with practical considerations. The art and architecture of the CAR remain obscure outside the country because of the relative isolation of the nation and its overshadowing from its southern neighbor, the Democratic Republic of the Congo. The art and architecture in the CAR underwent changes that were both organic and external, but they are still alive and well. Centrafricans produced art to suit their own needs: religious, judicial, agricultural, aesthetic, societal, and more. The historical artistic record is difficult to recreate because much of what has been produced has been lost to the elements in the degradation of the materials and because the art was taken out of the country and placed into the hands of museums and private collectors. Art is well integrated into everyday life; it is found not only on canvases and in masks, but also in musical instruments, religious objects, architecture, textiles, and in tools for everyday use: all strive to bring beauty into people's lives.

ROCK ART

The first art found in the CAR were rock paintings and other forms of rock art. Through this evidence, archeologists and historians have dated the presence of human societies in the region. There is rock art in the north, south, and west of the country in a total of 8 areas, some with up to 30 specific sites. Kaga Tallu in the north is perhaps the best-known site, where sandstone serves as the canvas for the red ochre, white, and black paintings. The figures are of humans (some of whom hold throwing knives in aggressive poses), and there are geometric patterns and shapes as well as animals. In the south and the west, instead of paintings, there are mostly engravings in the laterite stones. Because of the environment, other ancient applications of color on surfaces have not survived.

PAINTING

Painting in the Central African Republic is not limited to canvas; other surfaces are used as well. Houses are frequently painted in ways that are not seen in the West. The house is not the single solid hue, perhaps accented with trim or shutters; rather, the outside walls of the house are used as tableaux. As these homes lack window frames and coverings, the embellishments are found on the buildings themselves. As the country's famous painter Jérôme Ramedane found in his early years, the mud-brick walls are suitable painting surfaces, and this in turn made building in this material more attractive. The rectangular thatched-roof houses of the Gbaya are painted on the exterior; typically, the top two-thirds of the exterior wall is painted in white, and a second section that begins below that. The lower part is painted in blue or brown, or sometimes both. On top of these solid colors are figures of flora and fauna, painted in an abstract manner that recalls the ancient images painted on rocks.

Jérôme Ramedane is one of the few Centrafrican visual artists known outside the country. A Banda man, he was born in what is now Kaga-Bandoro to a poor family and grew up in the savanna of Mbrès, eventually becoming a catechist in the town of Sibut. Because he was small in stature, he was teased relentlessly by his peers, and he took refuge in his secret world of art. Ramedane was inspired by the same influences that other Centrafrican writers and artists have found irresistible: nature, social life, and the history of his country. His style was "naïve" or "primitive." When he began painting, the exteriors of houses were his canvases, and he created images of chiefs, military men, and other notables as well as scenes from everyday life, such as hunting and people working in their fields. When he received more recognition, he was able to buy more and better materials; he later used oil and canvas, but his inspirations remained the same. His studio was not inside of a building; he preferred to sit in the open air under the shade of a roof while looking at what moved him to paint.

Ramedane painted what he knew. Sibut's influence on Ramedane's life is clear, and he did paintings of both the town center and its Catholic Church. The scenes of rural life and the countryside that he depicted demonstrate his great feeling and empathy for rural people and their lives as well as the physical environment in which they lived. He drew on his experiences in the vast savanna in creating his images. "The Animals of the Forest" is an idealized scene of wildlife with a majestic lion as its centerpiece. The lion is accompanied by a water buffalo in the foreground, and there are two duikers behind them. A degree of abstractions finds giraffes and birds in the far background that are perched on top of hills. A stream and a spring are found in the lush grasses of the foreground, and a brilliant blue sky (a component of many of his paintings) features prominently.

Ramedane also produced representations of people, especially political figures. One such work is the painting "Président V. Giscard d'Estaing in a Hunting Village," in which the French president stands out among the villagers—his prominence in the painting comes from his height and his very different clothing. He is a somewhat startling figure in the midst of Centrafricans, much like the colonists who preceded him in the country. Another painting of elites is that of a meeting between Charles de Gaulle, the leader of the Free French movement who later became the president of France, and Barthélemy Boganda, the first leader of the Central African Republic. Although de Gaulle is larger in the painting, he was in reality a tall and physically imposing man, and Boganda is represented in a way that does not diminish the Centrafrican's stature. De Gaulle is in military garb and Boganda in Western clothes, including a long jacket and a briefcase as his only accessory. The French Resistance during the Second World War owed an enormous debt to the whole of Central Africa for its role in the conflict, which this work demonstrates as the two men meet as equals on this canvas. Europeans were certainly not the only subjects of Ramedane's work, as Africans featured prominently in his scenes of rural life. There are paintings of traditional dancers. In "The Fire," the focus is on a man who has climbed on top of a roof and is throwing a pot of water on the thatching, trying to extinguish the fire inside. There is a group of people that stare horrified at the burning house while others move to help, including a second man who is scaling the same thatching. Both men and women are actively trying to combat the fire by bringing calabashes of water and lifting them up to the roof. In this tragedy, the people of the village are uniting to save a neighbor's home and perhaps their own.

ARTISANS AND THEIR PRODUCTS

The objects of daily life have long been produced by those who use them, even after the sometimes inexpensive imports became widely available.

Some imports might be too costly, or not aesthetically pleasing. For some products, there has been a long and proud history of their being made in rural areas. To learn their craft, artisans go through a period of apprenticeship. Artisans have a degree of freedom, as they work for themselves in time-honored and necessary jobs. Other people produce these goods within the home economy, not as a profession, but out of necessity. Artisanal products can be quite simple, as with the *marmite,* or works of art themselves, as with musical instruments and earthenware. The gendered division of labor also exists in the making of these products. For example, in each ethnic group, basket making is done either by men or by women, and pottery is made by the opposite gender.

Pottery, especially Gbaya pottery, is considered to be some of the highest-quality indigenous artisanal product on the continent. The ubiquitous streams in the CAR provide the necessary raw material: clay. Among the Gbaya, it is women who make pottery. The pots are not made on a wheel; instead, the shape is formed by hand, and a broken calabash is used to manipulate the wet clay into the desired form. The pot is then polished with a smooth stone or with a piece of calabash. Decorations are added with implements, perhaps an iron ring for a pattern or a stick to add a freehand decoration. Gbaya women do not bake their pots in an oven. Instead, these urns sit inverted in an open space where they are surrounded by piles of dried wood, and a fire is started. The fire burns intensely and quickly. If the woman wants to add a dark hue to her pottery, she will add some leaves to the burning wood, or she may tint the pot with black graphite paint. Pottery is used to make earthenware dishes and storage containers for foodstuffs.

Gbaya women make the pottery and the men do the weaving. Weaving is not limited to baskets, but includes the mats used for the walls of homes, storage rooms, and yard fencing. There are close to 20 types of baskets that the Gbaya create, and each one has a specific use. The exceptions to the male-made baskets are the ones that are dedicated to *manioc,* and as food is the production of women, the women make all the baskets that are used in conjunction with this food.

METAL WORKING

Metal working is always done by men. Iron smelting is arduous work, and the entire process takes about four days. Forgers heat their furnaces with charcoal so that they are hot enough to remove the ore. Young men operate the bellows by hand or by foot to constantly feed air currents into the fire to keep it burning at a very high intensity. Lively music accompanies their grueling labor and when one is exhausted, another takes over for him. As the process of purifying the metal continues, the iron is taken out of the furnace and beaten;

it is then returned to the furnace and the process is repeated until the pieces of ore have been reduced to iron. It is then placed in a hole in the ground into which water is poured and the iron eventually cools. Then the iron is ready for the blacksmith to transform into an implement or an adornment.

Other types of metals such as copper and bronze are produced, but iron is the one that has made the biggest impact on Centrafrican societies. Iron produces many of the goods of everyday life, such as *marmites,* but it is also important for the pleasure and symbolism that its products bring as well. Musical instruments, objects of authority and status, items of a religious nature, and adornments are all made from metals, including bronze. Iron farming implements increased the amount of land that one could put under cultivation, and iron weapons increased the warrior's effectiveness: Iron allowed for societies to increase by being able to produce more food to support larger populations and by providing the ability to conquer more peoples as well. Like the forger, the blacksmith is held in reverence yet feared for the transforming work that he performs. Without the forger and the blacksmith, farming tools would be far less durable, weapons less effective, and there would be less adornment of the body.

TEXTILES

The making of cloth by hand is an artisanal work that has mostly been replaced by industrial production. In Bangui, there is a textile factory, L'Ucatex, that weaves cloth with "African" patterns. The cotton that L'Ucatex uses comes from Chad, even though the CAR is a cotton producer as well. Although most people would prefer to wear rich imported damasks, L'Ucatex cloth is of a good quality and the patterns are pleasing to its buyers. For some traditional ceremonies, people prefer to wear cloth that is not only local, but that also has historical and cultural significance.

Textiles are enormously important in their function and their fashion. Cloth that is made from the bark of trees, beaten until soft and supple, is very hard to find today. Cloth woven from raffia is also rare, but locally grown cotton is still woven by some. The weaving in the CAR is done on horizontal looms, much the same way as it is done in West Africa. The handwoven materials have become less common, more expensive, and harder to obtain. To some, handwoven cloth is a sign of luxury; to others, it is a sign of poverty.

WOODWORKING

The abundance of trees, especially in the more southern part of the country, means that woodworking is widespread. Ivory was a popular medium for carving until the 1989 Convention on International Trade in Endangered Species of Wild Fauna and Flora ban on taking the material out of the country effectively killed that art form. Most ivory carvers turned to wood instead. Numerous tropical hardwoods are highly prized locally and sought-after on the international market as well.

The sacred and the profane are both produced in wood. Wood is transformed into the tools of quotidian life: *marmites,* pestles, cooking implements, bowls, shelves, and the like. The work in wood with which most people are familiar are masks, but wood was also the material of choice in the carving of animals, ancestor figures, and other objects of art. Other wooden items in everyday use include plates and platters, shelves, and tables. A market for African art developed when the West "discovered" African art and when people were willing to exchange their cultural objects for money. In some cases, carved pieces that are of ritual or personal significance make their way into the hands of collectors and tourists, but replicas of significant pieces are created for sale. The same items carved for everyday use are transformed by artists into luxury items, such as a serving spoon embellished with an animal head on the top of the handle. Instruments of augury, for example, those of the Zandé, could be both everyday objects and works of art. Friction oracle boards are quotidian accoutrements of Zandé males, and these simple boards are exquisitely made by the men who use them.

Currently, a good amount of the artisanal production in the visual arts is made for the small tourist market, or it is aimed at the elite. Wooden carvings cross the line from what people want and use in the villages to what tourists want to bring home. For those artists who do not display their goods in the Artisanal Center, the most popular alternative is to show their wares in front of large stores and hotels in Bangui. The *Centre Artisanal* in Bangui, popular with visitors to the city, centralizes the products of numerous artists; the crafts at the center are of local and regional origin. It no longer is a place to buy ivory, but there are all types of wooden objects, especially masks, and animal statues, and gold jewelry. These items are usually produced for sale rather than being cultural items that are later sold. One of the most popular types of art produced in the CAR, certainly for foreign buyers, are pictures made of butterfly wings. In October and November of each year, the skies are filled with butterflies at the end of their life cycles. They die and fall to the ground, and people gather the wings to use in their creations. The process of placing and gluing each wing in place is painstaking, but the results are stunning. Like other Centrafrican artists, people who make butterfly pictures are inspired by and produce pictures of nature, people, animals, and rural life.

An interesting new development in artisanal production is the use of recuperated materials to create art and other useful objects. In these cases, necessity can be the mother of invention. The rubber from tires that are no longer safe for use on automobiles is used to make sandals, and the spokes from defunct bicycle wheels are turned into skewers used to cook *brochettes*. Kitchen utensils are now being made from previously used and discarded metals. In the increasingly tight urban space, the ingenuity of Centrafricans not only saves scant resources, but it helps to protect, at least to some degree, the fragile urban environment.

ARCHITECTURE

Centrafricans create architecture that responds to their need for shelter and reflects their ideas about what is visually pleasing while taking into account the resources available for construction and other practical considerations. Because of the different geographic spaces that Centrafricans inhabit, there is a variety of housing styles and village patterns. Village layout often echoes the cosmology and always the aesthetic principles of the people who lived in them. Imperialism had an impact on the ways that houses and villages were built, and the postcolonial era has seen the resurgence of some precolonial patterns. The West's impact remains, but it is negotiated with time-honored principles.

Colonialism's Impact

When the French had established themselves as the colonial rulers, they then turned an eye toward making changes in their colony of the Oubangui-Chari. Certainly, the colonial officials wanted to make the colony profitable and compatible with Occidental ideas; thus they decided to make all possible changes to accomplish this goal. The alteration of indigenous architecture and settlement patterns was one of the methods the administration tried. The colonial government wanted to regulate the way that Centrafricans constructed houses and arranged their villages. The result is that architecture during the colonial era was standardized and made less complex.

The administration did not appreciate the various settlement patterns that Centrafricans used. The first nuisance to the colonial government were nomadic pastoralists and hunter/gatherers, whose lack of a fixed residence obstructed the accuracy of census projects. Even those with permanent dwellings posed challenges to the administration: The ways that villages were laid out represented peoples' cosmologies and sense of aesthetics, but they appeared disordered to outsiders. People were encouraged to build their homes in villages that lined the new roads. This system and layout worked well for the French because it allowed officials to more easily keep track of people, but for those who lived in these villages, it meant living in houses that were foreign to them and in a physical environment of communities that held less meaning for them as well. In a testament to their adaptability, the people found features in their new dwellings and spatial layouts that they could parlay into coinciding with their social organization and cosmologies. They made their new physical environments make sense to them. Officials deemed the vernacular to be inefficient and sometimes immoral.

Architecture reflects people's values as well as their tastes, and it is the same with people's reactions to architecture. European sensibilities were offended by parents and children sleeping in the same room, with the children being exposed to their parents' sexual activities. The colonials advocated and enforced the change from building round houses to rectangular houses that had separate bedrooms for parents and children. This modification was considered a part of the civilizing mission. It did not take into account that there were not only aesthetic, but also practical, reasons for people building the type of housing that they did. Rural housing is a bridge from the precolonial past to the present.

Rural Architecture

The architecture in the countryside varies according to the resources available for construction and the needs of the community. Today people who are settled in villages in the savanna usually build round houses from sun-dried mud brick. Those who are settled in forest areas build rectangular houses with walls constructed from bark panels, broad leaves, or woven reed, and straw mats, as well as earthen-based materials. Hunter/gatherers also construct their homes from the materials that surround them by using sticks and leaves from the rainforest as the components of their houses. Because all these dwellings are made of highly impermanent materials, the need for upkeep is constant, yet properly maintained houses that are not constructed from leaves can last for generations. When houses are built from locally available materials, when the walls and roofs have been built from mud and leaves and other flora, these artificial constructs truly come into harmony with their natural surroundings. The resulting lack of visibility in the eyes of the colonizers that these houses had gave the colonizers the idea that they were in a space that was not in use.

The hunter/gatherers of the rainforest needed to build homes that corresponded to their two most pressing needs: keeping the interior of the home dry while in an area of high rainfall and their transhumance. When walking to set up a new camp, women move household goods in very large baskets that hold kitchen gear, clothing, reed sleeping mats, leftover foodstuffs, and bundles of leaves. Women construct the houses when they arrive in the new camp. The frame is built with thin, supple poles that are placed a little less than two meters (6.6 feet) apart. Then crosspoles are added that create a sort of lattice into which *ngungu* (megaphyium) leaves are woven. The shape of these leaves directs the rains away from the interior of the house. If the leaves at the former site are still in good condition, the women collect them and carry the leaves to the new camp, where they will be used until they crumble. It takes approximately two hours to put a house together. The people's lifestyle renders the notion of durable housing moot, and they are willing to "sacrifice" durability for mobility. Women need to be able to build quickly because the sun sets with alacrity in Equatorial Africa, and rainstorms are frequent occurrences. Because the leaves are ubiquitous, any repairs that need to be made to the house can be done quite quickly. It is important to keep a fire going inside the house because it helps to desiccate the air and keep the home free of insects. On a platform that sits over the fire, meat is smoked to preserve it. Much of the smoke escapes through the leaf roof of the house and more exits through the door. The size of the door determines the amount of smoke that wafts out of it.

Often the whole band moves together, but there are occasions when smaller groups travel for short periods of time, and they require protection from the elements as well. Special shelters are needed for the hunting trips that can last many days. If it is a hunting party of men, there is just enough room in the shelter for all to sleep. Even if the shelter is built for a couple, by the woman, it too is quite small. There are also larger, more permanent shelters built at strategic points in the forest that can last for months. It takes several men to build one, and they are almost always built at the end of the day. Men also construct the bamboo clubhouses found in large encampments where widows, bachelors, and visitors without spouses share a common sleeping space.

Sedentary forest dwellers traditionally live in rectangular houses. These homes were built without central walls in precolonial times, but the French influence led to the creation of rooms. It is more common now to have an inner wall that stretches along the length of the house to split the public room from the bedrooms, which are at the back of the house. In this type of house, there are two doors, one in the front and the other in the back, with the door facing the front yard the larger of the two. There are no windows in the home because they are considered to be dangerous. Ventilation comes from the doors and through the walls themselves.

These rectangular homes are made from a variety of materials: bark panels, woven reeds and straw, broad leaves, or mud brick. These materials are widely available, people have a long history of building with them, and they can be had without monetary cost. The materials that are less dense allow for a greater circulation of air, while at the same time being less permanent. A more modern version of this type of home is one made from concrete. The trade-off for cooler interior temperatures was the need to repair and rebuild more often. Gbaya houses on the edge of the forest are rectangular with saddleback roofs. These houses typically measure up to 10 × 7 1/2 meters (32.8 × 24.6 feet). Gbaya houses farther from the forest have a hip roof and are smaller, usually 8 × 6 meters (26.6 × 19.7 feet) or 6 × 5 meters (19.7 × 16.4 feet). Houses become successively smaller as one moves from the forest.

Currently in revival after its colonial suppression is the conical Gbaya house of the savanna. The walls are usually 1 1/2 half meters (4.9 feet) high and 30 to 40 centimeters (.98 feet to 1.3 feet) thick, and there are no windows. There is one doorway with a door step that is about 40 centimeters high. In these houses, the floors are somewhat below the level of the ground upon which the house rests. The floor is ground covered with a combination of earth and material from a termite mound that is fairly sticky and used as a glue. The flooring material is the same in rectangular and round buildings. In the traditional round house, the sleeping area is separated from the living area by a *pagne.* Typical furnishings on the sleeping side include a bed and containers made of wood and woven straw for storage and clothing. The other side contains a table, chairs, cooking utensils, and often a large *marmite* with drinking water.

Thatching was the norm for roofing in both the savanna and the forest. Strong poles are needed to support the roof and to ensure that the roof does not rest directly on the house. This preserves the walls by keeping rain farther from the delicate organic interior partitions; it also creates a shaded porch. Sometimes the roof is thatched in two layers with the outer layer providing an added degree of protection against the elements. The trees of the forest create a barrier against the wind. The roofs of rectangular houses are much more prone to damage in severe windstorms than the conical roofs of the savanna because the corners where walls and thatch meet are likely to get caught by the wind and raised, whereas the other form disperses the force of the wind. Metal roofs are preferred by those who can afford them, but they too pose problems. The metal roof on a rectangular house can also be lifted off, and a more constant concern is that they raise the interior temperature of the houses. Solutions include weighing down the metal roof with stones for the first problem and covering the roof with thatch or reed coverings that act as sunscreens for the second.

Many of the rooms that are inside a modern Western house are physically separated from the main house in the CAR. For example, kitchens are outdoors, built from the same material as the house, which maintains their architectural cohesiveness. For people who do not have indoor plumbing, anything that involves water is also done in a place that is removed from the house. Bathing areas are constructed in ways that allow people to maintain modesty, and still farther away from the house are the latrines. People who have the resources have individual latrines; others may share them among the extended family or with neighbors. The toilet area may simply be a corner in the concession, or it may be more elaborate with walls made from planks, mud bricks, mats, or palm fronds. The result of having separate places for discrete functions is that people from different sections of the household come into greater contact with each other as they move from house to kitchen to storage area. This fosters a greater connection between the disparate parts of the household and the wider community as well.

House-buildings are community events. For the house itself, it is the man who bears the responsibility, along with other men from his immediate family. Although it is the duty of men to build the home, women participate as well by hauling the water used to make the bricks and in the paintings on the exterior, and by making the floors. The raising of the heavy roof was what required the real labor. Men from the neighborhood or greater community supplemented the labor of the man's lineage in getting the top on the house. This is done with some festivity, as singing accompanies the labor itself and drinking beer and eating are the reward for a job well done. The notable exception to the construction of houses by men is found in the dwellings of the nomadic hunter/gatherers of the rainforest, whose women are charged with the construction of the homes. The homes of the nomadic-pastoralist Mbororo are built for the purpose of providing necessary protection from the elements as well. The few possessions of these groups also reflect this need: Clothing, hunting implements, and items for food preparation are among their scant material goods.

Royal settlements and households reflected the societies they ruled in that they mirrored those of their subjects, but at an amplified level. The Zandé king was at the physical center of his settlement, and a number of paths led to the house of the king. Chiefs' residences very much resembled those of the king, but on a smaller scale. They also featured an inner and an outer court, and while the Zandé empire existed and there was a need to have military men and information carriers quickly at hand, there were houses for warriors and pages. Like their subjects, the homes of the elite were round with conical roofs.

The furnishings of the homes of sedentary people are simple and most are locally made. There are two types of beds that people use, one is mobile and the other is fixed to the floor. Many beds used to be made from clay, but this material has given way to more pliant substances. Shelves, benches, stools, and chairs are all made out of various kinds of wood; earthenware pots for storage of food are set on pedestals and line the walls of the house. A table may also be found in the house. There are wooden storage containers, but people without many possessions do not need to devote much space to their goods. Interior decorations are minimal, hunting gear may hang near the door, and earthenware food containers are adorned. If someone in a rural area is lucky enough to have a photograph of, perhaps, the family, that will certainly take center stage.

Polygynous Households

Polygynous households are arranged in such a way that their space represents and enhances their functioning. They also adhere to the norms of the ethnic group. When a family has more than one wife, there is a special concern about space. The group lives in a compound in a communal area made up of very separate spaces. The husband's house is for him alone, and it is in the physical center of the family. Each of his wives and their children live in their own small family unit in a house; all their houses are arranged around that of the husband. The co-wives need to have separation from the others, and each has her own quarters that consist of a house and other buildings, including a kitchen and usually a latrine and food storage unit. The women's quarters are separated by their kitchen gardens, which provide not only food but some much-needed visual distancing as well. In rural areas, the polygynous household often has abundant space, but this arrangement can create special problems in densely settled areas.

Urban Architecture

The French created the urban centers of the Central African Republic, so it is not surprising that one of the most visible marks on the cities' landscape is colonial architecture, most evident in the capital. What the French constructed in Bangui for its government and its personnel was what it constructed in its tropical empire across the globe: ample offices and homes with large rooms and hallways that are encompassed by whitewashed outer walls that can be found in Africa, Asia, the Caribbean, and Pacific Islands. Some buildings and homes had a second story, although this was not too practical in the heat and humidity, especially without climate control. Currently, the European section of town has a fair degree of activity during the day, but at night, it is practically deserted. It is the nighttime when the always-busy African sections of town can be at their liveliest.

Urban planning separated the colonized from the colonizer. The French feared that contact with Africans would threaten their physical safety and their health. Because malaria, diarrhea, and acute respiratory diseases were so persistent, Europeans feared that proximity would lead to their "contamination." Africans were relegated to certain sections of the city, where they lived among themselves.

As Bangui expanded and more people moved into the "unofficial" areas of town, more homes and buildings were constructed in these sectors of the city.

After independence, numerous buildings were erected in the somewhat universal style of the 1960s with concrete, steel, and glass structures that appear to be in stark contrast to the physical environment. These edifices were minimalist, which also made them seem oppositional to the more gracious design of the colonial architecture at the center of the city, almost as if they were rebuking the older buildings for their excessiveness. They are also very different from the homes in the African quarters on the outskirts of town.

The years have not been kind to Bangui physically, as many of the older buildings retain their structure but are in need of repairs, paint, and upgrades. Even the surroundings have declined: the once well-paved streets buckle and break. The mango and palm trees that provide shade along the large avenues are ruptures in the sometimes bleak atmosphere of downtown Bangui.

The wealthy Muslim merchants of Bangui built large houses that are conducive to conducting business. Just as Islam does not dictate that religion and commerce should be separated, home and business life often coincide. In these merchants' places of business, there is a small door reserved for men that connects the courtyard of the house to the commercial enterprise next door. The courtyard is covered in mats, and the merchants can welcome guests, share meals, drink tea, discuss business, and pray with their guests. There is a second courtyard for the women of the household, where they receive friends, cook, and do housework. Women are not supposed to leave the home without the permission of their fathers or husbands; in these quarters, some women have chiseled a little hole in the wall of the compound or even in the house to let them see what is happening on the outside.

Although colonial architecture as well as urban and village planning had organization and regularization as their most fundamental principles, the outlying areas of Bangui certainly changed that trend. In the *kodro,* it appears as though rural Africa has transported itself to the urban milieu. Yet there are some distinct differences from the countryside. In the rural areas, people are starting to build round houses again, although the opposite is true in Bangui, where this kind of house with the conical roof has almost disappeared. Rectangular homes in Bangui have windows, which goes against the tradition of believing that these portals were actually dangerous. This is just one example of recent change. In the city, tradition meets modern ideas and circumstances to create new living arrangements.

The *Kodro*

At the end of the Second World War in Bangui, an interesting housing and use-of-space trend developed: the *kodro. Kodro* means "place of lineage, origin, area, or village where one resides"; in Bangui, it is form of neighborhood. The *kodro* resembles the rural villages in its use of space, the kinds of houses it contains, its leadership, its population, and even the names used to designate a specific area. The neighborhood is often named after its founding migrant, his descendants form the core group of the area, and allegiance in the neighborhood is based upon these people. Centrafricans migrate from the countryside to Bangui to escape rural poverty and to find work outside of the agricultural sector. When they get to the city, the new arrivals look for a place to stay, and the most logical option is with family. With many people following the same pattern, areas fill with members of the same ethnic group. Ethnic similarity is a hallmark of the *kodro*. As in the countryside, the family in the *kodro* is an extended one. New arrivals to Bangui stay with the urban part of their families, and they start their own as well.

Boy-Rabe is a *kodro*. Oral tradition tells that Gbaya people moved there under a chief named Gbafio, who, in 1946, was a replacement for another chief who had committed financial abuses. The Gbaya had been living in an area that abutted a French neighborhood, and while the French were worrying about the unrestricted development of African neighborhoods, a fire broke out and destroyed many homes in the Gbaya settlement. The French encouraged the Gbaya to decamp to some distance to create their new community. Thus, the Gbaya moved into the hills in the northeast part of the town, the area that corresponds to the present-day settlement of Boy-Rabe.

The *kodro* is a spontaneous space. It is often far from the center of town where the bureaucrats work and few foreigners visit. The *kodro* are not on the tourist map. The boundaries of these areas are undefined and only those who are initiated know what they are; for those who are not in the know, it falsely appears to be in chaos. The broad avenues of the old section of the city are not replicated here; the streets are unplanned, unpaved, and traveled by foot. The organization of the houses varies according to the traditions of the ethnic group. The building materials are of local origin. Houses are made from unbaked mud brick, built by the owners, their kin, and friends. The vast majority of these houses are rectangular; the round house with the conical roof is fast disappearing from Bangui. The architectural form is simple, and the house is basically a succession of rooms.

The *kodro* is the reality for many of Bangui's residents, and existence in these places is not easy. The sanitary conditions in the *kodro* are quite poor. Electricity exists along the main axis and in some public establishments. Water service is rare, and most people rely on the distant springs. Discarded tires that are no longer safe to use are salvaged by *kodro* residents, who turn a number of them into bridges that help them navigate rain-swollen passageways that regularly flood their neighborhoods. People sometimes refer to the mosquitoes as the air force and the rats as the land army. There is economic disparity in the *kodro*, more so than in the villages. The size of houses varies enormously, as well as what they contain. Those who are well-off have more and bigger rooms, more doors and windows, cooking sheds, showers, and wells.

The men who live in the *kodro* do not work in office buildings. Instead, they are day laborers, assistants to mechanics, domestic servants, night watchmen, and gardeners. Sometimes, men perform work that they would not dream of doing in the villages; for example, working as a domestic or houseboy is not uncommon in Bangui, but it would be out of the question for a man in a rural area to wash clothes. Most of the men in the *kodro* do grow some kind of food crops. Women who live in these sections of town are also not participating in salaried labor, and they perform different types of work to piece together a living.

As the quarters and their populations expand, it becomes increasingly difficult to find work, fuel, and food. Even though many migrants to Bangui go to the city because they do not want to farm, having a plot of land that produces food is vital to the families that live there. Newly arrived wives of junior sons get the land that is most distant and often the least productive. Women have small gardens that they keep at their homes; *manioc* and sweet potato plants surround homes. Women too are involved in this peri-urban farming. The women who live in Boy-Rabe have a group that grows and sells *manioc*. Often their farms are a good distance from their homes, and they go on foot, every day. The food produced is destined for family consumption, with any extra marked for sale, perhaps in a market or maybe just sold by the woman in front of her house. For women who are unmarried with children, the need to work can be more pressing, as many of the women who have children out of wedlock often do not receive any paternal support.

The *kodro* demonstrates not only how tight the lines are between the peoples of the *kodro* and the people of the villages, but it also illustrates the continuity in living patterns, leadership, and lifestyles. Modernity is not something that is attained by moving to the city, nor is it always desired. The replication of age-old housing, living patterns, and authority figures is out of necessity and choice. The two areas are in a symbiotic relationship where the lines of influence flow in both directions. More and more people who live in the *kodro* refer to it as "the village."

In the past as in the present, architecture reflects the status of those who dwell or work within the walls, although sometimes the distinctions are subtle. The nod to the past often trumps what is new. There is continuity between the urban and rural areas when one looks at the *kodro:* The inhabitants' give continued allegiance to a clan head and their chiefs continue to direct the communities from their houses in the center of the settlement, where young children gather to play games. In the village, the center of power is the chief, and he takes a parallel physical space; the situation is the same in Bangui, as those with more economic and social power reside in the center and the marginalized live on the ever-growing outskirts. Today, the houses of chiefs or other notables and buildings that have political and social purposes still reflect the technical and symbolic achievements of the past. In art and architecture, often the past is the present.

5

Cuisine and Traditional Dress

THERE ARE SOME GREAT differences between cuisines and eating habits in the Central African Republic and the West, and there are similarities as well. Like people everywhere, Centrafricans enjoy food, its preparation, and its consumption. For Centrafricans, meals are a time to relax and reenergize. Not only about nourishment, food brings the pleasure of sharing a meal with friends and family. In some cases, it even has ritual significance. Food has a great many links to various aspects of Centrafrican culture. For example, Centrafrican languages have great vocabularies for food and drink, which show the centrality of these consumables to their cultures.

Dress is also important to Centrafricans: They have more ancient ways of dress, and there are recent influences, such as Western styles. Textiles in the CAR are of different qualities and origins, and the patterns and colors can be very different from what is seen in the West. Hairstyles are also important as a part of traditional dress and life. Dress is not just a method of self-expression but also a statement about culture, tradition, and one's position in society. Both food and dress seem homogenous to outsiders, but they are far from it.

FOODS

People in the Central African Republic are as interested in preparing and eating good food as people are elsewhere; the lack of numerous types of food means that they have to be very creative to have variety in their diets. The staple starches are the most important part of the meal in terms of providing bulk and calories for people who do physical labor all day. Vegetables and the many ways that they are prepared provide the diversity in meals. Proteins in the form of meat and fish are less abundant than what Westerners are accustomed to, and creativity once again comes into play, as Centrafricans find and prepare alternative sources of protein. Food preparation is considered to be one of the essential skills of women.

Girls learn how to cook at their mothers' sides. They do not use cookbooks, but train through observation, trial and (it is hoped, little) error. To be a good cook is a highly desirable trait in a woman and makes her sought after as a wife. A woman should be prepared to demonstrate her good cooking skills on a daily basis for her family and guests. Centrafricans like to prepare extra food in case guests should visit at mealtime. This is not wasteful—as all parts of animals are used, all food will be eaten.

The foods that are consumed in the Central African Republic are of African and non-African origin. Staple foods before the year 1600 were sorghum, millet, yams, and bananas (originally from Asia). New crops were introduced with the arrival of Europeans. The foodstuffs that came from the Americas—maize and manioc—were some of the staple crops that allowed for more plentiful food supplies and the expansion of populations. Other items that crossed the Atlantic include groundnuts, beans, and hot peppers, which widened the pool of protein-rich foods and added new flavors to many dishes. But it is the starchy staple foods that supply the majority of the calories that a Centrafrican consumes.

The staple foods vary according to region. Millet and sorghum, indigenous to Africa, can survive in harsh environments with limited water. Both sorghum and millet are quite nutritious, high in vitamin B and protein. These grains are not harvested all year as tubers are, but millet and sorghum have the advantage in that they can be stored, so that even though the supply is not constant, they can provide for a longer time than just the time at which they are reaped.

Plantain, yam, and rice grow in the wetter southern regions. Plantains, often referred to as bananas, are a close and very starchy cousin to sweet bananas, and they are valued as a basis of a meal and as a snack. Bananas are nutritious and particularly bountiful in vitamin B. Bananas grow best in areas with high rainfall, making them impractical and expensive to consume in many areas in the CAR. *Foutou* is a staple food for banana farmers. To make *foutou,* plantains are boiled and beaten in a mortar until it results in a mixture of a firm and smooth texture. The *foutou* is served with a sauce. Plantains can also be boiled and cut into disks that are topped with a sauce. As a snack, plantains are prepared in a variety of ways, including boiling, grilling, and frying. The latter is particularly delicious. Sweet bananas are the only type of bananas that people eat without cooking.

Yams (*ignames*) are indigenous, and some new varieties arrived with Europeans in the middle of the nineteenth century. Yams are more flavorful than other tropical tubers. They grow in areas where the rainfall is high; the soil does not have to be well drained; they can survive the occasional flood; and they also thrive in shade. Yams are more easily digested when they are grated or fermented, but they are often served boiled, fried, or beaten into a solid and malleable mass like the *foutou.* All the tubers and bananas can be beaten into similar forms and consistency, yet it is *manioc* that takes center stage in the culinary life of the CAR.

Manioc, or cassava, is very important to the Centrafrican diet, and its product, *fufu,* is something of a national staple food. *Manioc* arrived with Portuguese explorers and made its way from the shore to the interior of the continent. Even though its price has almost doubled recently in Bangui, *manioc* is the least expensive staple because it grows so well. It has replaced millet and sorghum in importance because it produces in less nutrient-rich soil, requires less labor, and is fairly productive. *Manioc* is also less nutritious than yams or bananas, and it leeches the fertility out of the often already-poor soils in which they grow. *Manioc* also has an inherent danger. *Manioc* naturally absorbs cyanide from the soil in which it grows, leading to the potential for cyanide poisoning, known as *konzo,* for those who consume it. *Konzo* can produce headaches, dizziness, stomach pains, diarrhea, and vomiting. It also leads to neurological complications, which result in the paralysis of the legs. As people who consume *manioc* regularly have learned to process it to remove the toxic substance, cyanide poisoning is a very rare event. The process, described later, is complex and time-consuming, but necessary.

Food Preparation

In the balance between eating to live or living to eat, Centrafricans lean toward the former. This is because of the great amount of labor that goes into food production, not from a lack of interest in it. Growing, preparing, and consuming food are central to life in this country and its economy. In the CAR, these are low-technology tasks that are enormously time-consuming. Virtually everything is grown and prepared from scratch by the woman of the household. Even with some modern conveniences, women in urban areas also spend far more time dealing with food than their Western counterparts do.

Food is the domain of women. The growing of crops and their transformation into food consumes much of their lives. While women work and cook, small children are underfoot, and girls are in apprenticeship. Little girls learn how to cook by watching and imitating their mothers and older sisters before trying their hand at preparing food. In rural areas as well as many traditional urban settings, kitchens are not a part of the main house. They are separate buildings or open-air stations where all the food preparation takes place. Appropriate for the hot climate, this arrangement allows for the clearing of the smoke from the open wood fires, and it lessens the chance that the house will catch on fire. In urban areas, those who live in the Westernized sectors have modern kitchens inside their homes that are outfitted with ovens, stovetops, and sometimes, refrigerators that are either kerosene or electric.

The washing and cleaning of food before its preparation is very important because food does not come sanitized as it does in Western grocery stores. As in all hot climates, there are pests such as weevils that attack grains and worms that are attracted to mushrooms and other vegetables. Cleaning food, such as washing rice, reveals imperfections in foods, and these are rejected for consumption. Tainted grains of rice, millet, and sorghum will join unusable fruits and vegetables and peels to make organic food for the chickens that eagerly await all edible cast-offs.

Food preparation is very much a group activity. Much of the preliminary work, such as the soaking of cassava, is done with others. When a woman gets ready to cook, she usually goes to the house of a neighbor who has already started her cooking fire to get a light. Also, if a woman does not have all the ingredients she requires to prepare a certain dish, she will ask someone in her lineage or her village to give her what she needs. In the past, reciprocity was the norm in this type of transaction, although today cash may be preferred. When a woman has an abundance of a perishable food item or she is making a highly prized dish, she will share it, especially with the women of the lineage whom she would like to please.

One of the most time-consuming, yet necessary, culinary tasks is making *manioc* edible and transforming it into *gozo, manioc* flour. Although the process described is specific to the Gbaya 'bodoe, there are many similarities in its preparation with other ethnic groups. The first step is unearthing the *manioc* tubers. Then women put the tubers into a basket and carry everything to a pond where the tubers will soak to remove the cyanide. The pond is shared by a number of women, each of whom gets her own section. The warmer the water is, the faster the *manioc* is ready. When it has soaked for enough time, the *manioc* is removed from the water, peeled, washed, and placed on a slab for crushing. Using special mallets, women beat the *manioc* into crumbs and set it out to dry. When the *manioc* is dry, it is beaten into the flour, *gozo.*

The *manioc* is sifted so that it can better continue to desiccate. Once it is sufficiently dry, the flour is swept into a basket and taken back to the village. In the village, the *gozo* is beaten in a mortar by women who are sitting either on the ground, a small seat, or even with their heels resting on their buttocks and knees on the ground. The beating of the *manioc* is done by one woman per mortar, although many women may be performing the task at the same time. Usually women hold the pestle in one hand for a while and switch to the other; sometimes two hands are used when more force is needed. The hand that is not beating the *gozo* with the pestle pushes the flour to the center of the mortar. Then the flour is sifted again. This *gozo* will be the basis of the *fufu*, which is so popular. The flour must be transformed into an edible state, and the *boule*, or ball, of *manioc* flour mixed with water to form a gelatinous orb is the mainstay of many meals.

To prepare the *boule*, a woman puts water into a *marmite* (large cooking pot) and waits for it to boil. To be sure that the water is hot enough, she drops a pinch of flour in the water and if it falls to the bottom, it is not ready. If she thinks that it is necessary, a layer of flour is then delicately placed in the *marmite* to create a cover to accelerate the boiling. When the water is hot enough, the woman will add all the flour that she wants to cook. When the flour takes on a grey tinge, it is ready to be stirred. At this point, some women take the *marmite* off the fire, but others do not. The woman stirs the mixture in a circular motion, while holding the *marmite* immobile between her feet (she wears flip-flops or some other protection for her feet). Once the mixture is free of any unmixed flour, she will sprinkle fresh water on the mixture. When it "makes a block," it is ready.

The staples are not numerous nor are the variations in their preparation. Therefore, the sauces (soups, stews) that are served with them become enormously important for creating variety. Attention is paid to the proper preparation of *manioc* and other bases, but it is the accompaniment that attracts the most attention. Sauces accompany all staple dishes.

One of the most highly consumed sauces is *manioc* leaf, in part because the plant is ubiquitous and because the leaves are picked when the tubers are harvested. *Manioc* varieties are categorized as sweet or bitter, and both types are used for sauce. People believe that with the sweet variety one should not talk while the leaves are being prepared or else their taste will turn bitter. The leaves' stalks are removed and cleaned, and finally, the leaves are torn. Then they are cooked to make them wilt; usually salt and *piment* are added at this point. The combination goes into a medium-sized *marmite* and is covered with water. It is then stirred and cooked for a long time. Oil is added at the end; the most common type of oil for *manioc* leaf is sesame. The *manioc* leaf must be cooked long enough or those who eat it can have vertigo, headaches, or upset stomachs to the point of vomiting. Many people believe that eating undercooked *manioc* leaves can lead to death. The texture of well-cooked *manioc* leaf is not only considered to be healthy, but delicious.

Manioc leaf can be eaten plain or enhanced with added groundnut or sesame flavoring that would be added in the middle of cooking. Sometimes in the dry season, the Gbaya 'bodoe will add a glutinous substance such as eggplant to the *manioc* leaf; the *manioc* leaf is prepared separately and the glutant is prepared at the same time. When the plain *manioc* leaf has cooked and cooled, the liquid is removed from the leaves and put into a container. The glutant is beaten into the juice of the *manioc* leaf, and then the mixture is added back to the leaves themselves.

The sauce that a woman chooses to serve depends on the tastes of the cook, those of the diners, and what is available. Sauces are often vegetable or nut-paste based with *piment,* salt, and oil added. Groundnut sauce has protein and is widely eaten. Of African origin, okra is one of the most common sauces in the CAR; one reason is that okra's slippery texture allows eaters to swallow the beaten tuber dishes with ease. It is also ubiquitous. Garlic and onions are consistently used as flavorings in sauces. Many sauces are cooked for a long time. This is quite true when meats are added to sauces, especially because the animals have neither been bred nor fed for tenderness.

Although meat is sometimes grilled for solo consumption and fish may be fried for the same use, meat and fish are most often used to flavor sauces. Most people do not have enough money to eat much meat and fish and those who have vegetarian meals do so because they lack the funds to buy meat. Because meat is a luxury of sorts, people consume as many parts of the animal as they can. Children may eat the chicken's feet or the neck, and people suck the nutritious marrow of chicken bones. The fish *capitaine,* pulled from the Oubangui River, is highly prized in Africa and Europe. Chicken (which also has ritual uses) and beef are popular domesticated meats. Some people prefer game meat varieties, claiming that they have a better flavor than those raised by people. There are many varieties of game meats, including monkey, warthog, antelope, and crocodile.

The vast majority of Centrafricans are much closer to the process of an animal becoming a meal than their Western counterparts are. When an animal is killed, the hides or feathers must be removed along with bones, cartilage, and fascia. Fat is not meticulously eliminated from meat because fat is a highly coveted part of the animal and most Centrafricans do not have high levels of fat in their diets. When a fish is prepared whole, the head, including the eyes, is not removed. Meats are sometimes cut into bite-sized pieces and cooked on a charcoal grill: *brochette*s are very popular at roadsides and bus stops as well as being a favorite bar snack. Most of the time, meats and fish are cooked in sauces. When the meat or fish is a part of the dish that accompanies a *boule* or other starch, it is cooked until it is very tender and the meat is falling off the bones, which makes it easier to share and consume from the communal platter. No matter what kind it is, or how it is prepared, meat is more of a condiment than a main dish.

Other Foods and Condiments

A number of agents and condiments are used to enhance flavors. Salt, as a product distilled from saline water, is not always readily available in rural areas, and Centrafricans have found ways to substitute for it. Although there is "Hausa salt" from a saline source in Adamaoua, local variations are quite popular. Vegetable salts are made from herbs, trees, and aquatic plants. The plants are collected, dried, and piled up before burning them to recuperate the ashes. The potash is then put into a funnel basket. Traditionally, Gbaya women made salt only once a year. The salt would be kept in a small piece of pottery.

Piment, hot pepper, is one of the most important items added to food. *Piment* is added to food while it is cooking. Women also make a sauce that is used to cut down on preparation time and so that people who like their food hotter than it was prepared can add some more heat. The varieties of peppers used in the CAR are very hot. The small seeds are extremely hot and must be removed before they are mixed into the food. People have to be very careful when working with hot pepper because even the slightest touch to the face, especially the mouth, nose, and eyes, can result in excruciating pain.

Condiments are very important for variety. *Yàké,* made by the Gbaya 'bodoe, comes from the berries of the *amblygonocarpus andongensis* tree. Women gather the pods during the dry season and remove the hard covering from the berries with the same instrument they use for pounding wet manioc. The berries are extracted and cooked for about three hours before they are cooled. The juice from the berries becomes a jelly, and people drink it with great relish. Then the women wash the berries and put them into a little basket that is lined and covered with leaves. The berries ferment in the basket for three or four days before being set in the sun on a mat to dry. After they are desiccated, women form the berries into little balls and wrap them in leaves. In the future, when they are used to flavor foods, they will be added to cooking water. The taste of these fermented berries resembles *gruyère* cheese. *Yàké* had become less used by the Gbaya; by the 1970s, only elderly women prepared it because many people held it in low esteem, and young men commonly avoided it. But the Mborro pastoralists started having personal and trading contact with the Gbaya, and they really appreciated the taste of *yàké.* Thus, it became revalorized in the eyes of the Gbaya, who started producing and consuming it again the way that they had in the past.

Oils are also flavorings for dishes, adding much needed fats to the Centrafrican diet. Because the *fufu* and other pounded starches are very firm, oils in sauces help the morsels be chewed and slide down the throat easily. Some sauces, such as a groundnut sauce, do not require additional oil, but the vegetable dishes do. Groundnuts and sesame are expressed for their oil, sometimes by hand. Palm oil is also used in areas where these trees grow. Very high in vitamin A, palm oil is orange and has a very strong flavor. Many Westerners do not like palm oil when they first taste it, but later they often grow to crave it.

The groundnut and sesame residue left over from oil making are turned into pastes that are added to dishes. Also, they can be used to make sauces, adding both flavor and protein to dishes. *Manioc* leaf, an often-consumed dish, not unusually has a ball of creamy groundnut or sesame paste placed in the center of the leaves while it is cooking. Groundnut and sesame paste can also be mixed into chopped vegetables or into wild mushrooms that are placed in leaves and cooked on the side of the fire.

Some of the forms in which protein come in the CAR are very different from what we find in the West. Americans are used to buying meat and fish in markets, usually covered in plastic and cut into ready-to-cook pieces; Centrafricans start with the live animals. Another difference is that one form of protein comes from insects. Some types of insects, especially termites, are highly prized as food. Abundantly available, they can be consumed fresh, dried, or roasted; they are a dish in and of themselves, and they are used as an accompaniment. Fresh termites are washed and often sprinkled with salt and *piment.* Some people will not eat fresh termites and only consume them when they are cooked. For one type of cooked termites, the insects are washed, rinsed, and put into the *marmite* with salt and *piment* and cooked until they are crackling. Some people grill termites (and often take them to add to a watered-down sesame sauce), or cook them in leaves. Dried termites, desiccated in the sun, are eaten as an appetizer, or they are added to food that is being reheated prior to serving it as a way of making leftovers more interesting. Related to termites as food are larvae. They must be washed, cleaned out/voided before preparation. Smaller larvae are often boiled, with salt and *piment* added to the mixture, and are consumed immediately or after they are dried. Some prefer to cook larvae in leaf packages in fires, and large larva can be grilled. Additionally, crickets, cicadas, and grasshoppers (with wings removed and usually the heads as well) are all eaten in the CAR. Insects are easy to prepare and eat.

Manioc leaves are cooked in a number of ways. Although straight into and out of the *marmite* is the most common way to prepare them, they can also be cooked in large leaves. With this method, they are cooked for a very long time, resulting in a food that is preserved well enough to last for three to ten days. Another method of preparation that is good for travelers is for the *manioc* leaves to be cooked and dried in the sun, which allows them to stay good for up to three months. This is done in the rainy season when the leaves are most abundant. The cooking of these dried leaves is also quite easy: Once the water boils, one simply adds the leaves and a bit of oil.

Manioc tubers make more than *fufu*. They are also prepared for quick consumption and to be eaten while traveling. The paste of *manioc* flour can be fried as well. In the rainforest, people make a sour *manioc* bread, *kwange*, and another variety, *mangbere*. These are breads that are wrapped in leaves and baked underground in embers until firm and translucent, or just steamed or boiled, especially in urban areas. The former can be preserved for up to six months, and the latter can stay fresh for days when it is packed in sterile leaves. This food is important, especially for hunters who travel far from home in search of game and when the group moves to a new camp.

"Fast food" is a reality as much in the CAR as in the West. This food is not quickly prepared, but it is made so that it is portable and easily consumed while on the go. Such foods can be prepared at home before a trip, or they are available on the streets or in places where people pass by, prepared by a woman who makes her living selling this sort of food. One such food is *kanda*. One type of *kanda* is made from squash seeds that are roasted and pounded into a paste, combined with termites and rolled into a rounded bar that is wrapped in leaves and grilled. *Kanda* refers not as much to the content, because it also can be made from tender *manioc* leaves or other stuffing, as it does to the leaf-wrapped form. Often *kanda* is eaten with *mangbere*, the fermented *manioc* flour roll. The combination of *kanda* and *mangbere* has been compared to the pairing of a burger and fries. Groundnuts are not just used for sauces, they are also snack foods. Many people enjoy groundnuts, boiled fresh in their shells, or roasted after they have been dried in their shells.

Although they are not in exactly the same category, porridges (*bouillie*) are also popular, in part because they do not require a long cooking time. They are often made from corn or rice; the main ingredient usually depends on what is most readily available and least expensive. A rice porridge is cooked until it is a gelatinous mass, and it is usually sweetened. Some people add groundnut butter to the mixture. Porridges are often prepared by women to soothe the hunger of their families who are waiting for the evening meal. Porridges are also good food for children, who are often hungry and always around food when it is being cooked.

Eating Habits

Eating habits and manners in the Central African Republic, which are quite different from those in the West, are influenced by whether or not one lives in an urban or rural area. One noticeable difference is that men and women do not eat together; men and older boys eat as a group while women and young children form another. Although women and men eat separately, these groups are often seated in close proximity to each other. Also, one's social position can dictate with whom one eats. For example, a son-in-law who is visiting his wife's parents to help them clear a field eats with the younger brothers of his wife, not with his father-in-law or men in his age group. Similarly, a woman visiting her in-laws does not eat with her mother-in-law or her husband's older sisters, but with the younger sisters.

This division in who eats with whom continues in the more immediate family setting. At the beginning of a marriage, a couple is likely to share the same *boule* on a regular basis (and perhaps the wife makes another *boule* for her husband's parents), but that changes as their family expands. The woman eats the *boule* that she prepared for herself and the children, and thus, both girls and boys observe the food taboos of women. (There are also specific food taboos for children.) Her husband will get his own *boule*, which he will share with older boys and other men if he wishes. Sometimes, if there is not a lot of food or it is very late, the whole family will eat together.

There is no set place where people dine, they do so inside and outside, depending on the elements. Visitors are served separately from the family members who are eating together, although for the guest, the meal is the same that everyone else eats. This is part of the hospitality that Centrafricans display. It is not that the guest is not welcome, it is just the opposite. It is considered rude to look at someone while he or she is eating, and eating alone is supposed to make the person more comfortable.

The timing of meals and the number of meals people eat depends on their work schedules. Many people, especially those who farm, eat two meals a day. They may snack between meals, on things such as fruit and nuts, when they get hungry. If people eat a mid-day meal, a period of rest after eating is in order. It both promotes better digestion and offers a respite from laboring during the hottest part of the day.

Before eating, all people must wash their hands. The point is both to clean the hands and to moisten them to facilitate eating, especially if it is *fufu*. A bowl of water is circulated and shared by those who will eat. Normally, they plunge their hands into the bowl. Sometimes, the bowl that holds the water for washing hands is also used for drinking, and in that case, water is poured on the hand that the diner will use for eating. Children always have both their hands washed. If someone has dirty hands, he or she will go somewhere and thoroughly wash them. People eat with the right hand exclusively, as the left hand is reserved for toileting. When people are sharing food consumed with their hands, hygiene is very important and a point of etiquette.

The group of diners eats from a communal platter. There can be anywhere from two to fifteen people sitting together for a meal, but five or six is more common. In general, people sit, but if there are many people, squatting accommodates a larger number. When the *boule* is ready to eat, the woman who prepared it will divide what is in the mortar according to the number and size of the groups. Before the *boules* are served, they will be placed on a plate and covered with *calabashes,* little baskets, or leaves to keep them moist. A woman prepares what she needs for herself, her children, and any others, including guests, who may eat with them.

Everyone cuts a bit of the *boule* with his or her fingers. The piece is stretched into an oblong shape and dragged through the accompanying sauce. Often a person will take enough of the *fufu* to fashion a spoon of sorts with it, so that he or she can scoop up even more of the sauce. Sucking one's fingers during the meal is considered to be gauche. If one's hand is too dry to manipulate the *boule,* it can be rinsed again in the washing water, but this is very rare.

When the sauce contains meat, people appropriate what they can at the beginning of the meal and either place it directly in front of them on the platter or hold it in the hand that is not being used for taking bits of the *boule*—this hand never goes into the communal platter. In the case where there are things such as wild mushrooms in the sauce, people often alternate between a bite of *boule* with sauce, then a bite with a mushroom. If there are a number of people sharing the platter, an adult, usually a senior woman, will divvy up the meat before people start eating.

Meals are generally silent and not lengthy affairs. People sit in a circle, around the *boule* and the accompanying sauce. Water is consumed at the end of the meal; the idea is that, especially at times of food insecurity, one should not fill up on water, but eat as much as possible. Again, a bowl is passed from which all may drink. In urban areas, for people with disposable incomes, it is becoming more common to drink a cold soft drink or a beer with the meal.

Eating Habits in Urban Areas

Food and its consumption in cities, especially Bangui, can be very different. The influence of the West has not affected basic culinary tastes, and most people greatly prefer to eat Centrafrican foods. Even though women in African neighborhoods maintain small kitchen gardens, people in Bangui are dependent on buying food from local markets. For those city dwellers who are involved in agriculture to make a living, they often have to walk many kilometers to their fields. One difference in rural and urban areas is the ability to buy prepared food.

In urban areas, most people eat at home, but there is the option of "street food" from vendors who sell all sorts of foods, such as boiled eggs, *beignets,* and grilled meat. There are also small restaurants, *maquis,* that serve a limited number of African dishes at reasonable prices. One can get in and out of these restaurants quickly because all of the staples and sauces have been prepared in advance. There are also Lebanese restaurants that specialize in shwarma for a quick meal; here the French fries are wrapped into the sandwich. At the top end of the scale, there are high-end restaurants in Bangui that cater to African elites and foreigners; these restaurants serve both African and Western dishes.

The French have impacted the culture of eating. In urban areas, especially Bangui, there are more imported foods, mainly from France, but also items such as Asian rice. Especially among the assimilated, one finds a nuclear family sharing a meal at a table with chairs and people eating with Western utensils instead of their hands. Perhaps the greatest legacy of French cuisine is the *baguette,* the long, white flour baton of bread that is called "French bread" in the United States and is a staple in Bangui. Roadside stalls serve cups of hot, sweet, milky coffee along with half a *baguette* slathered in butter to hungry commuters. Another change is that people consume three meals a day. Some Banguiois, especially those who work in offices, have a higher daily caloric intake than their rural farming compatriots do.

Food Taboos

In the CAR, the food taboos are specific to ethnic groups, social groups, gender, and specific situations such as pregnancy or mourning. Taboos are also tied to clans and allegiances. The totem is the protection for the living members of the family and consuming the flesh of totem animals is the first taboo of the group. Not solely a means of social control, taboos are meant to ensure the smooth functioning of society. People believe that eating certain foods will have a negative impact on people, especially babies who are in utero. Food taboos for women often concern meat. Gbaya 'bodoe women should neither eat snake or fish; they also abstain from baboons and birds that are strictly carnivorous and thus constitute "game for men."

What constitutes food for men versus women? In part, it is the frequency with which the game appears, with the more rare animals being considered masculine. Other game that has a strong taste is in the "food for men" category.

People will say that women do not have a taste for such food. In general, game is considered to be more masculine and domesticated animals more feminine. Because women are not supposed to eat certain types of food, men are the ones who cook "food for men." The very food that is being cooked changes the nature of the gendered division of labor. These dishes are cooked in special pots that women do not use, lest they contaminate the regular cooking pots and expose women to taboo foods. Although men will prepare the meat, the *boule* with which they consume it is made by women.

Fecundity and the health of the baby are of the utmost importance to Centrafricans. Gbaya 'bodoe women are not allowed to eat hens. This is one of the items offered to a woman's future father-in-law to be consumed by the men of that family as a way to seal the union of the marriage. Symbolically, for a women to eat these items would be for her to consume her own fecundity. For this reason, women also do not consume eggs. After a child is born, the mother protects its health by eating and not eating certain foods. Often both parents eat a prescribed regimen. If a man remarries, he does not have to follow food taboos after the birth of his first child with a new wife, but a woman must do so after the birth of the first child with a new husband. Restricted food for new parents among the Gbaya 'bodoe are the popularly consumed *boule* of *manioc* and *manioc* leaf. Instead, "sweet" *manioc* tubers, yams, and banana make up the bulk of the diet at this time.

Food taboos rarely involve insects and vegetables, even though they make up a significant part of the diet. Controlling the consumption of meat is more important. People want to eat meat and getting it requires labor, skill, and luck. Among the Banda, people believe that women who eat tortoise will bear children who are sickly, puny, and prone to premature aging. Women are not allowed to eat monkey because it could make the baby's face contort and be prone to grimacing. Also, no woman wants the mouth of her baby to resemble the big mouth of the monkey. Antelope and gazelle will give the baby skinny legs, and tortoises, reptiles, snakes, and eels are to be avoided because the way they move could influence the child's locomotion.

DRINKS

The Central African Republic is a country where water is plentiful yet scarce at the same time. A safe water source is sometimes difficult to find, and even suspect water sources can be distant from home. Yet, cool water is usually the only drink that accompanies meals. Indigenous fruits such as lemons are juiced for drinks. One drink is the juice of the *Landolphia,* to which sometimes salt, *piment,* a finely chopped onion, and slivers of mint are added. The consumer spits out or swallows the nuts in the juice, depending on his or her preference. Ginger beer (imagine very strong, spicy, and noncarbonated ginger ale) is popular, and its high ginger content is a stimulant of appetite and energy. People who herd or have contact with herders consume milk, but it is often considered to be nonnutritious. For example, the Gbaya drink milk because they exchange one of their commodities for it, but they think that the Mborro are very thin, so it cannot be so good.

In the past, hot beverages were consumed for health reasons, but now people have hot drinks for pleasure. Many hot beverages are concoctions of leaves, roots, or barks chosen for their therapeutic effects in fighting pains, rheumatism, coughs, and fevers. The notion that hot beverages are enjoyable to drink came about when the French introduced coffee at the beginning of the twentieth century and with the commercialization of sugar production under Europeans. Now lemon grass teas, along with "Russian tea," can be purchased in towns in packets. Coffee is also purchased in packets; it is the powdered variety that has been processed outside the country instead of being brewed from beans harvested in the CAR. People now consume coffee socially, often sipping the beverage while sitting around a fire, conversing.

Centrafricans who do not follow the Koran's proscription of alcohol enjoy spirits. They sometimes have ritual significance, as when alcohol is an offering to the ancestors. There is also the social aspect of sharing a drink with family and friends. Additionally, beer is a staple part of nightlife, whether relaxing at home or dancing in a club. There are both imported alcohols from Europe and indigenous alcohols. Red wine and European beer are called "white alcohol" and are available for the few who can afford them. More commonly consumed, especially in rural areas, are alcohols made from locally available stuffs.

Hydromel is a honey-based drink and a traditional alcoholic beverage. Part of *hydromel*'s appeal is that it is not always available. People drink *hydromel* only during the time that honey is harvested, the last month of the dry season and the first three months of the rainy season. Only honey from bees that make the sweetest kind is used. Men collect the honey, and women prepare the *hydromel*. To begin, the honeycomb is crushed into hot water, then germinated sesame seeds are added to begin the fermentation process. Also, for symbolic value, a woman may add a couple of coffee berries or a couple of crushed groundnut shells. The mixture ferments in a pot that is made specifically for this purpose. Traditionally, *hydromel* was a beverage that a couple would share with friends and neighbors, a very local production and consumption, but in the 1980s, the need for money led to its commercialization, and some women specialize in its sale.

Stronger spirits are also made from local ingredients. Today, there are distilleries in many rural areas. Corn and *manioc* are the main ingredients.

Dried grains of corn are shelled and put into cold water to soak for three days before they are removed and set out to ferment. Later the kernels are crushed and then placed into a container. At the same time, the *manioc* is prepared by roasting it before placing it in the water with the corn. It is distilled in a closed vessel, and the vapors escape through a tube that empties into a bowl of cold water that is regularly replaced. The alcohol condenses in a bottle placed just below.

Some foods and other locally available flora are used to make alcohol. Palm wine comes from certain types of palm trees. The trees are tapped, usually after being felled, and opened up with a machete, and the sap from the tree is collected. The palm sap begins to ferment when it comes in contact with air. Sometimes palm wine is consumed as soon as the tree is cut; when the palm wine is very young, it is quite sweet. The longer the palm wine sits, the stronger it gets in taste and potency. As long as one has a starch and a fermenting agent, beer can be made. Beer is prepared from millet, *manioc,* and bananas. These drinks are more refreshing than they are potent. In Bangui, there are two breweries, and the elite are beginning to enjoy a soft drink or beer with their meals.

TRADITIONAL DRESS

What is traditional for clothing for the CAR and what is not? This question is hard to answer because of the creative ways that Centrafricans have assimilated certain aspects of Western styles, along with textiles, and adapted these to forms that make sense to them. Clothing made from imported European cloth is often in the category of "traditional" dress because it is constructed into African styles. Indigenous clothing has changed along with their cultures to produce a vibrant fusion of hues, textures, and styles. In our increasingly close world, African food and African clothing, like African music has already done, are becoming more available and appreciated in the West.

The earliest outfits were minimal. The heat and humidity of the region meant in many ways that less was more. Men and women wore *cache-sexe,* or a loin cloth (although the French version of a "genital hider" is a more accurate description) for everyday life. This provided protection for the reproductive organs and a sense of modesty while not overbearing the wearer with cloth. These were made from soft fibers held by a corded belt that had, for men, another, tighter one underneath. Men also wore belts that held the knives they used in agriculture or hunting. Women often wore belts of leaves that had a tuft in the back as well as one in the front. Cloth was produced from the bark of trees, which was pounded with a hard wood or an ivory club

to remove the fibers and make the bark pliable. Certainly, Centrafricans produced textiles, but often their wearing was reserved for social occasions.

Traditional dress for men included wrappers, *pagnes,* that were securely
folded around the waist. Women also wore *pagnes.* A *pagne* is about 175 centimeters (5.74 feet) long and 120 centimeters (3.94 feet) wide; it is the name
for both the length of cloth and the cloth itself as it is worn. Traditionally,
women wore *pagnes* folded around the waist or sometimes around the chest.
Some women wrap *pagnes* around their waists and wear tops with them.
Women were often bare-breasted. Wearing a *pagne* without a top is not considered scandalous or disrespectful in any way. Breasts are not as sexualized in
traditional African society as they are in the modern West. The clothing of
the denizens of the rainforest was and remains minimal. Because they live in
the hot and humid rainforest and spend their days in hunting and gathering
activities, their clothing must be functional and appropriate. This also reflects
the nonmaterialistic nature of and egalitarianism in their culture.

One outfit that does not make an attempt at egalitarianism is the *grand
boubou;* indeed, it is one of the items that men who want to become businessmen list as an inspiration. This is a three-piece outfit with loose ankle-length
pants, a long-sleeved shirt (that men sometimes do not wear when in an
informal situation), and a large overshirt that could measure as much as five
pagnes of cloth; the rich, imported damask is preferred. The shape of the top
shirt is rectangular with an opening at the neck and the width runs from
fingertip to fingertip. The wearer can pull the material up on the shoulders to
increase air circulation and improve mobility. Often the very fancy cloth is
embellished with detailed embroidery around the neck, wrists, and in the
front where the *grand boubou* has a large pocket. A small hat, embroidered
and of the same material, completes the outfit.

For traditional styles, embroidery is used to embellish clothing and to
complement and enhance the colors and patterns of the cloth. The embroidery can draw the eye up and down or from side to side. It can frame or pull
the eye away from the face. Embroidery patterns are as complex as the fabric
upon which they are sewn. Most often embroidery decorates the opening at
the neck and sleeves as well as the opening of the bottom of the garment.
Especially when the cloth is lightly patterned or unpatterned, embroidery
may be in the middle and the focal point of the garment. Even the material
most often used for the *grand boubou* is patterned. The damask, called *bazin,*
has patterns that are woven into the fabric itself. This increases the richness of
the material and enhances its natural sheen.

Including *pagnes* and other traditional outfits, most women wear the
equivalent of dresses and skirts. Pants are worn by young girls and single,
"evolved" women. Women do not wear shorts. Thighs are considered to be

more sexually suggestive than they are in the West; thus, it is not appropriate to be seen with exposed upper legs. The equivalent to the *grand boubou* for women is the *kaba,* an ample garment worn by *grandes dames.* It is made very similarly to the men's outfit, but there is a skirt instead of pants, and there is no matching shirt worn underneath. There are also more fitted, luxurious outfits made for women with tops and skirts. Both types are crowned by a head-tie in matching cloth. These styles signify a high social status. In Bangui, a woman who wears a *kaba* is called "Mama Kouloutou."

Just as the consumption of meat and fish indicates the wealth and social status of the consumer, clothing reveals the same. Some of the differences in what is worn depend on the quality and origin of the material used. There is a textile company in Bangui, but people in Bangui prefer to wear foreign-made cloth. Some of these are indigo cloth that comes from Togo, Bénin, and Côte d'Ivoire. From Europe comes damask, which is often made into the fancy *kabas* and *grands boubous.* There is also fancy wax cloth that comes from England and the Netherlands. There is cloth that is made, including textiles made in Europe, specifically for the African market in colors and patterns that one does not see in the West.

The fancy wax cloth and the locally produced cotton fabric are specifically made to accord with African aesthetic ideals. Ideas about combinations of colors and patterns are quite dissimilar from those in the West. Imagine seeing an Englishman covered from head to toe in shiny banana yellow cloth. Deep red, bright orange, olive green, dark blue, kelly green, and canary yellow may grace the same piece of cloth. The patterns are quite complex, with angled and soft shapes used together. Animals often appear on locally printed cloth, and there can be a variety of shapes with the animals as well. Festivals, baptisms, and the like are reasons for people to buy new outfits. Cloth is printed for special occasions, such a papal visit or a celebration on the part of a company. A local governor may have the faces of himself and his wife appear on cloth that will be used for a regional celebration.

Western clothes have certainly made an impact on the ways that Centrafricans dress, and the impact is most profound for the urban elite when they are in the workplace. Some have suggested that traditional African clothing is not conducive to the nine-to-five workday (because its comfort leaves people too relaxed to be productive all day long), but it is also because these workers are more likely to work in Western organizations and with Westerners. Also, the level of education (sometimes attained in the West) that these workers have has exposed them to a wider range of tastes. It is not unusual to find men who work in offices in coats and ties or the African version of the leisure suit. This suit has long pants, a matching short-sleeved shirt with a collar, and is not made from material that has traditional African patterns. Women may also wear Western-styled clothing, eschewing miniskirts for a more culturally acceptable length. When people arrive at home, they trade in their suits for more comfortable African clothes. For many people, the wearing of a three-piece suit during the day is a signal that the wearer has "arrived."

The foreign impact on clothing is not limited to the urban elite. People who live in rural and urban areas wear clothing that comes from the West, sometimes clothing that has been donated to charity that people purchase in local markets. Manmade fibers have also become popular. Although the material does not breathe as well as cotton, men find that synthetic pants are good for walking through the savanna; people also wear shirts and shoes of nonorganic materials.

In the countryside, many people do not wear shoes on a daily basis. For working in the fields, going to fetch water, or walking to do an errand, Centrafricans are usually barefoot. They are accustomed to going about without shoes and develop calluses that protect their feet. For hunting, some men do wear sandals or shoes, which was traditional, because there are more dangers in the high grasses and in the rainforest. In the city, more people wear shoes, especially those who work in offices, who may sport fancy imports from Europe.

ORNAMENTATIONS AND HAIR

Ornaments are important accessories to complete an outfit. In precolonial days, ornamentation was as important as it is now. Scarification, the making of patterns on skin through a series of small cuts, was popular and available to all. Tattooing was also done, with pastes of pulverized woods and oil that was not permanent for special occasions; herb paste was rubbed into small incisions to create permanent body art. Jewelry was also worn, and it sometimes indicated one's status. Early ethnographers reported that among the Gbaya people, only old men had the right to adorn their ear lobes with ivory or polished ebony plaques and that while men regularly wore iron bracelets on their arms, only chiefs were permitted to wear an iron bracelet around the ankle. Another manner of body alteration is the filing of front teeth that is rarely practiced today. Ornaments and ornamentations continue to have symbolic and aesthetic significance today.

Like ornaments, hair is decorative. As in the West, hairstyles can consume much time in their preparation and are often done in a group setting. Hair's presentation varies from the quotidian to the special. For special occasions, Gbaya men used to completely shave their heads. For everyday, young men used to let single tufts grow from the top of the head that they would allow to grow and braid into three or four sections. Adult males had the same tuft, but they would let it grow without treating it. Old men and young boys kept their heads completely shaved. Mature men wore beards that they sometimes twisted into two points and some chose to shave their moustaches. Today Centrafrican men wear their hair short, and some choose to have facial hair. Men did not and do not have as many options for hairstyles as women.

Braiding hair is the norm for women, and there are many hairstyles that women produce. Gbaya women used to add colorful feathers, shells, and beads to their hair on special occasions. Today women still want to have their hair done for a special occasion. In Bangui, there are hair-styling stations on practically every corner. These are not veritable salons, although there are places where one can have her hair relaxed and where Western styles are done, but more popularly, there are tables and chairs set out for the stylists and customers. These places, along with their counterparts for men, are advertised with brightly colored, hand-painted signs with pictures of the styles available. The prices vary according to the style and the amount of time that it takes to produce it, and some can take more than seven hours. Fidelity to a stylist is rewarded with lower prices. The results of these braidings varies from the plain to the spectacular. Sometimes braids are done in neat rows straight back from the hairline to the neck; this is more typical of the braiding that girls do while resting in the shade after lunch. Some are complex with patterns that have twists and turns, some have parts that are elevated, some have pompons, and some require thread to keep the styles in place. No matter what her socio-economic class, every girl learns to braid hair.

Despite the elaborate hairdos that many women sport, a head-tie often covers their creations. Head-ties are practical because they keep hair clean, especially during the dry season and in urban areas. Head-ties are attractive as well. Sometimes women will tie their hair with a simple *pagne* or piece of cloth, usually in an emergency, but it is often part of an outfit, especially traditional styles and the *kaba*. In this case, the cloth is of the same material as the rest of the outfit. The head-tie should not be confused with a bandana. It is made from a much bigger piece of cloth, and its tying is more elaborate. Ridges and peaks are created to accentuate the face and complement the cut of the outfit. When they are well done, they draw a person's attention to the woman's face.

As is the case with cuisine, the West has had an impact on indigenous clothing, but it has not altered the way most people dress. One of the differences that is most apparent between the way people dress in the United States and in the Central African Republic is the level of casualness or dressiness in what people wear. African traditional dress, especially the dressier items, is conservative. Centrafricans do not subscribe to the notion of casual chic or dressing down the way Americans do. For example, a Centrafrican would not wear flip-flops or a T-shirt to a meeting because that would be interpreted as a sign of disrespect on the part of the one who was casually dressed. Also, although most Centrafricans may not have the money to buy fancy outfits, personal appearance is still very important. Someone's clothes may be patched, but they will be scrupulously clean and impeccably pressed. The way that a person dresses is indicative of what the person thinks about himself or herself and those the person encounters. To dress well is to demonstrate respect.

Food, drink, and dress have all been impacted by the West, but people return to their African roots for inspiration. Food, especially for people in the countryside, is the same as what their ancestors ate, and it is eaten in the same manner in which they ate. Even urban elites who have the most exposure to and ability to consume Western food usually prefer traditional dishes. The case is the same with clothing. Centrafrican ideas about what is and is not appropriate for clothes are adapted to aspects of Western clothing, but most people choose to wear the indigenous styles that have served people well for centuries.

A field in the outskirts of Ouango. Courtesy of Molly Smith Mullally.

On the road from Bema to Ouango. Courtesy of Molly Smith Mullally.

A stop for repairs on the road to Bangassou. Courtesy of Molly Smith Mullally.

A man, perhaps forging metal, in a village between Ouango and Bema. Courtesy of Molly Smith Mullally.

Workers in the middle of cotton production. © Barry D. Kass/Images of Anthropology.

Harps are very popular instruments in the CAR. This nineteenth-century Mangbetu (closely related to the Zandé) *kùndi* is made from wood, hide, metal, and beads. The anthropomorphized harp features intricacies such as jewelry, scarifications, and elaborately braided hair. Courtesy of Founders Society Purchase, Henry Ford II Fund, Benson and Edith Ford Fund, Photograph © 1982 The Detroit Institute of Arts.

Children sitting in an Aka Pygmy hut. © Barry D. Kass/Images of Anthropology.

Net fishing from a *pirogue*. Courtesy of Molly Smith Mullally.

Woman preparing cassava root. © Barry D. Kass/Images of Anthropology.

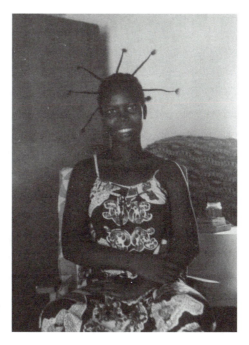

A woman in Ouango. Courtesy of Molly Smith Mullally.

A Chadian merchant with his children in Ouango. He is wearing an abbreviated version of the *grand boubou*. Courtesy of Molly Smith Mullally.

A family in Ouango dressed up to have its picture taken in front of the banana trees. Courtesy of Molly Smith Mullally.

A family in Ouango posing in their Sunday best. Courtesy of Molly Smith Mullally.

A classroom in Ouango. Courtesy of Molly Smith Mullally.

Students in a *sixieme* class in Ouango. Courtesy of Molly Smith Mullally.

Teenage boy in front of his house. The material that he is wearing bears the name and logo of MOCAF, the brewery in Bangui. Courtesy of Molly Smith Mullally.

A gathering of neighbors in Ouango. Courtesy of Molly Smith Mullally.

Aka Pygmies performing a ritual dance. © Barry D. Kass/Images of Anthropology.

Women and children in a small village watch a dance. © Barry D. Kass/Images of Anthropology.

6

Gender Roles, Marriage, and Family

In the Central African Republic, family is the basis of self-identification and a key building block of society. Because of the centrality of family, marriage is a key moment in the life of a Centrafrican, the event that allows the person to begin to fulfill his or her ultimate purpose in life: the creation of a new family. Kinship groups are large, complex, and fluid; some families are polygynous, others are monogamous. Gender roles in relationships are clearly defined. Every couple wants to have both boys and girls as offspring, seeing the combination of both sexes as pleasing and harmonious. Marriage and family are not only expectations from society, but they are social security for people throughout their lives. Lineage is a refuge for all, but the immediate family is the true safety net.

CONCEPTS OF GENDER

Gender affects many aspects of the lives of Centrafricans. In the CAR, as in other African countries, there are very clear ideas about what personal qualities men and women should have and what their roles in society are. Of course, colonization altered traditional gender roles. Marriage and family have undergone great transformations from the precolonial era to the present, and many people look to an idealized past as a way of envisioning the future. For Centrafricans, men and women have complementary roles; both are essential, even if men have more power and authority than women. This is understood as the natural and preordained order of things.

Gender was a way of organizing society on a basis that was both organic and mandated by a higher power. In addition to living creatures, gender was assigned to objects as well, based on what their nature was considered to be. For example, among the Gbaya 'bodoe, different types of wood are gendered because men and women light fires for different reasons: Men light fires to keep them warm as they sit and talk with other men in the evening and men select wood from the forest for this purpose; women light fires to cook and they opt for wood from the savanna. As in all societies, there is gendered division of labor: men's work and women's work. The rationale for this is that men and women had complementary roles and this way of organizing work and society ensured that everything necessary was done. One of the most evident ways that work is separated is in agriculture. Basically, men clear the fields and women tend them. Women are also involved in all aspects of changing crops into meals, from harvesting to food conservation and preparation. The food that they produce satisfies domestic consumption and any products that were in surplus could be traded for other goods.

In the precolonial era, gender was clearly defined. There was a parallel functioning of the genders and the rights of women were analogous to those of men. Women were involved in the running of those things that pertained to women; for example, if there were discussions about the use of a *manioc-soaking* pond, women would be the ones who made the decision about its use because preparing cassava was women's work and men should not get involved. Women had agency in their personal and family lives as well; they enjoyed sexual freedom, some even into their marriages, and could also initiate divorce. Females could own personal possessions and do with them what they wanted. Equally important was their ability to participate in decision-making processes. More than just allowing them to weigh in on the affairs of their immediate families, the society accepted their counsel on issues that affected the wider community because they were members of it.

WOMEN

The status of African women is a topic of interest for the West, where they are often portrayed as powerless and oppressed people. This is too simple an explanation for the lives of women in the Central African Republic. Their status is an inheritance from the precolonial era, combined with the new customs imposed on all Centrafricans by the colonization, and the more recent era in which people's ideas about how women and men should behave and what they should do is under discussion and revision. Traditional societies were certainly male-dominated, and women gained power and authority depending on their age, personality, and fecundity. As women progress in their life cycles, they gain highly cherished wisdom, and as they pass through menopause, they often are regarded differently. No longer capable of reproducing children, their essential feminine element is no longer in action, and they are seen as honorary men.

The Central African Republic is a male-dominated society, and its ethnic groups place women in positions that are subordinate to men. This is not to say that women do not exercise power, but they do so in less public ways. Women direct the activities of their households and influence the decisions that their husbands make on all levels, even if they must cater to the whims of their mates. Women are supposed to obey and be faithful to their husbands, raise the children, farm, and do housework. Women are supposed to be stoic, tolerate their husbands' infidelities, and follow the rules of their husbands, fathers, and other men. Although national law stipulates that married women have the right to work outside the home, this is often ignored by husbands who want their wives to stay home. This is particularly true among those of medium and higher means.

Women are supposed to display obedience, chastity, and stoicism. They learn to withstand physical pain in initiation to prepare them for the future. Women who yell or complain during childbirth are shamed and ostracized. Women are supposed to endure in silence all the difficulties and pains that life may bring. This training and inculcation translate into women thinking that they are supposed to be subordinate to men and to obey them. Women who refuse to submit to their husbands' authority are often victims of domestic violence. Many men believe that their wives should do as they say or be punished, and women have been taught that this is their lot in life. However, in recent years, women have begun to protest their ranking as second-class citizens and the results that this position afflicts on them. Bolstered by interest from the government and some legal changes, women's organizations work to better women's rights and voice in government.

The case of adultery is a good example of gender differences in the CAR, their legal and social ramifications, and how women often receive the short end of the stick. Legally, adultery is not permitted under the country's civil code. Socially, it is a serious transgression, especially on the part of a woman, and there is a certainly a double standard. If a woman commits adultery, her husband can ask her family to return the bridewealth. In the case that a man catches his wife in the act of having sex with another man, the murder of the wife and her sexual partner are excusable. Marital infidelity is not a serious offense for a man; rather, it is expected that men will look for a sexual partner outside of marriage. For the urban elite, the concubine is referred to as the *deuxième bureau* or second office; some women are kept by their married lovers, whose legitimate wives feel that they have no recourse and must accept the situation. Women "of a certain age" who allow themselves to look after a younger man are known as "mother superior." If an adulterous man is imprisoned for his affair, his wife usually brings him food every day while he is in jail. Because the position of an unmarried or divorced woman can be precarious, she often makes peace with her circumstances because of her economic vulnerability, to keep the family together, and to maintain her position in society.

Most women do not have steady jobs, and they have to piece together livings from various sources. Women rule the markets. Men sell certain items such as meats, but women sell the surplus food that they grow, textiles, and other key items. In the market at KM5, the city's largest, women sell their wares in friendly competition, calling out to shoppers to come see their wares. Women also sell food and alcohol that they make in their homes, along with cold drinks and cigarettes in an area that abuts the house. Restaurants are also in the purview of women, not the formal kind, but roadside that serve the same kinds of food that the average person would eat at home. Women tend to reinvest their small profits in their families by buying household necessities and by putting them back into their businesses. These small sums allow them to buy more necessities, such as firewood, food, medicine, as well as paying their children's school fees. Outside of vending, women's participation in the economy was basically through the production of foodstuffs, fishing, harvesting, and making some artisanal products. Some women resort to selling their sexual services.

Existence for women is precarious in rural and urban areas. Women suffer from a lack of accessible health care, which is most evident in the high rates of maternal and child mortality. Women are subject to domestic violence, rape, forced prostitution, and other sorts of violence as are women everywhere, but it is female genital cutting that is the most evident target of both international and domestic protest.

Women are sometimes considered to be dangerous. Their menstrual blood is reputed to be so powerful that women are not permitted to walk across fields while they menstruate because if a drop should fall, no plant would grow. Men cannot have sexual relations with their wives while they have their periods, nor can they eat food that they prepare. Some women may not cross the thresholds of their husbands' houses and some women even remove themselves from their normal place of residence. Likewise, the blood that accompanies childbirth is thought to be essential and dangerous, and women are not permitted to cook until the baby's belly button stump has fallen off.

Colonial rule's impact on Centrafricans was wide-ranging and that included gender relations. For women, the preexisting favoring of men was made more severe with Victorian notions of gender and the roles of women that were carried from Europe by imperialists. The superimposed ideas about the inferiority of women bolstered the idea that men were naturally in charge of all aspects of life. The complementary nature of the relationship between men and women was replaced by a gender construct in which women's contributions were less important. This can be seen in the laws that the French created.

Previously, land was not owned by individuals but meted out by chiefs or lineage heads, according to the needs of the community. When the French introduced the practice of land ownership and commercial farming, they prohibited women from having title to land. Land was owned by men who would control its use and the agriculture that it produced. Women were still the major producers of foodstuffs, but they were not involved with cash crops. These products, intended for the external market, were grown by men. Women were excluded from this sector of agriculture because the colonial government believed that wage earning was the prerogative of men. Also women were no longer allowed to divorce or to own private property. They continued to grow the food for their families. These legal changes were readily accepted by men who found that women were more and more dependent upon them, especially economically, and this suited the preexisting mentality.

Men's participation in cash cropping changed precolonial patterns in gendered work because the daily agricultural work had been women's work. Men accepted this new situation because they worked very different crops, and they earned cash for their produce. When women participated in cash crop production, their roles were subordinate, laboring when their husbands needed them, but rarely enjoying the economic benefits of their efforts. Cash crops were sold in a different way as well; they went to the local European purchasing agent instead of being bartered or used to support the alimentary needs of the family as women's production would.

When women began migrating to Bangui, it was principally to follow their husbands. Many men went to the city alone, leaving wives and children behind in the villages. Seeing the low number of marriageable men in the village, some young women moved to the city, hoping to improve their chances of wedding. This is still true today. Some move to escape the confines of family or village life. Once in Bangui, many females work in domestic positions, some marry and have traditional lives, and a few are able to go to school.

LIFE FOR WOMEN

The lives of women in the CAR can be quite constricted because they are supposed to obey their husbands, live with them, be faithful to them, take care of and raise the children. Their inability to act with autonomy, coupled with the lack of access to credit, greatly limits opportunities for women. Elite women have more opportunities available to them, and often, more autonomy and agency. For the majority, however, life is a daily struggle to keep themselves and their families happy and healthy. With education, some women have been able to find jobs in retail shops, teaching, nursing, and in the government. The majority, however, live lives that are similar to the ones they left behind in the village.

Despite the reputed glamour, urban life does not automatically mean a better life for women. They are still subject to physical abuse, rape, genital alteration, forced prostitution, and various forms of exploitation. Ideas about gender relationships and roles do not change, and, except for those who have achieved high levels of education, women are still relegated to their traditional professions. The woman in an urban polygynous marriage is often less happy than her rural counterpart because the living quarters are so close. Also, it is easier for a man to keep another woman secretly in the city, as there are more places for her to live where she will not encounter the legitimate wife.

There is an increasing recognition of the second-class status under which Centrafrican women operate. Since independence, there have been a growing number of studies that focus on the situation of women, and these are helpful in examining the realities of their lives and those of their children. Health care, violence, and women's status are focal points. In December 2005, the Minister of Communication, Fidel Ngouandjika, threatened legal action against anyone who broadcast songs that are misogynistic, claiming that popular culture is helping to further the notion that women are inferior to men. Critics claim that this is not doing enough, but it is a message sent through the most popular medium of news and entertainment in the country. Women's organization such as the Union of Centrafrican Women are important in local politics and work on issues relevant to females and the greater Centrafrican society.

Women often lack direct control over their lives; however, social status and religion can mitigate or enhance their agency. One factor is that, although they are allowed to participate in public meetings, women are unsure if they can attend and speak their minds; elder women are among a chief's close advisors, but their advice is usually limited to the area of conjugal affairs. Older women can claim authority because their roles as wives and mothers have helped to assure the survival of the clan, but often, younger women are too busy to attend village meetings. Peasant women are very much under the control of their fathers and husbands, but elite women have more freedom. For example, the princesses of the Bandia are not marred like other women, they are neither doweried nor exchanged, but instead select men of their own choosing. Additionally, the Bandia preserve the notion of the infallibility of women's intuition and caution men to take the counsel of their wives before making decisions. Women who follow traditional religions are supposed to stay at home if their husbands are there and they do not have chores outside the home, but they come and go as they please when the men are gone. Muslim women have less mobility and must often stay in their compounds. They should walk in public only with their husbands, speak only to men that they know, and leave the compound only if the father or husband has given permission.

Family Life

In the CAR, families are extended, and their structure means that family members are intimately connected through various means: bloodline, initiation, fraternal and sororal relationships, apprenticeships, marriage, and more. Because families live in compounds with many generations, aunts, uncles, grandparents, and cousins have daily contact with each other. Elders have great control over their kin: They are in charge of familial resources and make the decisions that impact the group as a whole. Elders of different families form a group that hands down decisions that impact the village. Although elders have great impact on the families' activities, ancestors do as well.

Ancestors are, in a sense, a part of the extended family. Those who have died become ancestors and continue to influence the lives of their families on earth. Ancestors exist in a parallel world, and their spirits may be found close to their graves on the family's land. It is important that family members remember the names of their ancestors and pay homage to them. They make sacrifices, either done by the head of the family on the part of everyone or people may make personal sacrifices. People may ask, for example, for the ancestors to bestow an abundant harvest or great fecundity on a woman. Neglected ancestors can be mischievous and cause their living relatives minor to major misfortune. People believe that infants are particularly close to the ancestors because of their very young age, and indeed, that ancestors can be reincarnated into their families. Children are a bridge to the other world.

Children are the future and the past. Children are highly cherished, as offspring are wealth, prestige, companions, and people's legacies. As a source of wealth, they provide labor to sustain the family, and they form part of the group of influence that the lineage has. Children will ensure the continuity of the family and the lineage; having children allows the group to perpetuate itself. It is also the way that an individual finds self-realization. Having children means that when one passes away, one's offspring will venerate the deceased, making sure that the individual will not be forgotten.

The *pater familias* is an essential role, and he makes the family's principal decisions. Although women are caretakers and educators, it is the family of the father, because most people are patrilineal and patrilocal, that takes primacy. Men can marry their children off at a young age, influencing the ability of the lineage to regenerate itself. Men are charged with providing for their families, ensuring that wives and children have what they need to sustain them and make them prosperous. Men must provide their wives with housing and conjugal visits.

The mother is central to the household and the family. In a polygynous family, all of the wives act as mothers to all the children, and the offspring are treated as brothers and sisters. A child must obey its biological mother's co-wives as the child would obey her. Older sisters take on the roles of mothers as they learn how to become adult women and mothers. These girls are called *mama kété* or "little mother." Mothers educate their children, provide moral guidance, nurture, and love them. Women are the primary transmitters of culture. Even though most Centrafrican societies are patrilineal, and in the case of marriages, across ethnic lines, women move into the culture of their husbands. This means that these women learn the cultures of their husbands and their families, including the language. Mothers are the ones responsible for all that pertains to the health and well-being of the children. This is her role as a woman and a mother. Women who have many children and raise them in a satisfactory manner may receive the "mother's medal" from the government.

CREATING AND SUSTAINING LIFE

Many Centrafricans understand their purpose in life is to have and raise children. Individuals are members of the community, and it takes vigilance on the part of the social whole to raise the person, yet it is the mother who is ultimately charged with the health and well-being of her family. From the moment a child is conceived, Centrafricans do all that they can to be sure that the child is protected and nurtured so that he or she can do the same for the preceding and future generations. For Centrafricans, children are life and continuity; without them, human existence would not have meaning or a future.

Fecundity

The ability to conceive and give birth to a healthy child is one of the most important aspects of womanhood. Centrafricans believe that even though it is the man who actually creates life, women are responsible for its nurturing.

An inability to become pregnant is the woman's fault; it is a lack of food and heat in her body that does not allow the fetus to properly develop. She who is unable to have children is in a precarious position in Centrafrican society, and although it is not uncommon that a couple cannot conceive, the man is never blamed for infertility.

There are many things that a woman can do to lose her fecundity, such as breaking a taboo. The legality of a marriage is supposed to have an impact on the ability to reproduce; if a marriage does not have the consent of the pair's families or they move away from the family, the capacity to have children becomes impaired. A lack of fecundity is a serious problem for a woman. Those who do not bear children are considered lesser women at least, and divorced and shunned at worst. The inability to conceive or to have a boy is considered grounds for divorce. If a woman cannot get pregnant or carry a child to term, she will often ask her husband to take another wife so that he can have children. Those who have many children are lauded for their reproductive abilities; their fecundity is seen as proof of their valor and correct comportment.

People also believe that a couple without children is not happy and that happiness corresponds to the number of children one has. It is difficult for women to try to limit their pregnancies; their husbands, their in-laws, and their parents all want the couple to produce offspring. The husband and his mother want to have children to increase the size of their patrilineal line, and her family wants to be sure that a lack of children will not give the husband cause for divorce or for a demand that part of the bridewealth be returned.

Controlling one's reproductive abilities is an issue fraught with difficulty. Many women are skeptical about modern methods of contraception, believing that they are irreversible and cause miscarriage or sterility. Yet a woman is supposed to be able to somewhat control her own ability to conceive in a traditional manner. A Gbaya-Kara woman who is menstruating or has just given birth can use some of this blood wrapped in a packet of leaves and bury it at the bottom of a firepit, saying:

> I don't want to have any more children
> Here is my fecundity which I bring
> I give it to you, *termitière kùsì*,[1]
> Keep it for me

When she wishes to recuperate her ability to become pregnant, she takes a bit of *manioc* that she has dried in the sun, taps the spot with the *manioc* and eats it to symbolize the return of her fecundity, and says:

I entrusted my fecundity to you,
Termitière kùsì,
I am taking it back
To become pregnant again[2]

This is a very private ritual; it has to be because what she is doing goes against society's norms in its first incarnation.

The goal of many practices is to ensure that a couple is able to have children and food taboos are an easy method. Proscribed foods for women include eggs and hens, both of which represent fecundity. Also these items are often gifts made by her family to the family of her husband in marriage rituals. Were a woman to consume the eggs or a hen produced by her kin, she would be figuratively eating her own ability to reproduce. Her husband is also careful about not consuming either of these products produced by his wife's lineage. If a woman looses children early in her life, sacrifices are made (often a goat kid) in the attempt to sway the spirits and the ancestors, imploring them not to let the same sad event happen again. There is also a notion that the legality of the couple's union impacts their ability to have children; ancestors who are upset that a couple has ignored the wishes of the family or had not had a legalized union may not help the couple conceive.

Pregnancy

The birth of a child is a most joyous time in people's lives. This is the case for the parents, the extended family, and the community as a whole. Giving birth and all that leads up to and follows the event are carefully orchestrated and ritualized to ensure that people are conducting themselves in ways that are pleasing to the families, friends, neighbors, and, of course, the ancestors. Having children is the realization of one's sacred duty to family.

The many ways to safeguard a pregnancy are all in the control of the pregnant woman. It is most important that she not announce her condition; even when her state is clear by the size and shape of her belly, a woman does not say anything about it. People look for signs that a woman is with child, especially a woman who has recently married, and it is exterior signs and behavioral changes that make her status clear to everyone. One of the indications is reputed to be that a woman will have more placid relations with co-wives and potential wives once she is pregnant. Her in-laws also keep a very watchful eye over her to ensure that she will not do anything that can adversely affect the fetus.

A woman who has committed some transgression will often go to a "medicine man" to confess her sins to the spirits. A pregnant woman also wears a charm around her waist. These belts can protect the fetus from malfeasance, and they can influence the gender of the baby. A woman who has many children of the same gender will exchange her belt with a woman who has had many of the opposite gender. This is usually done by women who know each other very well and have great trust in each other; in rural areas they are usually of the same lineage, in Bangui, the women can simply be friends or neighbors.

Although the woman is not responsible for creating life, she is entirely responsible for protecting the life that grows in her body. There are many superstitions surrounding pregnancy and signs are taken from the fauna with which a woman comes into contact. Some people believe if a firefly alights on a woman's arm, she will soon become pregnant and that the benevolent presence of a snake is indicative of twins. Pregnant women must observe strict food taboos, both of her own and those of her husband's lineage. There are definitely foods not to be consumed and restrictions extend even to the way that food is prepared and how it is consumed. The food that she eats must be prepared in a separate pot to ensure that no illicit food touches her lips. The woman should avoid the market and eat only what comes from her garden. If she does not cook for herself, the person who prepares her food should be her mother-in-law or a woman who has a profound desire to see her deliver a happy and healthy baby. For more about these food taboos, see Chapter Five. Women also take great pains to ensure that they will not be observed while they are eating.

Any case of uncertainty is also to be avoided. Pregnant women are distrustful of new things. Many people believe that the fetus develops at night, so women take care not to be alone at this time. A pregnant woman is vigilant about paying attention to her dreams and nightmares and someone who stays with her makes sure that she is not awakened at night. Waking suddenly can encourage malformed limbs or ear problems. There are definite ideas about how pregnant women should sit—on a mat is preferable to the low chairs that one finds throughout the country because people think that if the mother sits with bent legs, that is the way that the baby will present himself or herself at birth. There are also a plethora of ideas about things that are harmful to the developing baby. The mother being seen while bathing, drinking water while standing, and sexual intercourse too late in the pregnancy are among the many potential hazards.

A woman who is pregnant is considered to be impure from the time that people are aware she is pregnant to the time that she weans her baby. Thus, by ancient custom, women are proscribed from having sex until the child is of the appropriate age; it is at weaning for some people, at the infant's first steps for others. This allows women more opportunity to choose when they will become sexually active again. Often, though, an authority figure such as a lineage head or the mother-in-law decides when the couple resumes its conjugal life.

Birth

A conscientious woman anticipates the uncomplicated and quick birth of a normal and healthy child, but this is not always the case. Childbirth in the Central African Republic is riskier than it is in more developed countries. In fact, it is tied with two other African nations for the highest maternal mortality rate in the world with 1,100 deaths per 100,00 births. Infant morality rates (the number of children dying before reaching the age of one) is 92.15 out of every 1,000 live births, the 18th-highest percentage.[3] Women in urban areas can choose to go to clinics or hospitals, but few rural women opt to travel to give birth; most do not have the resources to do so. Some rural women give birth while they are in the fields, sitting on a *pagne* or banana leaf. However, they usually deliver their babies at home and are attended by the women of their community. The women present at the birth assure the mother, try to make her more comfortable, and make sure that all is done according to ritual.

Birth is an exclusively female enterprise and mid-wifery is an age-old and revered profession. When birth seems imminent, the woman usually stays with the family of her husband, but a few do go to their village of origin. She who has female relatives come to stay with her is usually giving birth for the first time, and the woman must often ask permission of her husband to have her mother or aunt come. As the delivery approaches, the pregnant woman drinks an infusion of herbs that helps to speed along the process, and sometimes herbs are rubbed into the vulva and onto the belly. This helps with the pain and facilitates contractions.

If a woman has a difficult birth or a long labor, community members suspect the woman of either having broken a taboo or having an adulterous affair. The difficulty is caused by the ancestors displaying their displeasure about her transgression by using the infant who does not want to be born into an unpleasant situation. The gathered women urge her to confess her sins. If she does confess to having an affair, but the birth does not progress, she must then name the man and explain how it happened. People believe that if she does not confess and she is guilty, the child will die in her womb. There is generally a code of silence among those in the birthing room, but a suspicious husband might ensure that his sister is among the women in attendance. Male adultery does not usually manifest itself in difficulty in birth, but if it does, the man should approach his laboring wife and tell her how many women he has had extramarital sex with, but he does not provide their names. He then washes her belly and tells her that because he has confessed, she can now give birth. The woman's mother-in-law may try to bring the affair to its rightful conclusion by saying to the soon-to-be born that it should be born if it is of the husband's lineage and return from whence it came if not.

The family of the father lays claim to the infant at birth. The mother-in-law is near the woman who is giving birth as a female representative of the husband's family; it is a way of laying the family's claim to the child. It is usually the paternal grandmother who catches the baby. The cord is cut, and, with the placenta, buried near the house. This affirms the connection between the ancestors, their land, and the newborn. The husband usually does not enter into the house until the cord is cut.

Villagers come out to welcome the newest member of their community. People bring presents to the newborn, often foods such as peanuts and fruits, and sometimes a chicken. Infants are passed around and everyone holds them, articulates their limbs, and listens to their chests, reassuring themselves that the child is healthy and introducing themselves to the new life. "May the ancestors give you beautiful children and have you give birth often" is a popular sentiment for visitors to exclaim to the new parents after the birth has been announced. It is not uncommon for a member of the husband's lineage to leave a basket at the door of the house with an offering (such as a white hen) to signal the pleasure of the family and to distance evil spirits from the baby.

The same principles about behavior that guide pregnancy are still at work postpartum. At the birth of a couple's first child, the pair must follow food taboos. If the mother has married more than once, she must do this for each husband with whom she has a child. Men, who are far more likely to have more than one wife because women can only marry serially, are obliged to follow the special diet only for the birth of the first child. Other methods of assuring the good health of the baby after birth include having the mother eat boiled vegetables, which is supposed to stimulate abundant lactation. Also the family visits the "medicine man" with a piece of each parent's clothing, from which a little band will be woven while saying ritual phrases. This cord is tied around the baby's wrist.

Depending on the ethnic group, the birth of an albino or twins is seen either as a precursor to happiness or sadness. They are feared and great attention is paid to them; they can be simultaneously respected and loathed. Twins are considered to be endowed with supernatural powers and knowledge that can render them dangerous when displeased. Twins are consulted before undertaking hunting expeditions or beginning a trip. Parents of twins often have to follow different food taboos after their births, and rituals for twins are also different from those for single children.

The social norm is for married women to get pregnant, but of course, that is not always the case. Being a single mother poses extra challenges. School-girls who get pregnant are usually expelled and once the baby is born, it is difficult for a girl to return to school because her need to care for the child conflicts with keeping up with her lessons. Even if she has the funds to go to school, the girl usually stays home after the birth of her child.

In Bangui, women who are in marriages recognized by the state and who are salaried in either the public or private sectors are guaranteed prenatal and postnatal periods of leave during which they receive their salaries, half paid by the employer and half paid by the state. When they return to work, these women are also allowed to leave their place of employment for up to an hour a day for 15 months to breastfeed. Children accompany those who are infor-mally employed while they work in the fields or in the markets, which at least eliminates the need for child care. These women also can have their babies in a hospital instead of at home. Women in the capital are discreet about their pregnant state and giving birth. Those who give birth in hospitals are less likely to make confessions about adulterous relationships because they are not surrounded by the critical eyes of their family and neighbors while in labor.

NAMING AND BAPTISM

The naming of the baby has great significance for the family and for the baby's future. The father's family typically chooses the names, and it is usually done by the baby's father or paternal grandfather; he often does so in refer-ence to the moment when the child was born or to a family ancestor. Gener-ally, if the infant is healthy, the naming takes place on the third day after birth for a boy or the fourth for a girl; this coincides with the approximate time that the infant's umbilical cord stump falls off. Usually, it is a godparent who announces the name to everyone else.

The godparent then brings a present to the mother. The present is gender specific and represents the kind of work that the child will perform as an adult. Presents for a male child include a machete and a lance, and for a female, a *manioc* baton and a fishing net. Both genders can receive a hoe. The godparents also give protective amulets to the baby. After the baby has been born, the mother can leave the house for the first time; often the mother and baby decamp for a period to stay in the home of a friend to escape evil spirits who may wish to do the child harm.

Baptism is similar to the naming process as it is one step toward attaining adulthood, and it is practiced by both Muslims and Christians. Christian baptism practices are similar to those in the West with a priest or minister in charge of the ceremony. The event is celebrated with friends and family who gather for food, beverages, and the giving of gifts to the baby. Muslims also have baptism ceremonies led by the *málùm*. His assistant shaves the baby's head seven days after birth. Women, including the baby's mother, are excluded from this ceremony. The baby's father keeps the women informed of the goings-on and announces the name that the women then shout three times. The ceremony is followed by festivities with food for the people of the neighborhood and gifts for the baby. The money that the infant receives is a sacrifice to the ancestors, and it is understood as the foundation of future prosperity.

THE EARLY YEARS OF CHILDHOOD

The newborn is considered to be a very close link to the ancestors, even the reincarnated spirit that has returned to the world. People believe that babies are capable of communicating with the ancestors, that the inarticulate sounds a baby makes are communications with those in the other world. This ability runs through the period when a small child is not effectively able to verbally communicate with adults. Once a child is able to speak, this supernatural communication ends, and the child must be educated and initiated into adult life as soon as possible.

In part because the father and mother cannot have sexual relations, the baby becomes the mother's sole concern. In this sense, the father and head of the family loses his primacy. The mother is considered to be responsible for virtually everything that happens to the baby. If the child should fall sick, the mother is immediately suspected; often people think that she had sex with the baby's father before the appropriate time. The mother is not solely responsible for the baby's health: If the baby's father has sex with another women, he must wash his entire body before picking up the baby or else risk the baby falling ill.

All precautions are taken to ensure that the baby is happy and healthy. Babies are bathed two or three times a day. The wearing of amulets ensures the baby's health and future. If a baby has a *gris-gris* that comes from an animal, it is hoped that the child will pick up that animal's main attribute. The most important way to keep the baby happy and healthy is to keep it close to its mother, and the infant is very much attached at the hip. Except for those who live in Bangui, it is extremely rare to have a mother who stays in the house to take care of the children and to do housework; it is simply not economically feasible. A woman with a baby who works in an office has family members who stay with the baby while she works. Rural women cannot afford the luxury of not working, thus, the mother in the countryside wears a *pagne* like a sling around the shoulders to carry the baby; the effect is similar to the wearing of a scarf and the baby is very tightly swaddled. In the second month, the baby is shifted to the back and during the third, the baby is allowed some movement of the head, arms, and legs. The baby is carried against the mother's body as she works on the farm, collects firewood and water, cooks, and performs any of the multitude of tasks that she does during the day. The securely fastened baby lies against the mother's body all day long, moving with her and feeling the beat of her heart. The proximity to her breasts means that she can easily feed the baby and keep working while she is doing it. At night, the mother and child sleep curled up together in the mother's house, and the baby can suckle when it wants. Until the baby is weaned, it has complete access to its mother.

Ending breastfeeding is a difficult process for both mother and child, and it often happens with the child is two years old. For a woman, weaning is important as a step in the life of her child and in her own as well. This is the point at which she can resume her life as a wife. Babies taste a bit of farina when they are about four months old and begin to try adult food when they are about 10 months, but they do not leave the breast until they are forced to do so. In preparation for the event, a grandmother will take the child to the "medicine man" for a new protective belt of *gris-gris* to distance any malevolence from the child. Then the mother refuses to give the child her breast. Weaning is done suddenly and completely, and the child is quite distressed by it. The mother tries to make her breasts unattractive to the child by putting *piment* or the juice of bitter leaves on them. In response, the baby cries, screams, throws fits, and refuses to eat. The mother will try to get the child to sleep with an older brother or sister to keep the baby from trying to suckle while she sleeps. After weaning, a woman is free to get pregnant again and the child moves on to another phase of life.

CHILDHOOD

From weaning to the onset of adulthood is a time when boys and girls learn what it means to be men and women. Far from being a carefree time of play and freedom, childhood is an apprenticeship of sorts, during which the child learns by watching, mimicking, and finally doing. The ties between the mother and child remain quite strong. The mother is the person who educates children when they are young, but when they get older, the gendered division of labor arises and boys begin to learn from their fathers. Girls learn about what women do: cooking, cleaning, and child care are at the top of the list. Child care starts quite early. A girl who is six years old may well have a sibling who was born to her mother; if not, a co-wife probably has a baby. The girl will start to care for the child, and she often carries her younger sibling. This is very helpful for the mother, especially for one who is trying to wean her child. Girls go to the *manioc* fields and ponds with their mothers and watch them as they work. As soon as they are old enough to do the work, they too will add their labor to that of their mothers. Boys follow their fathers, going on a hunt, for example, when they have reached the correct age.

When children are old enough to live away from their mothers, some spend time living with other family members. Some of them go to help older relatives with housework and farm labor; others live with kin who are closer to a school. This is in no way an unusual occurrence, and there is no stigma attached to it. It is understood as a mutually beneficial arrangement, a way to allow different family members to benefit from different resources that the family shares.

MARRIAGE

Matrimony is one of the great times of change in the life of a Centrafrican, and it is a state to which all people aspire. The real point of marriage is to have a family. Wedlock brings socially sanctioned sexual relations and gives children legitimacy. Because marriage is so common, one would think that it would be a simple process; nothing could be further from the truth. From selecting a mate who is acceptable to the family, to amassing the resources to marry, getting married involves many people, many goods, bargaining, and much patience. Marriage can establish or strengthen alliances or even heal rifts. Each ethnic group has its own traditions specific to betrothal, but the process is generally the same, and the compatibility of the couple is one of the main considerations. Marriage is not just the union of two individuals, it is the joining of two families.

Selecting a Partner and Getting Engaged

Couples come together either out of mutual attraction or by the work of their families. Some unions are begun by older family members; these arranged marriages are still commonplace. Even though the youngsters did not initiate the action, the interests and sentiments of the couple are quite important because no family wants to see a marriage end in divorce. The end of a marriage is not just the break-up of a union of wife and husband, but of a bond between two families and the extrication process can be onerous. If a woman of marrying age rejects all suitors, it is said that she is possessed by an evil genie that has control of her body and spirit. Girls are considered marriageable when they reach physical maturity, but often men are quite a bit older when they marry for the first time. The ability to provide bridewealth is the main obstacle to marrying. The marriage proposal comes from the man's family and is accompanied by gifts. If the answer is positive, it is at this point that negotiations begin.

Bridewealth

Bridewealth is what binds the families of a married couple to each other. Long called "bride price," it erroneously has been thought to be what a man gives to his in-laws to pay for his wife. Bridewealth is what a man renders to his in-laws to compensate them for the loss of their daughter's labor, the addition of her reproductive capacity to his lineage, and to reward the parents for having raised a daughter who is so marriageable. Reciprocity is the hallmark of bridewealth, the clan loses one of its women, but it gains the means to welcome a woman into the family as a new wife.

Bridewealth is the exchange of goods, visits, and labor between the families of the engaged. The family of the man makes a more sizable material contribution to the woman's family than vice versa, but both families give and receive. The point is to allow the families to display the resources at their disposal, to render service to the families through the labor of those who will marry, and to allow each family to learn about the other and its representative who will join theirs. It is a way to assess the potential for the marriage from material comfort to emotional support.

Bridewealth is considered by many to be a necessary evil to have a legalized union. With the economic problems in rural and urban areas, its fulfillment can be more difficult. The function that bridewealth serves is to further sanction the marriage. It indicates that the couple marries with the support of both families. Bridewealth is what makes a woman a wife and not a concubine; it provides legitimacy in the eyes of society and in the view of the law. Also, cooking for her husband makes a woman a wife and not a concubine. If a woman is found not to be a virgin when the marriage is consummated, the husband will often ask for a portion of the bridewealth to be returned.

Arrangements are made to spread out the process of rendering the bridewealth to coincide with other events in the life of the married couple, often the birth of the first child. If a child is born before the bridewealth has been finalized and the man is still at his future in-laws' house, the bridewealth will be increased accordingly, because her family has assumed the responsibility that should rightfully be that of the father and his kin.

In a traditional marriage, the bridewealth supports the woman's brother's betrothal and if her marriage has problems, she goes to him for assistance—his house is always open to her. The one who is the recipient of the dowry understands the profound debt that he owes to his sister and brother-in-law. He even calls his brother-in-law "father" in recognition of the important role that his resources have made to his ability to marry himself.

Courtship is spent in exchange of labor. The woman spends time with her husband-to-be's family, particularly his mother, and the man goes to his fiancée's family. Men do some heavy farm work, hunt, and collect wood. This is an opportunity for the woman's family to observe the man who will marry their daughter, to assess his kindness, trustworthiness, and ability to work. He typically stays at the house of the girl's parents until the bridewealth is ready. While in their house, the man owes complete obeisance to the family of his future in-laws, including the small children. The scrutiny is not one-sided; the family of the man can also assess the girl's suitability. She cooks, cleans, farms, takes care of the children, and performs many other quotidian tasks at her in-laws' house before the marriage. After the bride is living in the home with her husband, the reciprocity between the families continues, mostly in the form of visiting. When the first child is born, the husband will also offer presents to his wife's parents.

The expansion of the cash economy has altered bridewealth: Gifts are changing from goods to cash. Cash has been a way for those who do not have access to commodities or who cannot, because of work, do service at the future in-laws' house to present the bridewealth. Now some people prefer cash to presents, and the idea that one is paying for a woman is coming into people's minds. Money also allows a young man who earns a salary to marry without the consent of the family because he does not have to go to an elder to procure bridewealth.

Bridewealth becomes particularly difficult when a marriage ends. When a couple divorces, bridewealth becomes an issue for the two families. The family of the wife often must reimburse the family of the husband, especially if her adultery has caused the split. In that case, if the woman has the means, she will reimburse it herself. The family of a man can agree not to have bridewealth reimbursed, but that is a difficult decision to make because it affects the finances of so many people.

TRADITIONAL MARRIAGE

Traditional marriages are more concerned with rites before and after the marriage takes place; the marriage per se tends to be subordinate to the negotiations and rituals of exchange if it exists at all. However, knowledge of the rituals of marriage in Christian and Muslim communities is influencing people to have more elaborate nuptials. For a traditional marriage to be recognized by the state, the couple must be married by the village chief and two witnesses must testify to the veracity of the nuptials; this marriage is considered valid on the date stated by the couple. Because most ethnic groups are patrilineal and patrilocal, a woman leaves her parents' home and moves to the place where her husband lives. When women marry, they enter into the communities of their husbands, and they are more or less strangers in their new village. In the case of difficulties in her new home, the woman can make an appeal to the elders of her husband's lineage. Additionally, she is still a part of the lineage of her birth and can turn to them for help when she needs it.

Among the Biaka, marriage is a relatively casual affair. The tradition is for the young man to advise the parents before he begins courtship. He gives honey, meat, and labor to his perspective in-laws. If she accepts the suitor and the parents approve, the couple moves into their own house near that of her parents, and they begin having sexual relations. Often the night before she first has sex, the woman and the other women of the camp perform the *limboku,* wandering about the settlement singing and dancing sexually charged songs and dances. A central figure is surrounded, and she conjures up the spirit of *limboku,* a female spirit. *Limboku* is limited to women, and men and boys are confined to their houses during its performance.

Food is important in the early days of a marriage. Ritual consumption is meant to seal an alliance and to assure the women's fecundity. In the case of a first marriage among the Gbaya, the father of the girl accepts a hen from the family of the groom. Later, when the new bride has gone to the house of her husband, he gives his father-in-law a hen. Both of these hens are prepared in the same manner. When the marriage is consummated, the husband gives his father-in-law yet another hen, which is known as "the hen of knowledge." If the woman has been married before, a hen is also given to the father-in-law, but in this case, it is known as "the hen that ends the previous engagement," and it is cooked and eaten only by the bride's father-in-law. This is often the final step in the marriage process.

The bride must move into her husband's house. When she goes to her new home, she is accompanied by women of her lineage. One of her first tasks is to cook a meal for her husband, which she often does with the assistance of her mother. Much of what she brings to her marriage are wares for her new home. The woman is more or less a stranger in her husband's village. She knows her in-laws and their family, but her circle of support is initially small. Although her husband's family welcomes her, her labor, and her reproductive capacities, they also watch her like hawks, making sure that she does not break taboos, observing how she gets along with the other wives and the women of the lineage, as well as ensuring that she is doing what she can to make the clan prosperous.

Among the Manza, members of the bride's family ask the groom for compensation for arrears owed to them. A grandmother may want money because, for example, she claims that her granddaughter did not serve her with enough deference. An aunt may ask for a *marmite*. An uncle may ask for money because of all the work that he has done on the woman's behalf throughout the years. This is done among those who follow the traditional religion as well as by Muslims.

MUSLIM MARRIAGE

Converting to Islam does not erase a person's ethnic background, but it does have an impact on the way some ceremonies are celebrated. Muslim Manza marriages are more closely in line with the practices of other Muslims. With traditional Manza marriages, the woman's family has responsibility for making the nuptial arrangements: The dates, sacrifices, and the bridewealth are made by the mother of the bride-to-be. Muslim marriages put more responsibility on the family of the husband-to-be. The man's family is responsible for all the decision making and all the financial costs of the ceremony and festivities. In a Muslim marriage, the bridewealth goes toward the bride's trousseau. If she has problems with her marriage, her brother has the same responsibilities to support her as would a non-Muslim Manza.

Engaged Muslim couples are not allowed to see each other, much less go out in public or have sexual relations. Through the intermediary of his sister, the man gives his future wife gifts of jewelry. For her part, the woman goes the house of her future in-laws where she helps the women with their housework, and if they have fields, she works there with the other women. The interactions she has with his family are quite limited and always mediated by a liaison whose mission continues through the marriage ceremony. The individual's representative is of the same gender and usually a married friend or sibling to avoid any impropriety.

The night before the marriage, the groom's family brings everything that they will need to the house of the *málùm*. Laden with tea, kola nuts, mats, glass and flatware, and gifts for the in-laws, the groom's family displays its wealth as the items are borne along the route. This display is an assurance that the man can take care of his new wife, and it is also a way for his family to buttress its standing in the community.

The most important people in the wedding are not the young couple, but their fathers. The two fathers meet in front of the house of the *málùm,* and the holy man listens to the stipulations of the marriage agreement, which includes a promise of mutual assistance on the part of the two families. The engaged couple does not attend this meeting, but they are represented by two friends of the same gender who are already married or an older brother or sister who can speak for them.

A group assembles around the *málùm*. For Muslim Manza in Bangui, the language of the ceremony is either Manza or Sango, and the prayers are in Arabic. The woman's father gives his assent, noting the communality of their religion. Then they pray. The woman's representative comes out of the house where all the other women are and places herself along with the man's representative in front of the *málùm*. They both assure the holy man of the love that each has for the other. The *in absentia* vows are repeated three times. After the *málùm* has given a discourse of advice to the newlyweds, he admonishes the man to protect and respect his wife and the woman to obey her husband. He asks God to bless the union and to give them lots of children.

If the groom's parents have good resources, the post-wedding festivities will last for up to seven days. The festivities start with a large meal; women eat inside the house of the *málùm*, and the men are served outside. The groom and his friends eat and spend time together separately in the house of a brother or an uncle who lives close to the festivities. The new bride will go to her husband's house the night of the celebration of their marriage. In the morning, the nuptial sheet is displayed. This is done to demonstrate the honor of the girl through her virginity. If the groom believes that his wife was not a virgin, he either does not show the sheet, or he takes the sheet to her parents' house. At this time, he can repudiate his wife and demand the return of the bridewealth.

When a Muslim man marries a non-Muslim woman, he and his family must be sure that she will convert. For the ceremonies, they first celebrate their marriage in the traditional mode, and he takes part in all the rituals that consecrate the union in her ethnic group's tradition. Once the traditional marriage has taken place, her family takes second place to his. Then another marriage takes place, this time in the Muslim style with a *málùm*. Although these women must convert, they are considered to be more pure if they come from the countryside rather than the city. Muslim women are thought to be less promiscuous and have fewer faults than their animist counterparts.

Bangui and Modern Marriage

In the waning years of colonialism, the government passed legislation that tried to regulate marriage. Concerned about girls marrying when they were too young and about bridewealth, the government enacted a law in 1951, stating that a woman who is 21 years old could marry without bridewealth and that if her parents demanded it, the amount could not be excessive. Yet the net impact of marriage laws on Centrafricans was minimal. They did attempt to decrease the authority that a girl's parents had over her, but it did not always work, witnessed by the continuing practice of older men marrying younger women without their consent.

The great reliance on tradition for one of the most important days in someone's life is apparent in Bangui wedding rituals. First there is the practice of giving bridewealth. Living in the city changes what one values and what one can offer. In Bangui, bridewealth usually consists of cash, goats, *pagnes,* beer, and whiskey. The first gift reinforces the incorrect notion that bridewealth is purchasing a wife, but it really replaces the agricultural products and labor that people give in the rural areas. Some of these new gifts are prestige items.

Many people in Bangui have civil weddings and marry at city hall. People must announce it 15 days before the ceremony and either publicize or make people aware of the celebration of the marriage. The couple and their witnesses appear before an officer of the state, who is told their names, professions, place and date of birth as well as their address; they must also provide the names, professions, and addresses of their parents. If either one has been married before, that person must provide the name of the former spouse. If either person is a minor, the consent of the parents is necessary. Finally, the man and woman declare their intention to take each other as spouses, and the official pronounces the marriage. One benefit of the civil union is that it allows a couple to bypass disapproving families.

When it comes to marriage, Bangui differs from rural areas in a few respects. In Bangui, there are fewer people who are involved in polygynous marriages, especially younger people. Banguiois are also more likely to marry outside their ethnic groups because the entire spectrum is present in the city. There is a sentiment quite pronounced among Muslims that it is better for a man to marry a woman from the village of his ancestors than a woman from Bangui. The latter is thought to be more interested in spending money than in keeping the house in order. An increasing portion of the population is unmarried. The reasons for this are polygyny, a lack of resources for bridewealth, and cohabitation. Unmarried women are less and less marginalized by society because of these changes. There are more unmarried men than unmarried women, and the number of children born outside of wedlock is increasing for the same reasons that marriage is declining.

FORMS OF MARRIAGE

Marriage in the CAR is the union of a man and a woman or a man and women. Because the purpose of marriage is to create a family, anything that does not led to a family is inconceivable as marriage. Homosexuality is taboo.

Polyandry does not exist in the CAR. Monogamy is the form of marriage to which those who are Christian must subscribe. It is also favored by the Westernized, especially women. Monogamy takes place in both urban and rural areas. Many non-Christian monogamous men are in that state because of a lack of resources to have more wives. Many people consider polygyny to be not only acceptable but preferable. Having one wife may be the Western style of family, but many consider it to be going against tradition and even unnatural.

Polygyny is practiced in all regions of the CAR, both in rural and urban areas. A man is supposed to get the consent of his wife or wives before marrying another and the situation of the previous wives and their children is not be diminished by the taking of another wife. Polygyny allows men to continue having sanctioned sexual relations while some wives cannot because of the very young age of their children; it allows for the rapid proliferation of the family; and it increases the amount of land that can be cultivated. The situation is best for the first wife who has power over the subsequent female additions to the family; she may take advantage of her situation to become more active in marketing activities.

The reasons for polygyny are many. One reason is that taboos prevent a man and a wife from having sex at the end of her pregnancy and for a significant amount of time after the baby is born, and having multiple wives facilitates the opportunities for intercourse. Sometimes a woman who cannot have children will ask her husband to marry again as a way of maintaining her marriage, as having children is not only a desire but a cultural expectation. According to the Manza, a serious Manza man would never repudiate a wife because she was sterile—that is why polygyny exists. Because wedlock is so desirable, some women agree to polygyny because they find it more important to be married than to be in a monogamous relationship. Polygyny is the norm in many places and is politically expedient. Although many women who are in polygynous marriages would rather not be, they cite keeping peace with their husbands and keeping them at home instead of tomcatting around as reasons they participate in it. Some women simply prefer the arrangement to a monogamous marriage. For men, polygyny is prestigious because it is imperative that they have the resources to support multiple wives and many children. Theoretically, a man who practices a traditional religion can have as many wives as he can afford, but Islam caps the number of wives at four.

In the traditional setting, not only is there abundant land to support numerous wives and children, but the social structure with the control of male elders facilitates it. As heads of households and community leaders, older men control the financial resources of the families and communities. These men are able to control the youth because they have control over the family purse strings. If a young man wants to marry, he not only needs the approval of his family but its resources as well. Older men might have many wives before younger men are able to marry for the first time, and the young have to curry the favor of the elders to be able to do so themselves. It is not unusual for an elder male, instead of providing the bridewealth resources for the young man, to marry the youth's intended.

In the perfect polygynous world, the women all get along and submit to the authority of their husband. In the polygynous rural household, each wife has her own house in the same compound. A woman's headquarters consists of several buildings that were separated by family gardens. The husband's house is in the middle of those of his wives. He is the literal and figurative center of the family. Reality rarely corresponds with the ideal, and wives are usually rivals instead of being close, mutual confidantes. It is natural that people whose lives are so closely entwined would encounter some rough spots, and tensions and jealousies are common features of the arrangement. Women share the husband: He designates the nights that he will spend with each to enjoy their culinary talents and their company, sexual and otherwise. The first wife usually is second in authority in the family, and sometimes she makes use of her liberties to become involved in marketing activities. The other wives should have a rank that corresponds with their entry into the household, but this is not always the case. Although impartiality and the spending of equal time with each wife would be the easiest way for a husband to maintain a smooth running household, cooking ability, personality, and the number of children produced are some of the factors that can move a woman up or down on the list. One of the main reasons that women want to divorce is that they cannot get along with their co-wives.

In the city, there is an evolution toward nuclear families. There is a lower rate of polygyny in Bangui, especially in the areas of town where Westerners and upper-level bureaucrats live. Popular music often encourages people to be monogamous, but these lyrics are as much about being faithful to one's partner as they are about having only one partner to help stop the spread of AIDS. The notion that men should have more than one woman has mutated for the elite from true polygyny to the *functionnaire* with concubines. One of the most difficult aspects of the polygynous lifestyle in urban areas is that of space. Polygyny developed in rural areas with living arrangements that allowed for a greater degree of separation, but the often-cramped quarters of the city pose additional challenges. In monogamous households, there is a room for the couple, a room or rooms for the children, and maybe even a dining room. In polygynous households in the city, the man does not have the luxury of his own room, rather he is always in the room of a wife. He makes a schedule of whose room he shares and must take care to follow it scrupulously—if he does not, the conflict that ensues will be exacerbated by the players' close physical proximity to each other.

Many think that monogamy is contrary to the laws of nature, but it is becoming increasingly common, if not popular, for financial and cultural reasons, especially among younger people. When a man marries for the first time in a civil ceremony, he must declare his decision to be monogamous or polygynous. If he declares monogamy, but later adds another wife to his family, he is subject to a punishment that includes a jail sentence of six months to three years and a fine of 100,000 to 1 million CFA francs[4]. Additionally, the public official who performed the ceremony is subject to the same punishment. Although the finding does not automatically make the second marriage null and void, it does allow the woman to divorce for cause.

DIVORCE

When a situation between a married man and woman becomes untenable, divorce may be the remedy. Divorce exists in traditional and in modern society; although the reasons for ending a marriage are the same, the manner in which it happens is different. Divorce is the most difficult way to end a marriage. It poses obstacles because the couple has to be extricated from the bonds that were developed before the marriage that tie them and their families together. Not only is there the issue of the bridewealth, but there are usually children as well.

Couples separate because they do not get along, one wants to make a more advantageous marriage, sexual indiscretions, problems with in-laws, and because co-wives do not get along. A lack of fecundity is a very common cause of rupture in marriage in the CAR. There is also a twist that comes from living in a polygynous society: relationships with co-wives. Divorce is particularly difficult for women who lose their status and support for themselves and their children, but the marginalization of women who are single for a long time or divorced is decreasing.

Men have the option of remedying marital problems by taking another wife, and the fact that they live surrounded by their supportive extended families led to traditional society allowing women to initiate divorce. An Ngbaka man cannot instigate divorce nor can he send his wife home if she does not want to go. The recourse that he has if he is unhappy in his marriage is to make her more so, causing her to leave. If he returns her to her family, the bridewealth stays in her family. If the couple divorces because of her initiative, the man can decide not to ask for the return of the bridewealth. Ngbaka people have the custom of "buying back" the offspring on the part of the father's family because the matrilineal line is as important in lineage (although the father's line is taking more prominence today). In this case, more money is given for girls as they will someday induce a bridewealth payment. Some Ngbaka men have resorted to fleeing in such a way that their wives cannot follow them; the woman would be obliged to accept another man from his lineage as her husband instead.

In civil marriages, a judge tries to reconcile the couple, and if the judge is not successful, the case is sent to court. In court, the division of goods and visitation rights are established. The judges, often caught in a liminal space of their traditional upbringing and the law, make rulings that straddle both lines and fully satisfy neither. As a result of the proceedings, usually the wife is the one who leaves the conjugal home. If her husband expels her, she leaves with her personal effects, which sometimes the husband has set outside the home. This repudiation is part of traditional divorce and is not written into law. The idea is that the home belongs to the man, no matter what the woman has done to help find it, finance it, or build it.

In the case in which a couple ends their relationship, people consider that the children belong to the father, as the mother is but a temporary and a non–blood-related member of the family. The exceptions to this are in societies (such as the Ngbaka) that have a strong tradition of the importance of matrilineal descent, or if there is a special bridewealth consideration. In the case in which bridewealth has not been fully rendered before the couple ends its relationship, the man's family must often pay an indemnity to the family of the woman to claim the children as members of its lineage. In the traditional milieu, when a couple separates, the woman and the children are deprived of their rights of succession from the husband and father.

For a woman who divorces her bureaucrat husband and the husband is found to be at fault, she has the right to her husband's pension when he dies; if she remarries after his death, she is entitled to a portion of the pension. However, if she remarries or enters into another long-term relationship prior to his death, she cannot claim his money. For polygynous marriages, the pension is to be divided among the wives, or if she is also deceased, the money goes to her offspring.

The case of divorce is different for those who practice Catholicism or Islam. A Muslim husband or wife can initiate divorce proceedings; the man if his wife does not listen to him, if she leaves the house without his permission, if she does not tell him where she is going, and so on. The Muslim husband is supposed to forgive a wife's offense three times, but can assume that the fourth transgression means that she no longer wants to live with him. Muslims must see the *málùm,* who tries to reconcile the couple. If he is not successful, he absolves himself of all fault in the eyes of God and pronounces the marriage dissolved. The husband does not ask for the return of bridewealth.

Children over the age of two usually stay with their father, but their mother is invited to attend all activities in which her children are involved, and she can visit them as often as she wants. If a Muslim woman wishes to remarry, she must have the *málùm* annul the first marriage. The case is not as easy with Catholics. Because the Church does not permit divorce, the woman's family refuses to reimburse the bridewealth if the couple ends the marriage. In the case of divorce, people pretend that the wife left her husband, fell gravely ill, and died.

Remarriage is a common phenomenon, and polygyny and bridewealth make it more complicated. Men will marry the widow of a deceased brother because of social expectations. It was also the case that a younger brother would marry his deceased brother's widow. Widow marriage provided for the social security of the widow and meant that assets would not have to be reallocated if she remarried outside her deceased husband's family.

Social customs that have survived for years and are adapting to a new era are concerned with the maintenance of society and its structure to ensure continued functioning. In the face of unstable governments and economic situations, people feel a real need to keep families together. Family, as the basic unit of social organization, is the natural refuge for the Centrafrican. In the case of marriage, the exchange of labor ascertaining character and worthiness of the pair and the financial consideration of bridewealth are meant to ensure that couples stay together. Men and women have expected roles to fulfill, and boys and girls are in a continual state of preparation for their future roles as adults. The gendered division of labor and defined roles guarantees that all necessary work is assigned and performed. Girls and boys spend their earliest years at their mothers' sides, but boys spend more time with their fathers as they get older, and girls do the same with their mothers. Taken as a whole, these aspects work together to make sure that families remain intact and as prosperous as possible. Change is inevitable, but ancient customs do not disappear overnight, and society adapts to these alterations in the best ways that it can to keep its most important needs in the forefront.

Notes

1. The firepit is the place where the three logs on the fire or three hearthstones meet.

2. Pierre Saulnier, *La Femme dans la Société Centrafricaine* (Bangui, Central African Republic: n.p., 1984), pp. 30–31, quoted in Paulette Roulon, "Rites de Fécondité chez les Gbaya-Kara," *Itinérance* II (1981): 355–77.

3. NationMaster.com, Health Statistics, Maternal Mortality by Country, http://www.nationmaster.com/graph-T/hea_mat_mor; and NationMaster.com, Health

Statistics, Infant Mortality Rate by Country, http://www.nationmaster.com/graph-T/hea_inf_mor_rat.

4. Organisation des Nations Unies, Commission économique pour l'Afrique, *Le Droit et la Condition de la Femme en République Centrafricaine* (Addis Ababa: United Nations, 1985), pp. 24–25.

7

Social Customs and Lifestyle

THE PRACTICE, MAINTENANCE, AND DEVELOPMENT of social customs is very important to all cultures in the Central African Republic. Cultural practices reflect the past and desires for the future. Customs are specific to ethnic groups, although there is a great deal of overlap because of intergroup contact and because many of the reasons that practices exist are common throughout the region. For many, maintaining social customs is understood as a way to hold on to the values of the ancestors and to stem the tide of rapid change. Social customs bind together the people who practice them, link them to the places where they are performed, and connect them to the wider body of ideas that created the practices. Customs, like the cultures that produce them, are not static; although change is inevitable, it is bemoaned by those who have the most to gain by stasis and championed by those who have the least stake in the safeguarding of tradition. As life in the CAR undergoes rapid change, people look to traditions as a way to interpret the past, understand the present, and envision the future.

SOCIAL RELATIONS

In the CAR, social relations are very clearly delineated. Although some observers find this restrictive, others say that it gives people clear rules to follow and prevents social gaffes. The hierarchy of people is based on social status. Money does impact status, but one's gender, age, family, and deeds are more important. One of the most significant aspects of social relations is that the community's needs are paramount. A popular saying in the CAR is "If you don't live in a group, you will disappear." This speaks to the great importance of being a full-fledged member of any number of groups. These can be based on geographic location, religion, ethnicity, profession, or kinship.

Although families are of the utmost importance, the wider circles in which they live and participate are ethnic groups and villages. As ethnic groups are sparsely stretched across large areas, contact with neighboring groups combined with distance from others has engendered change. Ethnic groups can be further divided into subgroups, whose dialects are sometimes not mutually intelligible with those of others and whose customs differ as well. These subgroups are further divided into clans whose members trace their lineage to a common male ancestor. Within these clans are extended families. Some villages are made up primarily of clan groups, while others are larger and have a greater mixture of peoples.

Often organized villages lead to organized political structures with a village chief. Gbaya peoples, for example, do not subscribe to the notion that one elder was above others, and collectively, village elders make political and legal decisions for the community. The colonial administration found their rule easier with African chiefs and had them appointed where they did not exist before. The national government still works in concert with "traditional" chiefs. The role of the chiefs changed in their villages because of their interaction with and the demands of the colonial government. Instead of collecting tribute from people to sustain themselves and community work, chiefs collected taxes for the government and located laborers for colonial public works projects. Their authority has been diminished, but it still exists; its present configuration leaves the chief at the pinnacle of local government, even if he must submit to a higher authority.

Respect is the basis for social interactions. Wives must respect their husbands, students must respect their teachers, and everyone owes respect to the elders. Respect is due to those who are higher on the social scale, but it is a two-way street. The rules that govern the way that children are treated by their mothers is a manifestation of the respect that society has for young people as well. "Old" is not a pejorative word in the CAR. Traditional society has great respect for the elderly, who are seen as repositories of wisdom. The elderly, especially men, form village councils that hear disputes and render verdicts. Old people are consulted on every imaginable topic and receive preferential treatment; for example, young people always give up a seat (without being asked) so that an older person does not have to stand. This respect for age works for those who are not yet elderly; people are always supposed to defer to those older than themselves. Any adult should be able to sit on his or her veranda and ask a child who is passing by to take some money and go buy a cold drink from the nearest vendor and return with it. The child may also be asked to go get a glass from the kitchen and pour the drink. If the adult feels like allowing the child to keep the change from the errand, that is permissible, but the child should never feel that it is owed to him or her in response for having to do a favor for an elder—it is just a part of the normal way that relationships work. Children in the CAR look forward to aging because they will be able to enjoy this privilege in the future.

Despite the veneration of age that typifies society, recent social and economic changes have negatively affected the status of the elders. The cash economy is slowly eroding the ability of elders to control family finances. The adage "Your parents took care of you when you were cutting your teeth, you must take care of them when they lose theirs" is not always followed now. Popular songs lament the decline of this tradition and chastise the youth for being more concerned with themselves than their parents (see Chapter Eight). Family has always been the social security net for Centrafricans. The large family and lineage group meant that there were always people related by blood who would care for elderly family members. The multigeneration compound might include grandparents or great-grandparents. The children vie with each other to be able to do favors for the old folks, who often reward their work with great stories. As more people move away from their natal villages and make lives for themselves away from the extended family, the safety net becomes very thinly stretched.

RITUALS OF TRANSFORMATION

Initiation

One of the most important ways that people learn about their roles in life is through initiation rites. Children are constantly being molded to be ideal members of both their families and wider communities. The period of training that leads to initiation into the community is an ancient and important institution. Training people to be socially effective is not only beneficial to the wider group, it also provides guidance and security to individuals. Initiation is also a bonding experience; those who go through initiation together are a family of a sort and individuals identify themselves as a member of their initiation group throughout their lives. Circumcision and female genital cutting are often a part of the initiation process.

Initiation is necessary to become a full-fledged member of society. Each ethnic group has its own traditions for initiation. The society's rules and regulations and culture are transmitted; initiates learn the lore and legends, the taboos, the religion, and the history of the group. They learn about gender expectations and social obligations. These students often learn secret information that is not to be shared with those not initiated.

The group is made up of people of the same gender and approximately the same age. The segregation is based on the different knowledge that men and women are supposed to have, the age grouping allows all those who need the training to receive it at the same time, thus, being less taxing to the resources of the community. It also creates a natural group of people who are bonded to each other. Because this is such an important step in people's lives, young people look forward to initiation.

Although initiation is primarily for the young, older people can participate in it as well. For men and women who marry into the Gbaya-Kara ethnic group, there is an initiation ceremony through which they can go. There is not the same need for these adults to do so as there is for adolescents, and there are sessions solely for the older people. This initiation includes scarification and ends with a public ceremony. What these initiations for adults do is to bond them to the other people of their gender in the village.

Food taboos are observed during initiation as they are during other important times in people's lives, but they are specific to this process. Gbaya girls neither consume mongoose for fear that eating it would cause their bodies to swell nor certain kinds of birds that are important to the initiation ceremony. Often domestic meat or fish are not consumed during the initiation period because they symbolize weakness, a trait that initiation practices seek to eliminate.

Dancing is an important part of the social conformity and endurance required for life; it reflects the collective nature of society. Dances are structured, demanding that everyone play his or her role; conformity is necessary to participate. Dancing is a way of conditioning the bodies and building up endurance. Sometimes the initiates dance all night, especially the night before circumcision or excision. Fatigue makes it easier to endure the procedure performed the next day.

Education is the goal of initiation. This is an informal education that focuses on cultural transmission as well as the imparting of practical information. Initiates often learn a secret language that they must use while in the camp. Because the period of initiation is diminishing, aspects that require a great deal of time are slipping off the agenda. In some cases, initiation has ceased to occur. Older people believe that the absence of initiations has a deleterious effect on the younger generations; they blame phenomena such as the lack of understanding of the purpose of bridewealth and their lack of financial control on the loss of this tradition.

Surviving ordeals is crucial to the initiation process. Ordeals strengthen the body and mind and any signs of weakness are to be eradicated. Initiates observe special food taboos: Domestic meat and fish are considered to be signs of weakness; thus; they are forbidden during training. Also, the ordeals represent the difficulties that life will certainly present and passing these tests prepares one to survive life's difficult moments. The "Lake of Sorcerers" story provides a glimpse of the trials through which initiates go (see Chapter Three). Sometimes, the ordeals are relatively minor such as being swatted with sticks; other ordeals such as surviving alone in the forest or savanna can lead to death. If a Zandé boy dies in the course of his training, nothing is said to the mother until the day that he should have returned. At this time, the mother is given a stick of wood, which symbolizes death. This also demonstrates the separation of men and women, and the latter have nothing to do with the boys' initiation.

Circumcision and Female Genital Cutting (FGC)

Centrafricans believe that circumcision is a religious, moral, and social necessity as well as an indispensable step for attaining adulthood, and many people think the same about excision. People believe that these procedures are pleasing to the ancestors, and thus, they will take good care of those who undergo them. Those who go through the particular procedure know that its completion will allow them to become adults and move on to the next phase of life. Also, great attention is paid to them when they return to the village, and they receive presents at the end of initiation. Those who do not have the procedure can be mocked by those who have, and it can be more difficult for these people to marry. In many cases, the procedure is done at the end of the initiation; it is the last and most painful ordeal through which the new adults must go before they are presented to their villages. The operation for girls is a part of the international debate about the procedure worldwide; in some discussions about the origin of the practice, people claim that it was introduced by Muslims. For both operations, there is variation, depending on the ethnic group, and these differences account for the timing, number of participants, exact procedure, and significance for each group. Of course, these practices change over time.

The Banda tell a tale about the origin of circumcision for their ethnic group. Téré saw his children die when they were quite young, and he sought the advice of Brakalé, who told him that his children died and would continue to die because Téré was not circumcised. Then Brakalé circumcised Téré. When Téré's children continued to die, he went back to Brakalé, who told Téré that he in turn needed to circumcise his children or their deaths would continue.

Brakalé said, "You must circumcise everyone: man and woman." Téré did as he was told, and the deaths stopped. This legend reinforces the notion that one needs to listen to and obey one's superiors, and it makes clear the connection between circumcision, fecundity, and continued life.[1]

According to colonial official and ethnographer Félix Éboué, some groups such as the Banda did not practice circumcision before the beginning of the twentieth century. At that point, young men wanted to be circumcised, and they went to hospitals to have the operation performed. Apparently, young Banda women refused to have sex with men who still had their foreskins. This is an interesting twist on the argument made about female genital alteration and men not wanting to have sex with unexcised women.

The Manza ethnic group provides insight into how ancient traditions survive in the modern day in light of the introduction of new religions. Conversion does not equal the wholesale loss of the culture of the ethnic group, but old traditions are modified to fit into the precepts of the new faiths. For Manza Muslims, both aspects of their cultures indicate that they should be circumcised, but the Muslim community is far less tolerant of uncircumcised males than their animist counterparts. Muslims can choose whether to do the traditional Manza circumcision or the Islamic one. Muslims want boys to have the operation before they go to Koranic school, so that they can be pure when they address Allah. The traditional rite is opted for by those whose entire families have not converted, and it is especially common in rural areas. The Muslim circumcision ceremony differs from the traditional in that it is the *málùm*, or holy man, who is in charge of the event. The man who performs the operation invokes the name of Allah while it is done. As the initiates mend, the *málùm* teaches them prayers.

Many Muslim Manza believe that their ethnic group's traditional teachings and ideas about comportment are not far from the traditional ideas. Indeed animist, Muslim, and Christian Manza are all taught not to lie, steal, cheat, disobey, or show disrespect lest they be severely punished. Manza boys of all three religious persuasions live and learn in the camp together. The food taboos that the boys observe in the camp do not disagree with Muslim principles because abstaining from meat means that the boys are not eating pork, as dictated by Islam. However, some aspects of the process do not work with Muslim traditions. The new name that is given to the boy in the camp is ignored by the Muslim boy and his family. They also do not participate in the village festivities with the same degree of enthusiasm as the animists: They do not drink alcohol, and they leave the event early to go to evening prayers. Although Muslim Manza boys may participate in training and ceremonies with non-Muslim Manza, that is not the case for females for whom genital cutting is banned.

Female Genital Cutting

The female genital cutting of females is a debated topic, both in the West as well as in Africa. Supporters of the practice passionately argue that it is a cultural practice, and it should be maintained just as other aspects of culture are preserved. Girls, they argue, look forward to having the operation because it allows them to become full members of their society and bonded with the other girls who go through the procedure. Detractors claim that it causes mental and physical pain and can result in serious health problems. Some who oppose the procedure call it "female genital mutilation," and some who approve of it call it "female genital improvement"; here, it will be referred to as "female genital cutting" for a more neutral tone. Male circumcision almost never raises such a stir.

The incidence of female genital cutting in the CAR is waning. The government banned it in 1966, but national laws have not had a real impact on the practice, especially in rural areas. In the countryside, the decline results from people deciding that some practices are no longer necessary. In Bangui, fewer girls are being cut because of the closer arm of the law, contact with people who have not historically practiced FGC and "new" ideas about the practice. Muslim and Christian women are far less likely than their animist counterparts to submit to the operation. Another reason for excision's fading is that women and men are questioning the necessity of it. The voices of Westerners demanding change probably have the least amount of impact on its practice. Yet, there are people, male and female, young and old, who support the institution.

For the Manza who are animists, the girls spend three days before FGC dancing and being hazed by the older women who accompany them and submit to ordeals such as being criticized for what the elders declare as poor dancing. After the procedure is done, the girls' wounds are tended. They dance all night long and are finally allowed to sleep. The ensuing days are spent in work and ordeals. Some trials are mild, such as having to eat food prepared without spices without reacting negatively to physical tests; the pain that these young women experience is representative of the pain that women experience in life: leaving the family home to live with strangers when a woman marries, the pain of childbirth, and being subjected to corporal punishment. The girls are menaced by the elders themselves who chastise the girls for being lazy, mean, egotistical, and for stealing, lying, and not wanting to serve their elders. All these are characteristics that are not tolerated in women and whose presence can lower a woman's bridewealth. Initiation is intended to eradicate undesirable traits. When they rejoin their villages, the women receive gifts of clothing, shoes, food, and luxury items such as lotion. The young women may resume eating once taboos foods, except for fish from the *marigot* where the FGC took place.

These operations are meant to bond people of the same general age and gender at the same time that it brings them into the wider society on a different level. Intergenerational conflict can be tempered by people of different ages working together toward a common goal and because godparents are appointed for the initiates. Also, the older generation takes care of and tends the wounds of the initiates, where usually the younger ones must do for the elders. The initiates look forward to the day that they may be on the other side of the activities in the initiation camp.

The return to the village is a time of great celebration. The initiates have been away for a long time, and their friends and families are excited to see them again. The food taboos for the initiates have been ritually removed. When there are different degrees of initiation (levels of difficulty of the ordeals), the color the new adults wear indicates the type of initiation they had to the gathered audience. The jubilant and recovering young men and women are the centers of attention as they perform dances that they learned while in seclusion, and the community receives those who will help to perpetuate it.

Death

Death is a normal part of life in the Central African Republic; it is one of the three, and the final, of the most important life transformations. Life expectancies are much lower in the CAR than in the West. Infant and child mortality is higher, and more women die in childbirth. For people who follow traditional religions, physical death is understood as part of a cycle that does not mean that life is over, but that it is in a different phase. Death is mourned and celebrated; it is one of the causes for reunions of family, friends, and acquaintances that has very specific rules of interaction. Death for the elderly is considered to be natural. When a younger person dies, people believe that there was a malevolent force that caused the death: witchcraft. The reasons that witchcraft is used against someone include vengeance, a dispute with a neighbor, an unpaid debt, problems with inheritance, jealousy, and family difficulties.

The social impact of a death in the family can be grave. A widow is in an awkward position. She does not become the head of the family upon her husband's death; she is relegated to an inferior position. Tradition dictates that the eldest son takes his father's place as the head of the family, and he has the responsibility of looking after the wives and his siblings. The widow can choose whether to stay or to go, but she often chooses to stay with the husband's clan if she has children. Sometimes, the brother of the deceased marries the widow—and then he owes the customary work and presents to the woman's family. Presently, young men who refuse to marry a brother's widow risk not getting married at all: Their lineage sees this form of marriage as a way to retain its resources, both of people as well as material goods and funds, and they may refuse to provide him with bridewealth if he wants to marry in the future. A man can marry the widow of his brother, and a man can marry his father's widow as long as the woman is not his birth mother. Low rates of fecundity are blamed on younger men having to marry older women.

Inheritance is usually a contentious issue, particularly for those of lesser means. When a couple is separated, the woman and children are deprived of their right to the succession of the husband and father. The status and type of one's marriage make the death benefits vary. The widows of monogamous functionaries are entitled to their deceased husband's pensions provided that they were married in the eyes of the state and for at least three years. In the traditional milieu, usually a paternal uncle or eldest son takes an inventory of the man's possessions and is responsible for their distribution. The husband's family can strip the wife of everything, including her own possessions, and, especially if she is suspected in his death, shave and beat her.

When a child dies, all eyes turn to the mother. People question whether she has broken any sexual or food taboos or whether she has taken good enough care of her child. The death of a young member of the family creates stress on many levels, especially between the wife and the husband who wonders if this will also be the fate of future progeny. There are rituals whose goal is the discovery of the source of the death of children, which finds that either the wife and her family or the father and his family are to blame.

Funerals

Funerals mark the end of one's life on earth and the beginning of one's life as an ancestor. The transition from life to death is marked by funerals and periods of mourning. Funerary rites differ according to ethnic group, but worldview and resources are also factors. For the Mpeimu in the Sangha forest, the deceased is washed and wrapped in barkcloth to prevent its uncontained elements from doing harm to others, and the immediate family members receive ritual washings to keep the dead person's uncontained spirit from harming them.[2] When Zandéland was an independent polity, funerals included the internment, immolations, and deaths of subjects, household servants, and slaves. Funerals reveal a great deal about the societies that created them, and the rites reinforce cultural norms.

Funerals are an opportunity for the family to demonstrate the importance of the deceased and of the kinship group as a whole. Funeral arrangements may be elaborate, and all members of the lineage dig deeply into their figurative pockets to ensure that the guests are well received and will recount their good treatment to others. When people come to the funeral in the countryside, they often travel considerable distances, so ample food must be provided for those who travel to attend, and they must be billeted and made comfortable. This hospitality, as with all hospitality, is not resented, it is relished as an opportunity to display generosity. The reciprocal nature of Centrafrican society also assures that the family will not be bankrupted by what it offers its guests, and it is not uncommon for the family of the deceased to collect more from those who attend the funeral than it spent. Everyone procures new clothes for the event.

There are very specific rituals concerning the preparation and burial of the body. Among the Bondjo, when a man dies, the body is prepared by opening the belly, removing the entrails which are washed and stored in a jar, and stuffing the opened area with aromatic plants in the countryside. In urban areas, people use bottled perfumes. The body is displayed attached to a post at the entry of the house. For two days people come to pay homage to the deceased. The internment is fairly close to the house. A pit of approximately 50 centimeters (1.64 feet) is dug; the earth is pounded and heated in preparation to receive the body. The body and entrails jar are placed in the pit and covered with mats. The lamentations and drum playing continue for days. When the burial ceremony is over, the divvying up of the deceased's goods begins.

Funerals for the Gbaya-Kara are three-day affairs. The body is prepared for burial close to the deceased's house. The burial takes place the day after death; if the deceased is male, the body should face the setting sun and the rising sun in the case of a female. Mourners come to the site and participate in wailing and moaning. As an act of humility, they strip off their clothes. For the Gbaya-Kara, the mourning includes panegyrics performed by friends who extol the virtues and bemoan the shortcomings of the deceased. Criticisms of the dead are especially harsh if the person is suspected of sorcery. After a period of some months after the death, the brother (if the deceased was a man) or the daughter (if it was a woman) will have a mourning ceremony.

The Manza announce death by drums, advising friends and neighbors that a specific person has entered the next stage of life. The information will pass this way from village to village. The body is prepared, men wash the bodies of men and women wash the bodies of women, and the corpses are then perfumed. After the body has been prepared, men build a structure of branches and palm fronds near the house of the deceased where the body will lie. The age-cohorts of the deceased will attend the funeral and perform songs and dances that they learned together in initiation. Among the Manza, one can attend a funeral only if one has suffered an equal loss. If one has lost a father, one can attend the funeral of a man with children, one who has lost a child can attend the funeral of a child; breaking this taboo would result in a death in the family of the transgressor. The body is transported by friends instead of family because the deceased's relatives are too overwrought to do it themselves. The corpse is placed on the side of the grave and the widow says "If it is I who made you die through magic, may your soul come snatch mine in the following days. But if it is not me, you must cause the death of the one who caused your death. Travel well and rest in peace." Friends and family will stay with the family of the deceased for three days if a man has died, and for four days if it is a woman.[3]

When a married man dies, especially if he is young, the widow is the natural suspect. When the cause of death is supernatural, the method for discovering its origin is, too. Sometimes the family of the deceased man will visit a "medicine man," who will develop a plant-based infusion with which to draw out the answer. If the widow survives the concoction, she is considered to be innocent in her husband's death; if she does not survive, she is found guilty and has already suffered her punishment. Sometimes the divination of the cause of death is done by a family member through a sacrifice.

Because death is so often attributed to supernatural causes, the burial often begins an inquest into the reason for the deceased's departure from earth. *Gris-gris* may be placed upon the tomb to ensure that the death does not go unpunished. Also, a sprinkling of dust from the tomb may be taken to the village "medicine man" so that he can use it to discover the source of witchcraft that took this life.

Offerings are made to the deceased at the time of internment. A calabash of water or a bottle of whiskey may be placed on the earth above the dead to assuage the thirst or indulge the peccadillo of the deceased. Also, cigarettes and other items that she or he enjoyed in life may be left as well. This is both a paying of respect to the deceased and supplying the needed accoutrements for the journey into the next stage of life.

Mourning the dead is an important part of the process of death, and it is heavily regulated. Lamentation is a very evident feature of women's mourning activities and include wailing, crying, yelling, rolling in the dirt, jumping, beating their breasts, stripping, and pulling out their hair; sometimes they do bodily injury to themselves. There are very strict rules that people must follow when in mourning, and food taboos are among the most important of these. The period of mourning can last for months or even years, depending not on affection for the deceased, but the quality of that year's harvest. The entire clan mourns along with the spouse(s). The bereaved spouse(s) abstain from sexual relations; only the polygynous man continues to perform his conjugal duties. For the Manza, the widow's period of grieving finds her wearing somber and dirty clothes; bathing is rare and coiffing the hair even more so. When the time of mourning is over, usually signified by ritual bathing, the widow or widower can rejoin society. One of the last acts of lamentation by the widow or widower is to go to the grave of the deceased with the parents and in-laws. He or she tidies around the mound while reporting on his or her conduct during the period of bereavement. Taking a fistful of dirt from the grave mound, the woman throws it in a calabash of beer and drinks it, declaring that death will be the result of bearing false witness. One of the areas of behavior that a widow would report to her deceased husband concerns her chastity while in mourning.

When a person dies and is buried in Bangui, a representative from the family of the village of origin comes to participate in the ceremony. This person is charged with indicating to the deceased the way (a road, for example) back home so that the deceased may avenge himself or herself and demonstrate the power of the family. The person returns to the village with a small amount of dust from the tomb of the deceased to turn over to a "medicine man," so that he could pinpoint the person who caused the deceased to die.

SEXUAL TABOOS

Refraining from sex at certain times takes place for many reasons, and the goal is the smooth functioning of society. Virginity is considered to be a positive for unmarried girls, but it is not uncommon for them to have premarital sex. Married men have much greater sexual license than women, in part because of polygyny, but also because it is more acceptable for men to have sex outside of marriage. Yet married women do have extramarital sex. The taboo against a woman having intercourse with anyone but her husband is to ensure that the paternity is certain and that the lineage is not diluted.

Some of the taboos concern with whom one cannot have sexual relations; these rules concern kinship and reproduction. One cannot marry in one's own lineage, and attention must be paid to the mother's bloodline as well. A man must abstain from having sex with a woman who comes from the same lineage as his brother's wife, if she and the other woman have the same parents. If this occurs, a large indemnity would be demanded by the woman's family.

The taboos are mostly directed toward women. Pregnant women are not discouraged from having sex in the early and middle months of pregnancy; it is considered a way for the fetus to be in touch with his father's bloodline, but it is not permitted to occur at the end. Those who are breastfeeding are not allowed to have sex with their husbands, and if the couple resumes sexual relations, the mother must wean the child immediately. Sometimes, the resumption of sexual intercourse does not occur until the baby is able to walk. A couple must often receive permission from a lineage head or the husband's mother to recommence sexual relations. These taboos are supposed to encourage the child's good health. A woman abstains from sex while she is in mourning for her deceased husband, ensuring that a child born to her after her husband's death is part of his lineage and will be claimed and celebrated as such.

VILLAGE CELEBRATIONS

Festivals and celebrations play an important part in village and clan life. Many of these are based on age-old practices and precepts. Festivals are now also organized by churches and companies as unity-building devices; festivals of indigenous origin serve the same function, but the newer ones do so more self-consciously. Festivals are occasions for people to come together, to take a break from their normal routines, put on their best clothes, and spend time with other people of their communities. They reinforce the feeling of belonging to a social organization that is larger than that of the family or lineage. For this reason, national holidays are particularly important to the young nation.

Villages have spontaneous celebrations, for example, after the birth of a child. Planned celebrations include the festivals that mark the return of the new initiates to the village. Virtually any significant event is recognized and celebrated by the community as a whole. Food and drink are vital parts of the celebration, and women spend a great deal of time on the preparation of the victuals.

Festivals organized for reasons outside the parameters of the traditional fête display the power of the organizer. Churches, for example, use festivals and celebrations as a means to make their presence felt in a community. The church takes responsibility for feeding those who take part in the event, and its members provide and cook the food.

To sponsor an event of this magnitude, the organizers need to amass a great deal of resources in the areas of personnel and materials. To print the cloth, organize the space, and prepare the food, drinks, and entertainment takes time, money, and labor. Prosperous chiefs may also organize a village festival. Members of the village will help to provide the food and drinks as part of the homage they pay to their leader. A crowd of people with bellies full of food and drink indicates a chief who is capable of maintaining his people well and that the ability to mobilize resources is there. Some festivals are organized for self-promotion. A local government official may call for a day to celebrate his reelection. It behooves people to attend local political celebrations, as absences are easily noted. Very often cloth with the visage of the politico, and perhaps his wife, will be available for purchase. Supporters and others will have new outfits made from this material to be worn on the day of the festival, as they stand lining the street, waiting to greet the passing motorcade and hear the speeches.

HOLIDAYS

Holidays are eagerly anticipated because they are days of celebration and days of rest. Many holidays in the CAR are connected to religious festivals. Indigenous religions do not have holidays per se, so the presence of traditional faiths is not felt on the official calendar. Because of its colonial past, the country observes Christian holidays: Easter Monday, Whit Sunday (Pentecost), Feast of the Assumption, All Saints' Day, and Christmas are official holidays.

Muslim and Christian holidays are celebrated the same way they are throughout the world by their co-religionists, although Christians in the CAR are more likely to observe these holidays by attending church services. People also dress more formally than their Western counterparts for church services in general, and holidays are no exception to this rule. Muslims also make it a priority to look their best on the Islamic holidays of Korité *(Id al-Fitr)*, which marks the end of Ramadan, and Tabaski *(Id al-Adha)*, the Feast of the Sacrifice of Abraham. They celebrate these holidays the way other Muslims do, in prayer and by spending the day with family and friends. Food is an important aspect of these holy days, especially Korité, which signals the end of a long period of fasting. Holidays that fall on a Saturday may either be observed on the Friday that precedes it or the following Monday. Individuals or businesses may choose to observe a Muslim holiday that falls on a Friday on that day or the following Saturday. The dates for Muslim holidays are determined by using the *Umm al-Qura* calendar of Saudi Arabia.

A number of national holidays do not have a religious origin. New Year's Day is the first official holiday of the calendar year. Most of the other holidays are tied to events of the postindependence state. Boganda Day is celebrated on March 29, to commemorate the death of the CAR's first leader. The first anniversary of the government is celebrated on May 15, and Republic Day is the first of December. Other holidays include Labor Day, celebrated with many other countries on May 1, Prayer Day on June 30, and a National Holiday on November 11. Celebrations for events on the national calendar are elaborate and celebrated on the national and local levels. For example, on Republic Day, there are military parades, and national figures give speeches to large crowds. When the official events are over, people return to their normal routines, and perhaps they might enjoy a bit of leisure time.

There are also sporadic or spontaneous holidays. A visit from a dignitary such as the Pope is a major national event. In much the same way that an important national holiday might be celebrated, there will be special cloth produced at the factory in Bangui, and people will get a day off from work. People willingly celebrate an event such as this. There are also spontaneous holidays for events such as a victory by the national football team. This is a double victory, not only does the home team win, but everybody gets a sanctioned reprieve from work as well. These spontaneous holidays are most enjoyed by the few people who are salaried employees. For people who farm, the day is the same as any other, and for those who are paid by the day or by the hour, it is a day of lost wages.

DAILY LIFE IN RURAL AREAS

People who reside in rural areas have lives that are ruled by the seasons and full of hard work. Farm work dominates the activities of the women, and men have more infinitely more leisure time than their female counterparts. Men may be seen relaxing in villages during the day, but women do not have the same amount of free time. Great amounts of time are spent performing activities that are necessary for survival, and these are done in a family or community environment.

Daily life for women is very busy and starts with the rising of the sun. A typical day for a woman in a rural area is to wake up early, around five in the morning, and her first chore is to clean the outside of her house, using a handleless straw broom; it is not easy on the back but it moves debris effectively instead of just redistributing it. Then she will straighten up the inside of the house before heading off to fetch water. If she is lucky, there is a pump in the village or a spring close to her house; if not, she may walk a long distance. Even when pump water is available, some people use it only for washing clothes and bathing, preferring to use water from a traditional source for cooking and drinking; people claim that what comes from a "natural" source tastes better. The woman and her daughters carry what the household will need for cooking, face washing, bathing small children, and drinking. The water is collected in basins, some plastic, others pottery, and a cushion made either from vegetable matter or a piece of a worn-out *pagne* rests between the basin and the head. Women become so adept at balancing their water that they can carry their load with only a few fingers lightly resting on the basin while negotiating narrow and uneven paths. Even if a woman lives in her own house, she will fetch water for her mother-in-law.

When the water duties have been accomplished, the woman heads for the fields, about an hour and a half after her day starts. Women in the fields work very hard, carrying their babies on their backs as they plant, weed, and reap. The crops are selected and sown in a complementary system, so that there are crops coming to fruition throughout the year and plants that need shade are given protection from light by plants that need more sun. In the savanna, crop rotation is practiced, while people in the forest tend to move to previously unplanted land. During the harvest of grains, people sleep close to the fields so that more of the day can be dedicated to reaping instead of walking. Also, it is a way of keeping birds at bay. Women prepare a meal for those who go to the fields. The mid-day meal is light, and people eat and take a break during the hottest part of the day; girls will braid each other's hair, boys will play, and adults will rest. When women are not in the fields, they have other chores that they must do, including washing. They wash clothes and pots, using the same soap after the hottest part of the day, when the rivers and streams are alive with activity: Women do laundry and socialize while the children run and play.

Bathing usually takes place on the way home from the fields, in water sources, and less frequently, in designated bathing spots in the village. Men bathe nude, while women cover their pubic hair and their bottoms with leaves. Especially during the dry season, women apply oil to their skin. If adults choose to bathe in the village, they haul the water themselves. After they are clean, they continue on their way home, collecting firewood to cook dinner. Food is prepared, and children are cleaned, then the meal is eaten, and people relax before retiring for the evening, at about nine o'clock.

Men sometimes go to the fields with their wives, but men's role in subsistence agriculture is usually limited to the initial clearing of land. In the dry season, they cut and remove large trees. After the first rains (so that the fire will not spread), they burn the trees to remove the stumps and to make charcoal; they also burn the grasses to allow women to get along with their agricultural work. Also, once the rains start, the men cut a secondary field on previously harvested land, and this field is often closer to the house than the main one.

Since the colonial era, men are involved in the raising of crops geared for the export market. Although harvesting can be done by both sexes, men have the primary responsibility for crops such as coffee and cotton. This resulted in labor being diverted from the raising of crops destined to meet the alimentary needs of families and from hunting. The cash generated from the sale of these crops was used in part to pay head taxes to the colonial government. Today, these crops are still exported and have the same financial and nutritional impacts. Cotton and coffee have also solidified the position of men as the breadwinners, taking them out from under the usual financial control of elders.

This rhythm is fairly consistent throughout the year, as the country's position on the equator means that the sun rises and sets at about the same time every day. The tasks that people perform are quotidian occurrences, as water always needs to be fetched, food cooked, and children tended. The exact chore may change from season to season or day to day, but farming activities are constant. Rural life goes at a slower pace than that of the city, but it is a relentless and unending day. Women work incessantly; men and children do so intermittently.

LIFE IN BANGUI

One-fifth of the country's population lives in Bangui, a city that beckons people in the countryside with the promise of a better life and often dashes their hopes when they arrive. Bangui is a place of both exhilaration and frustration, and these sensations often happen at the same time. There are other urban centers in the Central African Republic such as Berbérati, Bangassou, and Ndélé, but "the city" is Bangui. The capital draws migrants each day, those looking for a better life and to leave farming behind in the villages. The city's creators saw Bangui as a counterpart to a town on the Belgian side of the river, and later, as an administrative center, but never as a site of large-scale African residence. Rural to urban migration takes place every day: The city swells and accepts more people. The capital suffers from a lack of sanitation with open sewers, poor housing and drainage, and hand-dug wells. The conditions of the *kodros* are at the same level or below those of rural areas. Despite the poverty and deteriorating conditions, people live lives that include joy. Centrafricans find ways to make livings and have some time to enjoy themselves as well.

Bangui is also a place of temporary migration, where parents send their children to live with relatives. This fostering is very common. People who live in cities, especially those who are formally employed, are perceived to be or truly are more capable of paying school fees than their rural family members, and it is part of the family obligation to take in the child and send him or her to school. In return, the child is expected to perform domestic duties. The rural family sends foodstuffs to the family in the city; these items can be expensive in Bangui, and they are welcomed on the urban table.

KM5, the neighborhood that is five kilometers from the physical center of town, is what many people consider to really be Bangui. It is one of the biggest and most popular neighborhoods in the city. The Church of Fatima and Notre Dame d'Afrique are both in this quarter, as is the city's largest mosque.

It is home to the city's largest market and many of the foreign merchants who control the trade in luxury goods. People of all ethnic backgrounds live and work in KM5. It is also full of nightclubs that pump music into the streets late into the night.

It is becoming increasingly difficult to find resources in Bangui. As more land becomes inhabited, fields for those in older neighborhoods are lost to the building of new houses, and people have to travel longer distances to farm. Also, as more land is cleared for homes and fields, trees are cut down. People have long been dependent on this nonrenewable source of energy for cooking, but it is getting to be more scarce and expensive. Petrol is always an issue; most of it comes up the Oubangui on a barge or is trucked from neighboring Cameroon. As the transportation from the coast greatly increases its cost, it is less expensive to buy from the roadside vendors who sell petrol in bottles than it is to purchase it at an official station.

Godobé

Godobé is the term for a child who lives by his or her wits on the streets of Bangui. The greatest number of this complex group come from fragile families in which the parents are struggling greatly and the children need to work; these children spend time with their families on an irregular basis. There is a group that comes from more desperate straits, who have either been abandoned by or have abandoned their families, or at least, have serious conflicts with their kin. These *godobé* are not solely the products of economically disadvantaged homes; some have good family ties. Children with physical disabilities are often left to the life of the *godobé* because their parents do not have the resources to care for them.

The *godobé* make a living by carrying packages for shoppers, watching parked cars, and helping women who run street stalls by fetching water and cleaning the grills. These tasks bring only slight remuneration. The *godobé* also sell plastic bags, cigarettes, bottles of gasoline and kerosene, or anything else that they can procure. As these young people spend more time on the streets, they turn to begging, thievery, prostitution, and drugs. Marijuana is the drug of choice for most of these youth, but sniffing is also popular: glue, gasoline, and other solvents. Also, antimalarials are crushed and snorted, and some of these children have graduated to opium or cocaine.[4] But not all are criminals or drug users.

The *godobé* live in a world that is very much their own. They are speakers of Sango, and with coded expressions onto which foreign words are liberally sprinkled. This version of the popularly spoken language allows them to communicate in a more clandestine manner, and it sets them apart from others in the city. The children band together for survival and safety, but their numbers can cause others to fear them for what these children seek. They live by their wits in the KM5 section of town, and the market in this quarter is their fiefdom, so much so that vendors have joined together to protect themselves from their criminal activities. Bands of children roam the streets at night and when they sleep, it is in groups with one appointed sentry. They do not fear for their physical safety as much as they do for their mobility. They can be arrested and made to work in public utility fields. Jails in Bangui do not have separate facilities for incarcerating adults and children. Prison in Bangui is a disagreeable place, and prisoners are subjected to isolation, physical violence, and lack of hygienic care. It is difficult for a child who has been incarcerated to return to a normal life, including going to school.

OVERALL CONDITIONS

The life of the typical Centrafrican is one of hard work and struggle, no matter if the person lives in the countryside, town, or city. People work, sleep, and play hard. Formal employment is the exception rather than the rule in the Central African Republic. The education system is plagued by many problems, including a lack of personnel and insufficient funding. Muslims send their children to qu'ranic schools. Agriculture is the field in which the largest number of people work. The informal sector is a powerful factor in urban areas, and it really drives the economy of Bangui. From market women vendors to taxi drivers to the little boy selling soap from a shallow basin held on top of his head, one can find just about everything one needs without going through any formal organizations.

The urban milieu as characterized by Bangui is a place where a very few do very well, some do moderately well, and the vast majority barely eke out an existence. There is little formal employment in Bangui, and the lucky few who have received formal educations and found government or private sector employment fear for their elite positions as the economy shrinks and takes jobs with it. The city is a place of chronic underemployment. Educated Centrafricans should be able to find good jobs; these jobs, however, have not materialized, encouraging the best and the brightest to find employment elsewhere, often in France. Industry is limited, and there is a small artisanal base. The light industries in Bangui include textile manufacturing, agricultural-product processing, a cooking oil factory, a soap factory, a sugar refinery, a sawmill, a cotton gin, a palm oil processing plant, a cigarette factory, a brewery, and a diamond-cutting facility. Most people are involved in some sort of agriculture and any of the multitudinous informal economic activities. The 2002 per capita income was USD260.

Men hold jobs from the highest levels of government to working in the informal market, but they have also been hit hard by unemployment. The kinds of jobs available to men without formal education are affected by the small industrial base in the country, and men often find themselves doing jobs that they would not have anticipated. Some recent male arrivals in Bangui find jobs doing domestic work. Other jobs for men include manual laborers, security guards, mechanics, and chauffeurs. The paucity of wage-earning work has led men to do work that they would not perform in the countryside because it is considered "women's work."

ECONOMY

Rural life is based on subsistence agriculture. Agricultural production falls into two categories, that for household consumption, which is done by women, and cash cropping, which is done by men. The major cash crops are cotton, tobacco, and coffee. Women produce the staples of *manioc*, maize, bananas, and yams, along with the other foods that make the sauces. During the harvest, men will work in their wives' fields, and women return the favor when the husbands' crops are ready to be reaped. People work long hours in the sun to feed their families and to earn extra cash.

This is a country where labor is cheap, and people are chronically unemployed and underemployed. Many of those who have struggled to get university degrees cannot find suitable work in the country. A good number of these educated people earned their degrees overseas, and they choose to stay there and work. Not only do they find work that is commensurate with their degrees, but the remuneration is much higher as well. These people send money to their families in the CAR. These funds are very important not only to the families that receive them, but also because they are a substantial part of the country's economy.

Mining and logging are also substantial contributors to the national and family economies. These industries' products are destined for foreign consumption and run by foreign interests. Employers often supplement labor from the surrounding area with recruited labor. These migrant workers are living without their families and among people they do not know, and the laborers' camps have high rates of alcohol consumption and prostitution.

Most commercial activity takes place in the markets. There are a few stores and boutiques in the cities, but the traditional format from the countryside continues to this day and has extended to the urban areas. Open-air markets are where people purchase everything from clothing to food to hardware. Larger towns may have a market open every day, but in rural areas, the market may be active as rarely as one day a week. Along Avenue Koudoukou, there are stores owned by ex-patriots from Senegal, Lebanon, Portugal, as well as "Hausa" people. The largest market in Bangui is Mamadou-Mbaiki in the KM5 section of town, and it is open all day long. It features specialties from each ethnic group. A standard feature of market shopping is bargaining. The seller proposes a price and the potential buyer counters with a lower one. There are some unwritten rules about bargaining: Certain items such as textiles do not have much wiggle-room, and a low counteroffer may result in the insulted snatching away of the material and an indignant refusal to continue negotiations.

LEISURE

Leisure time is something of a foreign concept for Centrafricans, especially for women. Most people work very hard, and the rest of their time is spent eating and sleeping. When it comes to "free time," people make the most of what little they have. The traditional telling of stories and time spent with the family encompasses the bulk of their time, but there are special leisure activities in which they participate. The Centrafrican's ability to do these other activities is as dependent on money as it is on unoccupied time. Music, discussed more extensively in Chapter Eight, is one of the major diversions in the CAR.

Most Centrafricans who are not Muslim enjoy beer. There are indigenous alcoholic beverages, and imported ones are often favored by the well-to-do. For those who have the time and the money, there are beer halls. These places are outdoors, and people congregate to listen to music and drink; sometimes, they drink to get drunk. Drunkenness was not tolerated in traditional society, where drinks were ritually produced and consumed. The introduction of factory-manufactured alcoholic beverages and alcohol for sale means that alcohol is no longer a community-oriented substance, a reward for hard work or a libation sacrificed to an ancestor, but a commodity. Alcoholism is an increasing problem in the CAR.

Because family is so important and members are increasingly scattered, travel helps to maintain the connections. Many people who work in cities try to visit their relatives in the countryside for weekends and holidays; it is rarer for the village-dweller to visit Bangui. Because there are no railways and other systems of mass transit, transportation is limited to the few privately owned vehicles and the vans and buses that ply the roads from place to place. Because road conditions are often poor and the crowded vans and buses frequently stop, road travel is quite time-consuming. When people visit, they bring what their area has to offer. People from villages bring produce, and city dwellers bring luxury items such as soap and perfume.

For those who have the funds, there are parks to visit. The St. Floris and Dzanga-Ndoki are two of the country's biggest nature preserves. Despite its abundant wildlife, St. Floris has received less than 1,000 tourists in its first half-century of operation, and many of those guests were foreigners. Obstacles include the difficulty and high cost of getting to the park and that local officials there prohibited tourists from taking pictures.

Sports are popular leisure time activities, and people do so both as spectators and active participants. Soccer, called football, is widely played and watched. There is a national stadium in Bangui where teams such as Tempête Mocaf, the team of musician Prosper Prosper Mayélé favored by the *godobé*, play. Football tends to be a bit rougher sport than in the West, and it is a good sport for people without a lot of means because very little equipment is involved. Basketball is also gaining in popularity. For those who can afford these activities, there is tennis, horseback riding, and golf. The clubs where these activities are offered have dues that are equivalent to approximately one-third of a typical person's yearly income, making it virtually impossible for the Centrafrican, even one with a good job, to enjoy such amenities, although the rates are very reasonable for the Western expatriate community.

Local cultural events have diminished in the rural areas as talented performers make their way to Bangui to reap the rewards of performing before large audiences and to have the potential to make good money. There are about five theaters and three large cultural centers, including the French and American Cultural Centers. One of the most attractive features of the centers is the staging of plays by youth. The theater is also popular, both live theater and film. Live theater is quite popular among the educated public. Bangui has a few movie theaters that show French-language films and movies dubbed into French; as in other places in Africa, films from Asia are popular. There is a nascent indigenous film industry. Its development is hindered by a lack of funds and a lack of equipment, not a deficiency in creative talent. Joseph Akouissone's 1983 film, *Zo Kwe Zo, Every Man Is a Human Being*, is the first film by a Centrafrican; its title comes from the principle of the same name put forth by President Boganda that declared that people must be assured of their dignity. It won the award for the best image/cinematography at the prestigious Panafrican Film and Television Festival of Ouagadougou. The CAR's first feature-length film, *The Silence of the Forest*, was actually a co-production with Gabon and Cameroon. Adapted from the Centrafrican Étienne Goyémidé's novel of the same name, the film is directed by Didier Ouénangaré and Bassek ba Kobhio. The European Union gave about 400,000 Euros for the project that focused on the problems of the Biaka people.

TECHNOLOGY

The lack of electricity in many areas precludes the use of not just media devices, but technology. There are 0.2 computers in use for every 100 people.[5] It is estimated that 5,000 Centrafricans access the Internet, one of the lowest levels of usage in the world.[6] The Internet is one of the best ways for Centrafricans to be in contact with the outside world. Most people in Bangui cannot afford to have Internet access at home, but there is a private company that provides Internet services and e-mail addresses. Although the number of people who have access to the Internet is limited, it is increasing in popularity, as it is a way to access information that has not been filtered by the government.

People do not spend a lot of time on the telephone in the CAR. One reason is that phones are comparatively expensive; another is that they are scarce. Although telephones were a missing part of the infrastructure for years, many people vaulted over the era of the land line and now have cellular phones. There are about twice as many portable telephones as there are conventional phones. Mobile phones can be purchased more easily and rapidly than conventional phones, which can take weeks to have installed.

HEALTH

Health conditions are often poor, especially in rural areas. There is a lack of funding for many health centers, which sometimes run out of medications. An attending lack of medical personnel only exacerbates the problems. Although all Centrafricans are affected by this situation, it is the most vulnerable populations that suffer the most: women, children, and the elderly are needier and underserved. The lack of doctors and nurses makes difficult births even more so. There are a number of endemic problems that are particularly difficult for children. The major causes of infant and juvenile morbidity are diarrhea, malaria, intestinal parasites, acute respiratory diseases, malnutrition, polio, neo-tetanus, tuberculosis, and anemia. Malaria is the leading cause of death of children from birth to five years. HIV/AIDS is also a grave threat to children in the CAR. Infected mothers can pass it to them *in utero,* but the disease is killing their parents and other relatives, and its spread threatens children in many ways. The country has one of the highest rates for HIV infection and is a leader in AIDS-related deaths.

Many of the statistical measures of life are lower in the CAR than in many other countries. Infant and mother mortality rates are among the highest in the world, and life expectancy at birth is less than 44 years.[7] Malnutrition is a major problem in both rural and urban areas. Challenges to maintaining good health in the CAR include HIV/AIDS, tuberculosis, hepatitis, meningitis, typhoid fever, and malaria, to name a few. There is one large government hospital, and dental care and optical services are available only in Bangui.

When people are ill, they seek out different types of healers; from the traditional realm, there are herbalists, spirit mediums, diviners, and "medicine men," and new religions provide Christian prophets and Muslim teachers. There are also physicians and other medical personnel who practice in the Western tradition. Indigenous traditional medicine is used to combat illness, both mental and physical. The patient is sick, and the diviner ascertains why. The illness is a physical manifestation of witchcraft, thus, the supernatural is used to combat the problem. In conjunction with fighting the supernatural, real physical medicine is used as well. Centrafricans are experts at finding medicinal plants and using them to cure all sorts of ailments; forest peoples have a deserved reputation for being excellent exploiters of healing plants. People in cities rely more on Western medicine, in part because the natural resources are harder to find and because people believe that Western medicine is better for some ailments. Some believe that Western medicine actually introduced illnesses (such as HIV/AIDS), while others believe that because Westerners were able to take control of Africa, their medicine is stronger than indigenous medicine. Diseases that existed prior to colonization have not been eradicated. Yaws, tuberculosis, leprosy, kwashiorkor, and dysentery persist, although there is one change today from the precolonial era: The health status of Centrafricans is lower now than it was then.

Social customs and lifestyles in the Central African Republic were created to support and reflect people's worldviews and social institutions, and they were shaped by the practicalities of history and environment. Many practices survived the colonial era only to be adjusted in the postcolonial world. For example, bridewealth is a means to the end of social cohesion and control. The French tried unsuccessfully to eradicate the practice by law, but their imported wage labor changed bridewealth's functions, as the new economy altered not only the way it worked, but the society that used it as well. Today, it is a cultural inheritance that many find unnecessary but impossible to escape. Centrafricans have adapted age-old institutions for reasons that are foreign and organic to make their worlds comprehensible and enjoyable.

NOTES

1. Félix Éboué, *Les Peuples de l'Oubangui-Chari: Essai d'Ethnographie, de Lingusitique et d'Economie Sociale* (Paris, 1933; repr., New York: AMS Press, 1977), pp. 48–49.

2. Tamara Giles-Vernick, *Cutting the Vines of the Past: Environmental Histories of the Central African Rain Forest* (Charlottesville: University Press of Virginia, 2000), pp. 80–81.

3. Suzanne Renouf-Stefanik, *Animisme et Islam Chez les Manza (Centafrique): Influence de la Religion Musulmane sur les Coutumes Traditionelles Manza* (Paris: SELAF, 1978), pp. 171–73.

4. UNICEF, *Analyse de la Situation de la Mère et de l'Enfant Centrafricains* (Bangui[?]: République Centafricaine, 1992), p. 162.

5. http://globalis.gvu.unu.edu/indicator_detail.cfm?IndicatorID=91&Country=CF.

6. http://www.nationmaster.com/country/ct/Internet.

7. http://www.cia.gov/cia/publications/factbook/geos/ct.html.

8

Music and Dance

IN ITS MANY INCARNATIONS, music is a fundamental part of the lives of people of the Central African Republic. Traditional forms of music that are still played today often sound strange to Western ears, but it is pleasing to the people who make it, and, just as important, to the people, ancestors, and spirits who hear it. Dance, spontaneous or orchestrated, often accompanies music, and its functions are very similar. Music is integrated into social life and the rituals, small and large, of people's lives; it is the foundation of dancing, an important form of entertainment, and an activity in which everyone participates. Music accompanies religious festivals; it is sung in the fields; it is used to lull babies into sleep, to entertain, to inspire, and to reflect and transmit ideas and values. Music is integrated into virtually all activities, from pounding *gozo* to funeral rites.

Music is a language of its own and an invitation to greater polylingualism and multiculturalism. Musicians from across Africa and the world have an impact on Centrafrican music. Lingala, a widely spoken language in the Democratic Republic of the Congo, is also a language in which many musicians in and out of the country record songs, so listeners are introduced to and can learn it through music. Also, musical styles from different ethnic groups are cross-fertilizing other traditions, infusing other groups' styles and influencing modern musical forms. The idea of "traditional" is complicated. What happens when traditions of one group are influenced by another? What if the instruments become electrified? What if a ritual is performed, not for its original reasons, but for an audience of foreigners?

TRADITIONAL MUSIC

In the Central African Republic, music and social life are inextricably linked, all aspects of life inspire musicians and lyricists. Music is very integrated into life; it is used for war, hunting rituals, and entertainment. A cappella singing accompanies many quotidian activities such as washing and beating cassava; the songs give a rhythm to the work and make hard labor less of a drudgery. Vital to special occasions, music accompanies the rituals that attend birth, death, rites of passage to adulthood, and all of life's processes of social transformation. Dancing is an activity in which all can participate, thus helping to strengthen the bonds of the community.

The places where music and dance happen vary from the private to the very public, and participation varies accordingly. Some performances can be limited in their scope, such as dances performed by those who are in seclusion for initiation, or very public, such as the dancing that takes place in a *bar-dancing*. There is a correlation between the degree of attendance and participation and the nature of the performance. Those performed with a more limited group tend to have greater social significance. To an extent, when, where, and what one dances indicates one's station in life; not all dances can be done by everybody. Certainly at a nightclub, it is expected that everyone will dance according to his or her wishes. The dances in initiation camps are limited to the participants. When the new adults leave and rejoin their villages, the celebrations will include dancing; some are done by those who have just been initiated, and the village may form a chorus around them; other dances are done by an ensemble. The audience may not be the focus of the performers; instead of dancing to entertain those who are in attendance, the performers may dedicate their dances to ancestors and spirits. There is gender segregation in dance too.

Traditional music in the Central African Republic expresses the joys and sorrows of daily life, as well as more notable events such as birth, initiation, war, and death. The instruments used are of indigenous origin, crafted to produce the sounds and emotive reactions desired to support the lyrics and inspire the dance. Sometimes a solo effort, traditional forms of music are often performed by two or more people and ensembles of all sizes.

Through music and dance, one can learn about the structures of discrete societies. There were dances for kings and for commoners. The *gitangi* dance, which probably originated with the Ngbandi, was adopted by the Bandia clan for the common people and was done purely for pleasure. Built on an asymmetrical pattern, the rhythm of the dance and its music give the feeling of perpetual movement. The *nbàkià* dance of the Bandia happens during celebrations that venerate the ancestors. The *limzana*, a Bandia dance, was associated with the ritual of the pipe or the throwing of the knife, during which a king or a chief was applauded while he either smoked a pipe or brandished a weapon.

Indigenous Musical Instruments

Music communicates ideas in much the same way that people do as they speak; instruments and singing convey the tone and the message. In the Central African Republic, traditional musical instruments mostly fall into the categories of the stringed and the percussive. Many of these instruments are intensely personal. Musicians craft their instruments with creative autonomy, allowing for variations in shape, size, and in decoration. Instruments are personalized and anthropomorphized to reflect the predilections of the player.

Some of the most basic instruments are the idiophones, the self-sounding instruments. An example of a friction idiophone is a stick scraped through a seed pod to produce sound. Struck idiophones include bells (also sometimes found on the end of an instrument such as the harp to provide extra rhythm) and drums. There are also tuned idiophones: the *sanza* and the xylophone. The *sanza* is a hand-piano made from wood; it has either a flat plate or a trapezoid sound box and lamellae, these are metal or bamboo strips of various lengths that produce different tones. The *sanza* is held in both hands by the player, who uses his thumbs to strike the slightly upturned ends of the lamellae. *Sanza* making is not at all specialized; anyone who wants to play the *sanza* makes his own. In tuning the *sanza,* the musician thinks not only of the pitch but of the overtones that the single lamella makes as well. The *sanza* is the accompaniment to Gbaya "thinking songs." Played only by men, the lyrics of these songs range from concerns about everyday life to special events and lamentations. As these songs are meant to promote contemplation, the quiet *sanza* playing enhances their reflective quality. These songs are often played by a sojourner who seeks to alleviate the ennui of the long walk or the night watchman who looks for a way both to relieve his boredom and to stay awake.

Drums

Drums are usually the first instrument that people think of in reference to African music. Drums are often the foundation for music, especially when music is supposed to induce people to dance. Drums are used not only for creating the rhythm for dancers, but they are also used as a medium of communication; for example, drums are used to announce a death. They can transmit messages from village to village as they also convey emotion to dancers. Drums are often part of a larger ensemble or can be played individually. Large drums are particularly powerful instruments. The importance of these percussive instruments has been enhanced by their inclusion in the representations that Occidentals produced of the continent.

Some drums are quite simple in form; for example, the wooden slit drum fashioned from a hollowed-out log with an aperture in the wood that creates two "lips." The two sides of the aperture are of different thicknesses and thus produce different tones. Although the slit drum is used across the globe, some of the largest are found in the CAR, where Banda subgroups produce very large and rounded varieties. Another type of drum is the slap-pot, an earthenware container with a hole pierced in the bottom.

Other drums are membranophones; one or two skins are stretched tightly over a resonator, almost always a hollowed-out tree trunk in the CAR, and attached with wooden pegs. The sound reverberates inside the drum and from the skin that covers the top. The skin vibrates when struck, producing a certain tone when the middle is struck and another when tapped near the edge. The thickness of the skin also affects the tone that the instrument produces. The drums are struck either with sticks or by hand.

The Babenzélé subgroup of the Biaka have two unique types of percussive instruments. One is the *koondi*, the water drum. While bathing, girls cup their hands and slap the water, creating deep percussive sounds that can travel long distances. They accompany these sounds with polyphonic singing and yodeling. The tone of the sound of the water can be roughly controlled by the movement of their hands. The Babenzélé also have an "earth drum" that is an exact spot in the forest where the earth is shaped in such a way that walking over it creates a profound resonation. Many are familiar with this place because knowledge of its existence has been passed down from generation to generation.

Xylophone

The xylophone is an instrument whose use crosses ethnic groups; one variation of it is known as the *balafon*. The xylophone is made of graduated wooden keys that rest atop a resonating chamber that the player strikes with mallets. The tone of the xylophone is consistent, as the keys do not vary from day to day, and it is used by harpists to tune their instruments.

In one type of xylophone, the pit xylophone used by the Zandé, the keys rest above the sound-emitting area that can be a box, a trough, or a clay pot. In another type, the keys are arranged over two banana stems. In a different variety, the keys are set atop a wooden frame, and resonators below amplify the sound. The resonator also varies in size, and its mass corresponds to the specific key that it enhances. Xylophones vary greatly in their sound, with the differences produced by the tuning and the material from which they are constructed.

The variations in xylophones can be seen among various ethnic groups. Among the Gbaya-Kara, the 10-bladed xylophones are made by experts who secretly cultivate the specific gourd that is used as a resonator. The portable xylophone of the Zandé is different from those in other parts of Central Africa because it does not use buzzers on the calabash resonators. This instrument could be played by chiefs or by the king himself. Among the Nzakara, this type of xylophone was used for the royal dance of *ngbàkià*. The *balafon* is a popular instrument in Ouham and Ouham Pendé areas; one well-known player is David N'gangue, who hails from Bossangoa. His music preserves the traditions of his area of origin, yet he sings in Sango. N'gangue and other *balafon* players improvise popular songs that are usually about the everyday lives of peasants and about common social problems.

Horns

Horns add melody to music and provide rhythm as well. Horns made out of animals reflect both the closeness of the relationship between humans and fauna and people's ability and power to take away and then use the weapons of these animals. Perhaps it is because of this symbolism that horns are used for important ceremonies and in court music. The horns of animals such as antelope are made into musical instruments, but not all horns come from animals, some are carved from wood.

Horns are used by Banda people in rites of passage into adulthood and in rituals of ancestor veneration. An ensemble of these horns is *ongo,* made up to 18 horns: 6 are higher-pitched, transverse, and made from the horn of an antelope; 10 are more centrally pitched and made from scooped-out tree roots played through a hole cut on a slant at the end of the horn; and the sound of the remaining 2 horns represents the bass of the ensemble's register. These last horns are made from the delicate trunks of trees such as papaya; these are end-blown and the mouth hole is a straight cut. Each horn plays at a specific time for each piece, and each player's horn produces a specific note; this results in the weaving of a tapestry of sound that is well orchestrated, polyrhythmic, and interlocking. The sound resembles the texture of the *hoquet* of the European Medieval era.

Wind instruments abound. Transverse horns are simply horns played in a horizontal position; horns made from animal horns and tusks are generally played this way. Sometimes, these horns are referred to as trumpets. Other horns are top-blown. Flutes are another type of wind instrument, and the

Zandé have a set of matched flutes that each have four finger holes. Whistles help to round out the aerophone category.

Harps

The harps of Central Africa are known not only for the music they produce, but also for their beauty. Both aesthetically and acoustically pleasing, it is a very popular instrument. The harp is an intimate instrument; the proximity of the harp to the player creates this reaction, as do some of the songs that accompany harp playing. Traditionally, the harpist holds his instrument vertically in his lap or between his thighs with the handle facing outward, a modern innovation that sometimes finds the player holding the harp so that the strings face him. The player uses two hands at one time and is thus able to create polyrhythms. Harps can be quite anthropomorphized: the body of the harp can resemble that of a human, legs are sometimes added to the bottom, and faces are common features—some even have eyebrows and pierced ears.

Harps from Central Africa are identifiable by their curved handles and the variations in the ways that their crafters attach the handle to the sound box. When the handle is placed into a socket in the sound box, the instrument is called a *kundi;* when the handle abuts the sound box and is attached to a projection from the box, it is called *ngombi.* The strings are made from vegetable matter. Harps must be tuned, and players are able to fix the pitch by putting resin under the pegs. Harps come in a great variety of sizes and dimensions. Harps can be made for children or adults, and harps made for court musicians reach an impressive size.

The harp has a sociocultural dimension and a prominent place in social satire. Because harp players often perform at rituals, they are important people in their communities. Those who play the harp are also poets whose words accompany the tunes they play. A contemporary musician who relies on instrumentation and the social context of the past is Bernard N'Zapayé, who accompanies himself on the *kundi.* He sings in Sango and three other languages so that his lyrics can be understood by a broader audience. He uses his lyrics to critique Centrafrican society, targeting men who frequent prostitutes and married women who dally with their pastors.

These popular instruments often have variations specific to the people who use them. In the Lobaye, harps are 10-stringed instruments of different dimensions that often have small bells attached to the head of the handle to reinforce the rhythm produced by the strings, and the songs are often syncopated. A large and sonorous instrument, it is often used to play songs of lamentation. In the Mobaye region, harps have six strings. Five strings are popular with many ethnic groups, including the Nzakara and Zandé, who call them *kùndi* or *ndàlà,* and *sàgiru,* respectively.

Pygmy Music

The music of different pygmy groups, such as the Biaka and the Mbati, is of great interest in the CAR and people in the West. One of the hallmarks of Biaka music is the very complex counterpunctive polyphony based on four consecutive voices. The songs allow for spontaneous or improvised additions. Those who are singing can, during the course of a piece, change from one voice to another, and these individual variations leave the listener with the impression of the sound of perpetual motion. Simultaneous melodic lines, rhythmic interlocking, wide intervals, and yodeling are also features of Aka music. Yodeling is the rapid switching between a "chest voice" and a "head voice" that results in a low-high-low-high sound pattern. Percussive instruments sustain the songs. The music of the Aka has become a local and exportable commodity, as they do performances in the country, especially for visitors, and travel to Europe and the Americas to perform their music and dance. The distinctive music of the pygmies is threatened by the current situation in the CAR. As the number of people diminishes and the forest is cut, the people and their inspirations are diminished in number. Also "progress" has had an impact, as fewer young people are interested in preserving their traditions and are looking at the potential of living outside the forest.

Court Music

In the societies that have monarchies, there is music and dance specific to these political organizations. One impact of colonization was to lessen the prominence of kings and their courts, and the accompanying musical traditions declined as well. The Zandé king had a court, as did his chiefs, and harps had a privileged role and status in the musical traditions of these courts. The great harps could exceed one meter (3.3 feet) in length from the bottom of the sound box to the tip of the handle, including the carving. Not only were these harps physically imposing, but what the harpists related could be challenging.

In these highly stratified societies, the king was an absolute ruler with power over the life and death of his subjects; criticizing the elite was difficult for the average person. In Zandé society, the musician of the court, the great harp player, had more freedom to do exactly that, although there certainly were limits to his liberties, and he had to be subtle about what he said.

This song from the former Bandia court demonstrates fealty to the power structure, while simultaneously representing the displeasure that could be generated on the part of people whose lives were controlled so tightly by the elite:

Walk on your own legs, do your errand yourself on your own legs, so that we can leave, [I hail] the courts, [I hail] the chief
 Walk on your own legs, so that we can leave
 Walk on your own legs
 Sovereign court! Do your own errand yourself on your own legs, walk on your own legs
 Walk on your own legs. Sovereign court, do your own errand yourself on your own legs, so that we can leave. Sovereign court, walk on your own legs
 Do your errand yourself on your own legs.

Interlude

Walk on your own legs, chief, do your own errand yourself on your own legs
 Chief, walk on your own legs
 Do your errand yourself on your own legs, father, do your errand yourself on your own legs

Interlude

Walk on your own legs, walk on your own legs, father
 Do your errand yourself on your own legs, chief, walk on your own legs, father, do your errand yourself on your own legs

Interlude

Walk on your own legs, sovereign court!
 Walk on your own legs, chief, walk on your own legs so that we can leave, sovereign courts, chief

Interlude

Walk on your own legs, walk on your own legs, father
 Do your errand yourself on your own legs, chief, walk on your own legs so that we can leave, descendant of Kule, chief, do your errand yourself on your own legs, father, do your errand yourself on your own legs
 Walk on your own legs, sovereign court, so that we can leave[1]

Funerary Music

As music is ubiquitous in the lives of Centrafricans, so is death, and music plays a vital role in the rites that accompany funerary practices. Drums are used to announce death, and they feature prominently in the music played in these rituals as well, often playing during the internment of the body. All ethnic groups have music that is reserved for funerary use.

The *mogbaté* is funerary music from the Lobaye region whose use has recently faded. The *mogbaté* should never be played except during funerary rites, lest the music provoke the death of another villager. The basis of the music is drums. The *mogbaté* is played by men whose goal it is to awaken feelings of sadness and joy in the family of the deceased. A group of wailers pick up on these emotions and sing funerary songs. The same rhythms attract people who dance until sunrise.

DANCE

Everyone in the Central African Republic dances: adults, teens, the elderly, and children of all ages. Babies are introduced to rhythmic movement when they are tied to their mothers' backs as they work in the fields and elsewhere. Women often accompany their work with song: to move with music is one of the first things that babies do. Because music, and especially singing, are a natural part of everyday life, the opportunities to dance are readily available. For ritual purposes, more specialized dances are performed. Also, people go out specifically to listen to music and dance; some say that going to dance clubs in Bangui is the best part of life in that city. In urban areas, dances, like the music that accompanies them, are very much inspired by traditional forms, and these are constantly being adapted as new influences arrive.

Dance is not at all static. As people move and come into contact with others and their styles, new forms arise. The *loudon,* a dance of the Ngbaka people, draws its inspiration from the Monte-Nguène. The Monte-Nguène, meaning "pleasure" or *joie de vivre,* is a style played by Ngbaka as well as Mbati and Monzombo peasants. The contact between and influence on neighboring ethnic groups is evident in the syncopated rhythms that derive from the polyphonic sounds of the neighboring pygmies. Dance styles are also particular to specific groups; for example, the dances of the Mbati have a hip-swiveling and rib-rotating action, and those of the Biaka are based on square-hipped chugging and buttock-bobbing. Christian missionaries often find these moves to be lewd.

Biaka dances are inspired by their principal activities, and a good number of them represent the behavior of the animals of the forest and the actions of the men who hunt them. Music and dance accompany and enliven hunting rituals; the participation of the community reflects the nature of Aka society and the importance of a successful hunt to everyone's well-being. For the ensemble of their dances, some are reserved for men, others are for women, and some are mixed.

The Biaka have a number of dances performed to ensure successful hunting. The *mabo,* specific to net hunting, features group dancing with intervals of rest that later sees the introduction of a solo dancer. This man wears a cone-shaped construction of palm fronds that are tied at the top of the head and drape over and away from the body. This dancer dons a mask of such a size that it requires skill to wear it and still be able to dance. During the dance, polyphonic singing is interspersed with percussive sections, and the combination spurs on the dancers to clap, make exclamations, and find other methods of reinforcing the dance beat of the music. The Biaka also have a dance for big-game hunting and for divination. The *ndambo,* an older dance that is more polyrhythmic than the *mabo* with a slower pace, features the yodeling style for which the Biaka are well known. The dance is circular but occasionally breaks into a snaking line. The dancers' steps sometimes resemble those of the game that the hunters will pursue. The Bangombe, a Biaka subgroup, have a men's society, the *jenge,* that performs a dance featuring a "masked monster" of the same name. *Jenge* is considered to be the ancestor of one of the oldest members of the camp as well as the luck of hunters. This masked monster dances publicly, performing rapid turning movements in front of the assembled women and children. The *mokondi* is a name for dances that fall into the genre of those involving spirits.

For the Mpeimu of the forest, the killing of a leopard is a significant event, and it is celebrated with dance. Leopards are believed to be beings whose occult powers transform them into creatures whose express purpose is to kill people. When a panther is slain, the event is followed by four days of dancing the *so.* The women vigorously dance circles around the village, and the men dance with their arms hanging loosely. This is done to represent the dead panther that is now mounted upon poles. The nights feature male dances that neither women nor children are allowed to observe.

Pygmy dances are at risk of disappearing for several reasons: the depletion of their forests, the dwindling numbers of the people who perform them, and the difficult cultural preservation in the face of increasing time spent outside of the forest with other ethnic groups. Yet there is an intense desire on the part of these groups and outsiders such as UNESCO to safeguard these traditions. The pygmies are famous for their music and dance, so much so that they often are brought out of the country to perform in the West. Their traditional music and dance are highly sought-after as a cultural artifact, and their impact on contemporary music is also remarkable.

CONTEMPORARY MUSIC

In a country with a limited press and production of literature, music is one of the most important media that Centrafricans use to express themselves in a way that is accessible to outsiders. However, the lyrics that they write and the music that they make are for themselves. They are a good way to understand the joys, frustrations, and aspirations of the people of the Central African Republic. The Democratic Republic of the Congo receives a great deal of attention for its contemporary music, while the CAR remains relatively unknown. New influences on the current music of the country are many, but traditional music continues to shape the forms that are currently being produced in the countryside and in the urban areas. Music from the Americas, especially African American and Cuban music, is very important. What the music of those who descended from slaves in the Western Hemisphere has in common with Centrafrican music is their African roots; thus, Centrafrican musicians are being affected by influences that may have originally come from their region, crossing the Atlantic twice before returning to them. In the late 1970s, a Centrafrican style of electrified band music developed, and it has taken off from there. Because of the cost of modern electric items such as guitars, it is not unusual for a few bands to share the same instruments.

In the 1950s and 1960s, the *baténgué* became a popular ball that was organized in some sections of Bangui. Its origin is in the folkloric traditions of the Gbaya-Kara in the western city of Berbérati, near the Cameroon border. The name *baténgué* comes from a small rectangular drum that produces a sweet sound. *Baténgué* music is spicy and weighty. The balls were often organized under the light of the moon and became a place for the Banguiois to meet. Modern dance halls have taken over the popularity of the *baténgué*. In the 1950s, Cuban rumba and Ghanian High Life, along with the Tchatchatcha, Méréngué, and the Mambo arrived. These styles came to the CAR with students who had studied in France, Cuba, Ghana, Togo, and Benin and inspired Centrafrican musicians such as Marcel Joachim Vomitiendé, Prosper Mayélé, and Rodolphe Békpa. From the fusion of these sounds and the addition of local melodies, the Congolese Rumba style was born. Although Brazzaville was the capital of the AEF in the colonial era, it was as the capital of the Belgian Congo that a music industry really took hold.

The themes of contemporary songs reflect modern society; they are slices of life that address the conflict between tradition and modernity, family, rivalry between and for men and women, the adversities faced by couples, negritude, and knowledge of African cultures, as well as exploring philosophical questions such as fate and the origin of evil. One example is the song "Fami tî zong-zing" that describes the tribulations of a widow whose in-laws strip her of all the goods her husband owned and her subsequent abandonment by her own family. Many of the songs are longer than their Western counterparts. It is not unusual for a song to last for more than 10 minutes, with long instrumental sections. Songwriters are rarely female.

The KM5 neighborhood is the heart of the music scene in Bangui. The quarter pulses with live performances at night. ABC is one of the most well known of the many "bar-dancings" in the neighborhood. This is a lively section of town at all hours, and the music from the bars resonates late into the night. Other nightclubs include Vis-à-Vis, le Rex, Cercle Mbi Yé, Bar Étoile, Coupole, and Tchatchatcha.

Bangui has been secondary to Kinshasa in the production of musicians, but the latter are no less inspired than the former, and musical acts began to proliferate. The band Tropical-Fiesta began in 1965 with Charlie Perrière, Elvis Evoko, and Baron. One of their biggest hits is "Profit When the Time Is Right," and their focus is on the relationships between men and women and love songs. Makémbé's origins were in another group, Amical Fiesta, which started in 1966. Ferreria and Ngoita were among the original members of Amical Fiesta, which morphed into "Los Negritos" when the members arrived from Mbaiki to Bangui in 1967. In 1975, the orchestra changed its name to "Los Négritos Makémbé," and José Ngoita became the leader of the band in this same year. By 1982, some of the group's members left the band to join Canon Star. In 1985, Makembé had six singers, three guitarists, two bassists, three trumpets, one organist, and one tuba player. The songs were written by different musicians in the band. The orchestra Centrafricain Jazz began in 1972 with Prosper Maylélé and ended in 1985. Canon Star is one of the most widely recognized groups outside of the CAR. It began in 1982 with singers who left Makémbé after a disagreement with the band's leaders; it was founded by Naïmo Christa, who directed the band's evolution away from the style of its parent. Solo guitarist Mombaza created a new style that launched the band in a different direction. In one of their songs, a man in the KM5 neighborhood of Bangui is stolen from shamelessly.

Kilomètre 5

Attention yeye yeye, attention dear
Attention yeye yeye, attention dear

Zone Cinq, popular neighborhood in Bangui
Kilomètre Cinq, the neighborhood makes people crazy
Kilomètre Cinq, the neighborhood of sin. Neighborhood of sin.

If you arrive at Zone Cinq, at Kilo Cinq
You think you will not die
You find some Centrafricans who are superb
You find some women who know how to dress
They can divert your husband
Without you knowing it. It's dangerous.

You find young chauffeurs, little models
You find "mother superior's"
Those who we call "ready to wear"
You also find "capable mothers"
Those who know to feed the men
You also find women who are pirates
Those who suck on men, drain men down to the marrow
Even if you leave with five thousand francs
You go home with five francs
...

If you want to have fun in KM5 fill your pockets
If not, your shirt will stay in KM5
Your pants will stay in KM5[2]

It is not only orchestras or band that have proven successful, individuals have as well. One example is Princess Leoni Kangala, the daughter of a politician and niece of politicians born in Bossangoa in 1953. She was a television broadcaster on TV Centrafricain for two years before joining the government. She and her brothers formed a band when she was in her twenties, and she was quickly pursued by other bands. She moved to Paris in 1981, and her first album appeared in 1991. Princess Leoni Kangala fuses the styles of funk, salsa, soul, rumba, and traditional Centrafrican music to produce her own blend. She sings in Yakoma, English, Spanish, and French. Sultan Zembellat was born Ghislain Jean-Baptiste Zembellat in Bangui in 1959. He was given his nickname because of his ability to recite the names and exploits of many of the sultans in his country's history. He began singing at the age of 15 and attended the fine arts school in Dakar, Senegal. After arriving in Paris, he became a member of two bands before beginning his own and starting on a successful solo career. Sultan Zembellat sings in Sango, Ngbaka, Lingala, Wolof (learned in Senegal), and French.

Songs reflect the values of the people who create them. With many of these contemporary songs, the relationships between men and women is a predominant theme. Women are often portrayed as being very critical of each other and interested in stealing men away from other women. Modern songs denounce many of the things that traditional society condemns, such as prostitution. In the 1980s, through the end of the twentieth century, there was a host of new bands: Zokéla, Super Stars, Tropical Fiesta, and Canon Star are just a few. The mid-1980s was the heyday of the Centrafrican music scene, but the economic crisis in the country meant that fewer people could afford to go out to bars to hear live music. Because of the deteriorating financial situation, many artists left for France. Princess Leoni Kangala, Sultan Zembellat, Canon Star (even though the departure of two of its members, Mombaza and Karawam, left the band with difficult holes to fill), and others migrated to Paris while some remained in Bangui.

Those who move to Europe, particularly France, do so to further their careers. The main reason that they cite for their migration is a lack of funds in the country to support their art. Some studios started to appear in the KM5 section of Bangui in the 1970s, including the Studio Vitanime and Bonga-Bonga, but their equipment could not rival what could be found in Occidental recording spaces. There is now a professional musicians' organization in the country, the *Union des Musiciens Centrafricains*.

Just as the traditional and the modern co-mingle in styles, old and new ways combine to create situations that cause people to reflect upon their culture. In a society that has long valued its elders and whose social security, especially for the elderly, is the family, not performing traditional obligations to the aged is denounced, but the practice is becoming more common.

The Old Man

My brothers, sadness has invaded my heart
Now I have become old
And I no longer have the strength to work
The children I engendered have now grown up
They finished their studies and are working
They all flee from me; I don't know why, my friends
You don't think of me anymore, my children
The rain has ruined my house
I sleep outside with the mosquitoes and the cold
Sickness and hunger are killing me
Really, I have lost a lot of weight my children
You drive air-conditioned cars
You have fun day and night
You sleep in hotels
You go to nightclubs
You party, you and your (girl)friends
But I am weak and without medicine
Hunger torments me, sickness as well

When you hear that I am dead you will organize a funeral so that you will not be
    ashamed
You will buy an expensive casket to bury me in
You will dress me in a jacket with a new tie
You will invite people, you will enjoy yourselves
You will eat chicken and *cabris,* you will drink whiskey and champagne
You will dance until dawn
Well, I'll be gone, adieu
Well, I'll be gone, adieu
…
My children, my children, I am your father, I sired you
What you are doing to me, God will give back to you
Your own children will give it back to you

All the bad that you do to me, my children
Later God will give back to you
Your own children will give it back to you
…
Later, you will become old
You will be sick and hungry
All the wrong you have done to me, my children
Later, God will punish you
Your own children will do the same to you[3]

The songs of the popular orchestras reflect urban society and are more
about the pain than the joys in life. But even when the subject of the song is
negative, humor often shines through. The orchestras that are popular in
Bangui and the rest of the country today perform songs that touch on the
themes of everyday life. Love, conflict between people (especially men and
women), the difficult circumstances of city life, and other issues that affect
people are the basis of these songs. Also songs explore philosophical questions
such as the origin of evil, fate as well as negritude, knowledge of and pride in
African culture, and the opposition of traditional and modern society. The
authors of the bands' songs are rarely women.

Zokéla music addresses themes common to the countryside, such as the
benefits and downsides to the life of the peasants who work the land. It is
inspired by the 10-string harp of the Lobaye and enriched by the polyphonic
rhythms of the neighboring pygmies. Modern instruments are used to create
the traditional low sounds of the drums and the higher-pitched sound of a
stick tapping a bottle as a percussive instrument. Two guitars play enmeshed
and repeating motifs that jump octaves and give this musical style an undu-
lating feeling. Zokéla's origin lies with the band Musiki, a rumba-styled
band based in Bangui that toured the country in 1981. The band spent a

few days in Mbaïki, the capital of the prefecture of the Lobaye, where the members met some young men who were interested in becoming professional musicians. These youth called themselves *zokéla*, which means "noise," "heat," "acclamation," and "ambiance" in the Mbati language; they thought their music sounded like water gurgling down a stream, or like the ululations of women at a funeral dance, or the sound of the life force itself. The original Zokéla players said that they were imitating Centrafrican bands that were emulating groups from Zaire. One night when an orchestra was in town, the young men convinced the players to let them play one song on their instruments. At two in the morning, the exhausted musicians agreed. The crowd's very enthusiastic response let everyone know that these boys had hit upon something great, and the band Zokéla was formed. The band enjoyed success singing about life in the Lobaye as well as in Bangui, and the introduction of songs sung in Sango only increased the band's appeal. Zokéla was at a disadvantage when it came to receiving financial support from the government because it originated in the Lobaye, as did the deposed Emperor Bokassa. Some bands shared instruments with the newcomers, and others tried to poach Zokéla members; the result of these pressures split the band.

Music has a political element, as musicians use music to make commentaries about the social life of the country and politicians use music to sway people's opinions. Bokassa tried to use the radio and musical groups as a part of his effort to create a cult of personality to support his rule. In an effort to ingratiate bands to him, Bokassa built a large recording studio and record production business in Béréngo. The bands Vibro Succès and Tropical Fiesta became "imperial orchestras" by Bokassa. Although these bands were used as tools of propaganda, they did benefit from the proceeds from concerts and material donations from the government. The repressive nature of the state ensured the compliance of these bands; otherwise, they could not exist. The name Super Commando Jazz accurately reflects the origins of the group. Bokassa asked officers in the newly created national army to form a band in the 1970s, during the era of government assistance for musical groups. There was a place for the band to play, and people came to hear it and dance all night.

HIV/AIDS is one of the themes that modern bands address. In the CAR, the phrase "nyàmà nà nyàmà" means "flesh to flesh," and a popular song uses this lyric. It clearly advocates not using condoms during intercourse. The phrase refers to idea that many people have that HIV/AIDS is propagated by whites as a way to keep Africans from having more children. This expression is quite popular among youth. Other songs advise against activities that spread the virus, as evidenced by the lyrics of this Canon Star song:

AIDS

AIDS, from where did you come to Bangui?
Everyone is afraid, everyone cries
People don't want to go out anymore
Everyone stays at home to read the paper
Sickness of the unfaithful, sickness of lovers[4]

This song reflects the local nature of the AIDS epidemic. There is the questioning of the origin of the disease, which some people believe was brought to Africa specifically to reduce the African population. Also, its focus on AIDS being a disease of lovers points to its method of transmission: In the CAR, this is a disease transmitted almost exclusively by heterosexual contact.

The power of music in the eyes of Centrafricans is clear when one understands its sometimes specialized performances and that it is considered to be so potent that funerary music played at an inappropriate time can cause death. It also has the power to entertain and enrich. Music reflects the culture of Centrafricans, not only in its inspirations, instrumentation, and lyrics, but in its growth. Much as people of the country have adapted modern introductions in the areas of education and living patterns, for example, their music has also adapted new influences. People are not abandoning the old ways; they are making changes that make sense to them. Pleasing influences from their neighbors along with electric instruments have encouraged music to grow, while ancient themes and rhythms persist. Centrafricans use music to express their newer anxieties about modernity as well as the age-old problems of social and political issues. The resiliency of music forms, like that of the people, during rough and better times, is a testament to their spirit and fortitude.

NOTES

1. Eric de Dampierre and Marc Chemillier, *Central African Republic: Music of the Former Bandia Courts*, trans. Peter Crowe (Paris, CNRS and the Musée de l'Homme, 1996), pp. 113–14.

2. Lyrics by Canon Star. Pierre Saulnier, *Bangui Chante: Anthologie du Chant Moderne en Afrique Centrale* (Paris: Éditions l'Harmattan, 1993), pp. 147–49.

3. Ibid., p. 93.

4. Ibid., p. 171.

Glossary

bagidi   male prophet (Zandé Mission ti Africa)

balafon   type of xylophone

bar-dancing   a bar that has live music for dancing

baténgué   organized dance popular in Bangui in the 1950s and 1960s

bazin   damask cloth

beignet   fried donut

benge   poison ordeal

binza   diviners who specialize in finding witches

bouille   porridge

boule   ball of prepared cassava flour, resembling a gelatinous mass

Brakalé   Banda god/spirit, one of the three sons of Ngandré, who often serves as counsel to his young brother Téré

brochettes   skewers of grilled meat, akin to shish kebab

cabri   kid (animal)

cache-sexe   literally a "sex-hider," a garment that covers the genitals

functionnaire   government employee

gitangi   Zandé dance for commoners

gozo   *manioc* flour

grand boubou   outfit for men commonly worn by Muslims, consisting of a very large overshirt with a pair of pants underneath and a hat

gris-gris   charm

hydromel   honey-based alcoholic beverage

iwa   Zandé friction oracle

jenge   Bangombe ancestor; luck of the hunt; dancer who performs as living embodiment of this entity

kaba   equivalent garment of the *grand boubou* for females

kanda   squash-seed-and-termite dish, rolled in leaves and grilled

Komba   supreme being of the Biaka

koondi   water drum

kùndi   harp that has a handle inserted into the sound box; generic term for a six-stringed harp from the Mobaye; Nzakara word for a five-stringed harp

kwange   sour *manioc* bread

limboku   Biaka dance performed by women before a marriage

loudon   Ngbaka dance

mabo   Biaka dance to ensure successful net hunting and divination

málùm   Muslim holy man

mânes   souls of ancestors

mangbere   sour *manioc* bread

manioc   cassava

maquis   small casual restaurant

marigot   (small) spring

marmite   large cooking pot, somewhat resembling a cauldron

mogbaté   funerary music from the Lobaye

mokundi   general name for Biaka dances that involve spirits

ngbàkià   Bandia dance performed during ancestor-veneration rituals

ndàlà   Nzakara word for a five-stringed harp

ndambo   Biaka dance to ensure successful big-game spear hunting

nebi   prophet (Zandé Mission ti Africa)

Ngandré   supreme being of the Banda

ngidi   female prophet (Zandé Mission ti Africa)

ngombi   harp with a handle that is wedged against the top of the sound box and fastened to a projection that may or may not be carved

Olokoda   Banda god/spirit

ongo   ensemble of horns

pagne   length of cloth, and the wrappers that are worn around the waist

piment   hot pepper

pirogue   canoe

sàgiru   Zandé word for the five-stringed harp

sanza   hand-piano

so   Mpeimu dance that celebrates the killing of a leopard

tam-tam   drum

Téré   Banda god/spirit of the land, one of the three sons of Ngandré

Selected Bibliography

Article 19 Research and Information Centre on Censorship. *Freedom of Information and Expression in the Central African Republic.* London: Article 19 Research and Information Centre on Censorship, 1989.

Barber, Kenneth B., Stuart A. Buchanan, and Peter F. Galbreathet. *An Ecological Survey of the St. Floris National Park, Central African Republic.* Washington, DC: International Park Affairs Division, National Park Service, U.S. Department of the Interior, 1980.

Baxter, P. T. W., and Audrey Butt Colson. *The Azande, and Related Peoples of the Ango-Egyptian Sudan and Belgian Congo.* Part IX, East Central Africa. Ethnographic Survey of Africa, edited by Daryll Forde. London: International African Institute, 1953.

Birmingham, David. "Society and Economy before A.D. 1400." In *History of Central Africa.* Vol. I, ed. David Birmingham and Phyllis M. Martin, 1–29. New York: Longman, 1983.

Boulvert, Yves. *Bangui 1889–1989: Points de Vue et Témoignages.* Paris: Ministère de la Coopération et du Dévelopement, 1989.

Bruguière, Philippe. "The Song of the Harp." In *Song of the River: Harps of Central Africa (29 May–29 August 1999),* ed. Eric de Dampierre et al., 107–13. Paris: Musée de la Musique, with the assistance of the Sociéte d'ethnologie, Nanterre, 1999.

Central African Republic. *Révision du document de politique nationale de promotion de la femme.* Central African Republic n.p., 1997.

Chants d'Orchestres Centrafricains: Orchestre Tropical Fiesta. Bangui: Centre Pastorale, 1989.

Chants d'Orchestres Centrafricains: Orchestre Makembé. Bangui: Centre Pastorale, 1988.

Chants d'Orchestres Centrafricains: Orchestre Canon Star. Bangui: Centre Pastorale, 1987.

Chemain, Roger, and Arlette Chemain-Degrange. "Tchicaya U Tam'si." In *Littératures Francophones: Afrique, Caraïbes, Océan Indien,* 258–72. Paris: Club des Lecteurs d'Expression Française, 1994.

Coguery-Vidroritch, catherine. *Le Congo au Temps des Grands Compagnies concessionaires.* Paris: Maton, 1972.

Cordell, Dennis. *A History of the Central African Republic.* Washington, DC: Peace Corps, 1975.

Cordell, Dennis D., Joel W. Gregon, and Victor Piché. "The Demographic Reproduction of Health and Disease: Colonial Central African Republic and Contemporary Burkina Faso." In *The Social Basis of Health and Healing in Africa,* ed. Steven Fiereman and John M. Janzen, 39–70. Berkeley: University of California Press, 1992.

De Dampierre, Eric, and Marc Chemillier. *Central African Republic: Music of the Former Bandia Courts.* Translated by Peter Crowe. C.N.R.S/Musée de l'Homme. Paris: Chant du Monde, 1996.

Dehoux, Vincent. *Chants à Penser Gbaya (Centrafrique).* Paris: SELAF, 1986.

Deverdun, René. *Jérôme Ramedane: Peintre Paysan, Peintre d'Histoire.* St. Maur: SÉPIA Éditions, 1995.

Éboué, Félix. *Les Peuples de l'Oubangui-Chari: Essai d'Ethnographie, de Lingusitique et d'Economie Sociale.* Paris, 1933. Reprint, New York: AMS Press, 1977.

Evans-Pritchard, E. E. *The Azande: History and Political Institutions.* Oxford: Clarendon Press, 1971.

Evans-Pritchard, E. E. "Some Zande Animal Tales from the Gore Collection." *Man* 65 (May–June 1965): 70–77.

Evans-Pritchard, E. E. "Zande Proverbs: Final Selection and Comments." *Man* 64 (January–February 1964): 1–5. http://links.jstor.org/sici?sici=0025–1496%28196401%2F02%291%3A64%3C1%3A1ZPFSA%3E.2.0.CO%3B2-B.

Evans-Pritchard, E. E. "Meaning in Zande Proverbs." *Man* 63 (January 1963): 4–7. http://links.jstor.org/sici?sici=0025–1496%28196301%291%3A63%3C4%3A3MIZP%3E2.0.CO%3B2-F.

Evans-Pritchard, E. E. *Witchcraft, Oracles, and Magic among the Azande.* London: Clarendon Press, 1958.

Feireman, Steven. "Struggles for Control: The Social Roots of Health and Healing in Modern Africa." *African Studies Review* 28, nos. 2/3 (June/September 1985): 73–147.

Gardinier, David E. "Schooling in the States of Equatorial Africa." In "Educational Problems in Africa," special issue, *Canadian Journal of African Studies* 8, no. 3 (1974): 517–38, http://links.jstor.org/sici?sici=0008-3968%281974%298%3A3%3C517%3ASITSO E%3E2.0.CO%3B2-9.

Gbenime-Sendagbia, F., J. Krief. "La Longue Route de Pierre Sammy." *Notre Librarie* 97 (April-May 1989): 70–72.

Giles-Vernick, Tamara. *Cutting the Vines of the Past: Environmental Histories of the Central African Rain Forest.* Charlottesville: University Press of Virginia, 2000.

Gillow, John. *African Textiles.* San Francisco: Chronicle Books, 2003.

Goyémidé, Etienne. "Le theater existe!" *Notre Librarie* 97 (April-May 1989): 88–92.

Goyémidé, Étienne. *Le Dernier Survivant de la Caravane.* Paris: Hatier, 1985.

Goyémidé, Étienne. *Le Silence de la Forêt.* Paris: Hatier, 1984.

Grootaers, Jan-Lodewijk. "Musical Universe of the Zande-Nzakara: In Search of a Lost Esthetic." In *Song of the River: Harps of Central Africa: (29 May–29 August 1999),* ed.

Eric de Dampierre et al., 121–27. Paris: Musée de la Musique, with the assistance of the Sociéte d'ethnologie, Nanterre, 1999.

Grootaers, Jan-Lodewijk. "A History and Ethnography of Modernity among the Zande (Central African Republic)." Vol. 1. PhD diss., University of Chicago, 1996.

Hardin, Rebecca. "Translating the Forest: Tourism, Trophy Hunting, and the Transformation of Forest Use in Southwestern Central African Republic (CAR)." PhD diss., Yale University, 2000.

Hewlett, Barry S. *Intimate Fathers: The Nature and Context of Aka Pygmy Paternal Infant Care.* Ann Arbor: University of Michigan Press, 1991.

Hilbreth, John. *The Gbaya.* Studia Ethnographica Upsaliensia Series 37. Uppsala: Institutionen för allmän och jämförande etnografi, 1973.

Hill, Robert William. "The Christianization of the Central African Republic." Master's thesis, School of World Mission and the Institution of Church Growth, Fuller Theological Seminary, 1969.

Igot, Yves. *Légendes Oubanguiennes.* Paris: L'École, 1975.

Igot, Yves. *Contes et Fables du Centre de l'Afrique.* Paris: Didier, 1970.

Kalck, Pierre. *Historical Dictionary of the Central African Republic,* 2nd ed. Translated by Thomas O'Toole. African Historical Dictionaries, 51. Metuchen, NJ: Scarecrow Press, 1992.

Kisliuk, Michelle. "Musical Life in the Central African Republic." In *The Garland Handbook of African Music,* ed. Ruth M. Stone et al., 681–97. New York: Garland, 1998.

Kisliuk, Michelle Robin. "Confronting the Quintessential: Singing, Dancing, and Every Day Life among the Biaka Pygmies (Central African Republic)." PhD diss., New York University, 1991.

Le Bomin, Sylvie. "The Banda-Gbambiya Harp." In *Song of the River: Harps of Central Africa: (29 May–29 August 1999),* ed. Eric de Dampierre et al., 129–34. Paris: Musée de la Musique, with the assistance of the Sociéte d'ethnologie, Nanterre, 1999.

Les débuts de l'Église Catholique en R.C.A; Notes et Documents rédigés ou recueillis par le Père Ghislain de Bainville cssp. Bangui, Central African Republic: Maison St. Charles, 1988.

Lumbala, Hilaire Mbaye. "An Inventory of the Comic Strip in Africa." http://www.africul-tures.com/anglais/articles_anglais/lumbala.htm.

Mabou, Michel. "Culture Locale et Organisation de l'Espace Urbain de Bangui (Centrafrique)." PhD diss., Université de Provence, 1995.

Maran, René. "Légendes et Coutumes Nègres de l'Oubangui-Chari. Choses vues par René Maran." *Les Oeuvres Libres* 147 (1933): 325–81.

Marwick, M. G. "Anthropologists' Declining Productivity in the Sociology of Witchcraft." *American Anthropologist,* n.s., 74, no. 3 (June 1972): 378–85.

Mayele-Sako, Léocadie-Milar. "La Problèmatique de la Reconnaissance Juridique et Politique de la Femme en Milieu Rural: Cas des Femmes de Boukou." Master's thesis, Université de Bangui, 1999.

Maziki.net. http://maziki.free.fr.

Morrill, Charles. "Languages, Culture, and Society in the Central African Republic." PhD diss., Indiana University, 1997.

Organisation des Nations Unies, Commission économique pour l'Afrique. *Le Droit et la Condition de la Femme en République Centrafricaine.* Addis Ababa: United Nations, 1985.

O'Toole, Thomas. "The Central African Republic: Political Reform and Social Malaise." In *Political Reform in Francophone Africa,* ed. John F. Clark and David E. Gardinier, 109–24. Boulder, CO: Westview Press, 1997.

O'Toole, Thomas E. "Shantytowns in Bangui, Central African Republic: A Cause for Despair or a Creative Possibility?" In *Slums and Squatters Settlements in Sub-Saharan Africa: Towards a Planning Strategy,* ed. R. A. Obubdo and Constance C. Mblanga, 123–32. Westport, CT: Praeger, 1988.

O'Toole, Thomas. *The Central African Republic: The Continent's Hidden Heart.* Boulder, CO: Westview Press, 1986.

Penel, Jean-Dominique. "La Litterérature Coloniale en Oubangui-Chari." *Notre Librarie* 7 (April–May 1989): 28–34.

Peters, Thomas A. "Appealing Cults in Central Africa: A Scriptural Perspective." Master's thesis, Grace Theological Seminary, 1987.

Philipps, J.E.T. "Observations on Some Aspects of Religion among the Azande ("Niam-Niam") of Equatorial Africa." *Journal of the Royal Anthropological Institute of Great Britain and Ireland* 56 (1926): 171–87. Stable ULR: http://links.jstor.org/sici?sici=0307–3114%2 81926%2956%3C171%3AOOSAOR%3E2.0.CO%3B2-Z.

Pigeon, Pierre. *Les Activités Informelles en République Centrafricaine.* Paris: L'Harmattan, 1998.

Poupon, A. "Étude Ethnographique des Baya de la Circonscription du M'Bimou." *L'Anthropologie* 26 (1915): 87–144.

Queffélec, Ambroise, Martine Wenezoui, and Jean Daloba. *Le Français en Centrafrique: Lexique et Société.* Vanves, France: EDICEF, 1997.

Renouf-Stefanik, Suzanne. *Animisme et Islam Chez les Manza (Centafrique): Influence de la Religion Musulmane sur les Coutumes Traditionelles Manza.* Paris: SELAF, 1978.

Rongier, Marie France Adrien. "Les kodro de Bangui: un espace urbain 'oublié.'" *Cahiers d'Etudes Africaines* 81–83 (1981): 93–110.

Rongier, Marie France Adrien. *Eveil à la Vie Centrafricaine.* Bangui: Ministère des Affaires Sociales, 1979.

Roulon-Doko, Paulette. *Cuisine et Nourriture Chez les Gbaya de Centrafrique.* Paris: L'Harmattan, 2001.

Roulon, Paulette, and Raymond Doko. "Un Pays de Conteurs." *Cahiers de Littérature Orale,* no. 11 (1982): 123–34.

Samarin, William. "Colonization and Pidginization on the Ubangui River." *Journal of African Linguistics* 4 (1982): 1–42.

Samarin, William J. "The Colonial Heritage of the Central African Republic: A Linguistic Perspective." *International Journal of African Historical Studies* 22, no. 4 (1989): 697–711. Stable ULR: http://links.jstor.org/sici?sici=0361–7882%281989%2922%3A4% 3C697%3ATCHOTC%3E2.0.CO%3B2-T.

Samarin, William J. "French and Sango in the Central African Republic." *Anthropological Linguistics* 28, no. 3 (Fall 1986): 379–87.

Sammy-Mackfoy, Pierre. *De l'Oubangui a la Rochelle; ou le parcours d'un bataillon de marche, 18 juin 1940–18 juin 1945.* Paris: L'Harmattan, 2003.

Sarno, Louis. *Bayaka: The Extraordinary Music of the Babenzélé Pygmies and the Sounds of Their Forest Home.* Roslyn, NY: Ellipsis Arts, 1995.

Saulnier, Pierre. *Bangui Raconte: Contes de Centrafrique*. Paris: L'Harmattan, 2000.

Saulnier, Pierre. *Le Centrafrique: Entre Mythe et Réalité*. Paris: L'Harmattan, 1997.

Saulnier, Pierre. *Bangui Chante: Anthologie du Chant Moderne en Afrique Centrale*. Paris: L'Harmattan, 1993.

Saulnier, Pierre. *La Femme dans la Société Centrafricaine*. Bangui, Central African Republic: n.p., 1984.

Speranza, Gaetano. "The Harps." In *Song of the River: Harps of Central Africa: (29 May–29 August 1999)*, ed. Eric de Dampierre et al., 59–94. Paris: Musée de la Musique, with the assistance of the Sociéte d'ethnologie, Nanterre, 1999.

Strong, Polly, trans. *African Tales: Folklore of the Central African Republic*. Mogadore, OH: Tell Publications, 1992.

Thomas, Jacqueline M. C. *Contes de la Forêt: Ecoutez le Claptois du Fleuve...* Paris: Conseil International de la Langue Française, 1975.

Thomas, Jacqueline M. C. *Les Ngbaka de la Lobaye: Le Dépeuplement Rural Chez Une Population Forestière de la République Centafricaine*. Paris: Mouton & Co., 1958. Reprint, Paris: Ecole Practique des Hauts Etudes, 1963.

Thomas, Jacqueline M. C., and Serge Bahuchet. *Encyclopédie des Pygmées Aka: Techniques, Langage et société des chasseurs-cueilleurs de la forêt centrafricaine (Sud-Centrafrique et Nord-Congo)*. Tome I. Paris: SELAF, 1991.

Thompson, Virginia, and Richard Adloff. *The Emerging States of French Equatorial Africa*. Stanford, CA: Stanford University Press, 1960.

Ugochukwu, Françoise. "Vie et Moeurs des pygmées par un romancier." *Ethiopiques* 5, nos. 1–2 (1988): 232–41.

UNICEF. *Analyse de la Situation de la Mère et de l'Enfant Centrafricains*. Bangui(?): République Centafricaine, 1992.

Vergiat, A. M. *Les Rites Secrets des Primitifs de l'Oubangui*. Paris: Editions Payot, 1936. Reprint, Paris: L'Harmattan, 1981.

Vidal, Pierre. *Garçons et Filles: Le Passage à l'âge d'Homme chez les Gbaya Kara*. Nanterre, France: Laboratoire d'ethnologie et de sociologie comparative, Université de Paris X, 1976.

Weber, Raymond Porter. "State Politics in the Central African Republic: An Original Study." PhD diss., University of Wisconsin–Madison, 1990.

Wright, Jennifer Lee. "Ritual Female Genital Cutting: An Ethnographic Exploration of the Cultural Context and Rite-of-Passage Ceremony Surrounding the Practice of Excision in One Tribe in the Central African Republic." Master's thesis, Yale University, 2000.

Index

About the Author

Jacqueline Woodfork is an Assistant Professor in the Department of History at Whitman College.

Recent Titles in
Culture and Customs of Africa

Culture and Customs of Nigeria
Toyin Falola

Culture and Customs of Somalia
Mohamed Diriye Abdullahi

Culture and Customs of the Congo
Tshilemalema Mukenge

Culture and Customs of Ghana
Steven J. Salm and Toyin Falola

Culture and Customs of Egypt
Molefi Kete Asante

Culture and Customs of Zimbabwe
Oyekan Owomoyela

Culture and Customs of Kenya
Neal Sobania

Culture and Customs of South Africa
Funso Afolayan

Culture and Customs of Cameroon
John Mukum Mbaku

Culture and Customs of Morocco
Raphael Chijioke Njoku

Culture and Customs of Botswana
James Denbow and Phenyo C. Thebe

Culture and Customs of Liberia
Ayodeji Oladimeji Olukoju

Culture and Customs of Uganda
Kefa M. Otiso